Marsilio Ficino: The Book Of Life

A Translation by Charles Boer
of *Liber de Vita* (or *De Vita Triplici*)

1980

Spring Publications, Inc.
Box One
University of Dallas
Irving, Texas   75061

First edition. Printed in the United States of America.

This book was designed and set by Gerald Burns at
national ShareGraphics, inc., Dallas.

The cover is an adaptation by Kate Smith and Pierre Denivelle
of Michelangelo's *Bacchus* (Bargello, Florence).

Manufactured by Sheegog Printing Co., Dallas, for Spring Publications, Inc.,
University of Dallas, Irving, Texas 75061.
European Agent: Spring, Postfach, 8800 Thalwil ZH, Switzerland

Frontispiece: facsimile of Latin text, *The Book of Life*.

ISBN 0–88214–212–7

CONTENTS

ACKNOWLEDGMENT

Since my text for this translation was the *Opera Omnia* Basel edition of 1576, notoriously full of errors, I have had to do much consulting in other editions, for which I am emphatically grateful to the staffs of the University of Connecticut Library and the Yale University Medical Library.

I must thank Professor Tom Moore, of Southern Methodist University, not only for making available to me the manuscript of his own forthcoming book on Ficino, but for his many suggestions for improving the present book.

Jay Livernois bestowed his vast Solar gifts on this project in many hours of reading and discussion of the manuscript, and the translation would have been abandoned many times had it not been for his encouragement and help.

I must also thank my two Italian Graces: Grazia Sotis of Minturno, for giving me considerable help with the names of Italian herbs and spices, and Grazia Giorgi of Florence, who seems to have been sent by the ghost of Ficino himself for inspiration.

Finally, it is perhaps in order here to offer a much belated acknowledgment to a distinguished teacher, Eugenio Garin, in whose classes at the University of Florence, twenty years ago, I first entered Marsilio Ficino's gardens. The Gods alone know how long and winding that garden path has been since those palmy days in an Italia *più calma,* but if the present work can be taken in any way as tribute to this great scholar, it is I who am honored.

INTRODUCTION

It is a singularly dismal comment on the state of Renaissance studies in the English-speaking world that so many of Marsilio Ficino's works are still untranslated. The *Symposium Commentary*, the *Philebus Commentary*, and some letters are all there is, except for spot translations of passages in general works on Renaissance Platonism. Why has Ficino, the most important *writer* in the Florentine awakening, been so ignored in English? Why do our universities attach so much attention to Pico della Mirandola's flummery *Oration On The Dignity Of Man*—already in several translations— and neglect Pico's master, the high priest of the Florentine Academy, the most adventuresome philosopher of the entire Italian Renaissance?

Ficino's genius, acclaimed in his own lifetime as the inspiriting force behind some of the greatest poets and painters, philosophers and statesmen of the era, has slept unread in the libraries of the western world for nearly five hundred years. It is surely time to disturb that sleep, not only for the sake of the historical record, our knowledge of Renaissance culture, or the tribute we clearly owe to this seminal voice in the western imagination, but even, as readers of the present book will, I hope, see, for the sake of knowing our own psychological past and the origins of what we still call our 'spirit' and our 'soul.'

Marsilio Ficino was born at Figline, near Florence, on the 19th of October, 1433, at 9 PM, when Saturn, as Ficino himself so often reminds us, was in the ascendant and making a gloomy horoscope for this first-born son of the town doctor and his clairvoyant wife.

Actually the horizon was far from gloomy, and foreign stars only slightly less influential than Saturn were soon gathering over Florence in the person of an eighty-year-old Greek scholar named

Gemisthus Pletho and his Byzantine Emperor, John Palaeologus. They were coming, in 1439, to a Church Council in which an accord would be reached for the first time in a thousand years between the Greek and the Latin Christian Churches. Gemisthus Pletho argued strenuously against the accord for philosophical reasons (the Greek tradition did not accept the Holy Spirit as an equal member of the Trinity, and Pletho himself hated the Latin Church), but with the Emperor needing western support in his losing battle against the Turks, Mars took precedence over the Holy Spirit, or at least over Pletho. In the bitter debates preceding the accord, Pletho enthralled the audience of scholars and clergy with his stunning erudition, but alienated them as well with an all too enviable display of his firsthand knowledge of Plato and the neo-Platonists. The Latin Church scholars had only a passing acquaintance with Plato, for Aristotle had long ago become their favorite, and only, Greek philosopher. What they had heard of Plato, through garbled Aristotelian sources, they didn't like. They considered Plato, and neo-Platonists like Plotinus and Porphyry, more or less anti-Christian. Some neo-Platonists, after all, had said that what was divine in Christ was also present in other miracle-workers like Apollonius of Tyana. Some of those present at the debates even grumbled that Pletho himself might be a neo-Platonist incarnation of the devil! But the devil could quote Aristotle too, for Pletho had read far more of him in the Greek original than the Italians had in their faulty medieval translations.

Fortunately, not all the Florentines present felt outraged by Pletho. Indeed, the single most powerful man in the room, though he was neither Churchman nor scholar, was enormously interested in what he was learning of the ancient philosophers. Cosimo de Medici, whose banking wealth controlled Florentine politics and Italian culture, invited the great Byzantine scholar to dinner. It soon became apparent to Cosimo that Florence must start a school for the study of Greek thought, especially this exciting new Platonic philosophy. Enough of the old Schoolmen and their Aristotle, who had an answer for everything. Cosimo could see that Plato was a crucial find, an invaluable opening onto the ancient world that was in turn now opening on the modern. Plato was a great undiscovered voice from antiquity calling out after centuries of Christianized Aristotelian pettifoggery. Cosimo, one of those rare men whom wealth deparochializes, apparently discussed with Pletho the idea of founding a Florentine *Acadèmia* (after the name for Plato's own school) for the propounding of all this fascinating new stuff coming out of Greece. But when Pletho left at the end of the Council, the plan went no further.

Byzantium fell to the Turks in 1453 and Cosimo's idea for a Platonic Academy came alive again only in 1457 when another great Greek scholar, John Argiropolos, emigrated to Florence to lecture on Aristotle and, on demand, Plato. But where was a man to undertake Cosimo's Academy? It was certainly not Argiropolos, whose official title was "Public Explicator of Aristotle."

Marsilio Ficino was a sickly boy, subject to quartan fever and, as he later wrote in a letter addressed to all his friends who kept asking about his health, "Stop asking—I've never had one entire day when my body was strong—I've been weak by nature from the beginning!" This is nothing unusual of course for the children of doctors, as everyone knows, and especially for the children of ambitious doctors. Doctor Ficino had treated Cosimo, and was on particularly friendly terms with Cosimo's son, Giovanni, to whom he once sent a couple of bottles of Trebbiano wine—the standard Ficino medicine for just about anything, as Marsilio himself would discover.

With a successful doctor for a father, Marsilio might have succumbed to his father's wishes and become a doctor himself, had he not also had a remarkably zany mother. She went around accurately predicting calamities for people—the death of her own mother, the suffocation by a nurse of her seventeen-day-old infant, and her own husband's fall from a horse, even telling him the spot. (Marsilio's explanation of all this was that some people can leave their bodies and see things because their souls are so pure.) Arnaldo della Torre, the superb Italian biographer of Ficino, attributes Marsilio's neurasthenic temperament, his mysticism, and his ecstasies to this much-pampered *gran signora,* who lived into her eighties and died only a year or so before Marsilio himself. That's a big ascription even for an Italian mama, but however they did it the Ficinos had succeeded in producing the last thing any parents want in a son, a philosopher.

Marsilio would have first heard of Plato from his Latin teacher, Luca d'Antonio de Bernardi, in the course of reading Cicero. From him he also learned music and his precious lyre playing. He learned the rudiments of Greek from Francesco da Castiglione.

His early education, however, like everyone else's, was Aristotelian. He studied under Nicolò Tignosi da Foligno, an orthodox Peripatetic philosopher averse to the practice of Argiropolos and others of mixing Platonism with Aristotelianism. Ficino's first real taste of Plato came from lectures he attended at the University of Florence by Cristoforo Landino, a friend of his father (as well as of Cosimo de Medici).

In 1451 (at age 18), Ficino was installed, with his father's help, as a cleric or seminarian (what else could you do with a kid who wanted to be a philosopher?) though the youth was hungry to explore Platonism and neo-Platonism. He started writing philosophical essays, some of which, in 1456, he showed and dedicated to Landino, who encouraged him to perfect his Greek and to continue Platonic studies. But suddenly, around the age of 24, just when John Argiropolos was beginning his lectures on Plato in Florence, Ficino had a 'crisis of faith.' All of this pagan study may have begun to shake the simple Christianity of his youth, but more importantly as a cleric he was suddenly forbidden by the Archbishop of Florence to attend Argiropolos' lectures. Instead, he was sent home to Figline. It seems certain that he wanted very much to study with Argiropolos but was the victim of the Archbishop's notorious hostility not only to humanism but to all antiquity. He accused Ficino of heresy and told him to read Thomas Aquinas instead. Back at Figline, however, in the winter of 1457 Ficino wrote, somewhat defiantly, a treatise on pleasure and a commentary on the Roman poet Lucretius, a sign of his budding Epicureanism. Then in the autumn of 1458 his father sent him to the Aristotelian-dominated medical school at the University of Bologna, where he stayed, no doubt unhappily, until 1459. He could have studied medicine in Florence and practiced with his father, but the Archbishop had told his father to send him far away from Florence.

He must have been wretched, yet as he would write later, Saturn, God of melancholy, offers compensations for the trouble he causes his philosophical children. Suddenly, in 1459, Marsilio was summoned by his father back to Florence and whisked into the august company of the great Cosimo himself. He had met Cosimo before, in 1452 (age 19), probably after asking Giovanni de Medici to arrange for a formal introduction (there is a letter from Giovanni, Doctor Ficino's erstwhile patient, to Marsilio, reminiscing about the friendship of their youth.) But Ficino made about as much of an impression on Cosimo at that original meeting as those beaming legions of sons and daughters people used to introduce to Nelson Rockefeller every year, and for the same reason. This time, however, Cosimo was summoning *him*. Though there is scant evidence, it seems that Landino, perhaps taking pity on what had happened to the boy, brought Marsilio's essays to the attention of the great man (another theory, more charming but less credible, is that Doctor Ficino himself did) and convinced Cosimo that this, at last, was the man for his Academy. Nonetheless Doctor Ficino, the worried father, wanted and got assurances from Cosimo that his son would be supported for life if he undertook this work. "You are a doctor of bodies," Cosimo is supposed to have said to him, "but he will be a doctor of souls."

Marsilio was enjoined to perfect his Greek, and Cosimo proposed he do this under Bartolomeo Platina (he and Landino seem to have thought Argiropolos too Aristotelian to risk with their young investment.) His first works, under Platina's training, were translations of the Orphic and the Homeric *Hymns*.

Cosimo purchased Greek manuscripts of Plato and gave them to Ficino to translate, along with a villa in the hills at Careggi, the new home of the Florentine Academy. Ficino decorated the place with astrological images (he thought such images of the Gods should be contemplated daily), with a fresco of the Greek philosophers, Heraclitus and Democritus, the one weeping, the other laughing, and with a bust of Plato, in front of which he placed a candle he never let go out. He had inscribed across the four walls of his study a Latin inscription reading, "All Things Are Directed To The Good By The Good, Be Happy In The Present, Don't Value Reputation, Don't Seek Prestige, Flee Excess, Flee Trouble, Be Happy In The Present."

By 1464 when Cosimo died, Ficino had completed a translation of much of Plato, which he was summoned to read to his patron on his deathbed. He had also completed the translation of the writings of Hermes Trismegistus he had been asked to translate even before Plato. It was thought that these mystical neo-Platonist writings, now known to be work of the first centuries A.D., had instructed Plato. They were considered a kind of 'ancient theology,' preceding Christianity and in many ways informing it.

Upon the death of Cosimo, Ficino worked for Cosimo's son, Piero, and tutored his grandsons, Lorenzo and Giuliano. The little villa at Careggi became a meeting-place for philosophers and artists, as well as for the bankers and statesmen of the Medicean empire. Ficino produced during these years his most famous work, *The Platonic Theology*, a commentary on Plato that incorporates all the neo-Platonist learning one could bring to bear on the task, as well as a considerable amount of his own imaginative approach. But anguish soon beset him, and from 1467 to 1469 Ficino was in serious despair. He had become so captivated, so exhilarated, by this new Platonic way of imagining that he found himself, like Pletho earlier, wanting to revive a pagan religion. But how far could he go with such ideas before the Church authorities shut him up? The *Platonic Theology* was, in part, an attempt to form a neo-Platonist religion, but it was also an attempt on the part of this deeply troubled man simply to understand the complex demands of his soul, to deepen the consequences of thinking about ancient Gods and the world around him. And somewhere between the conventional Christian religion of his day and the study of antiquity, Ficino crossed an internal boundary—indeed, he crossed over into that area Jung would have called psychology. After much anxiety about where this was taking him (he was singing Orphic hymns on his lyre and performing every pagan ritual he could think of), Ficino resolved the crisis in a remarkable way. He decided he would take the route of Augustine, who had been a Platonist before he converted to Christianity. Ficino now "converted" to Christianity again, but with a new perception of it. He explains this in his book *On the Christian Religion*, in which he claims that there are two ways of looking at religion, the common one (which he had trouble with), and a "rational" one based on Platonic enlightenment. Not permitting himself to practice an outright pagan religion, he would adapt the Christian one to his purposes. He began formal religious studies, and was ordained a Dominican priest in 1473.

He continued to live and work at Careggi, however. In 1474 Lorenzo, who after the death of Piero was his Medici patron, had him appointed rector of the Church of San Cristofano at Novoli, where he had no duties. Now, more energetically than ever, he worked to revive and interpret the *prisca theologia* or ancient theology, which he was convinced had been born in Persia with Zoroaster and in Egypt with Hermes Trismegistus, revived by Orpheus in Thrace, then by Pythagoras in Greece and Italy, and perfected by Plato. If Christianity was its outcome, and all there was, he was willing to take it from there.

When Pico della Mirandola arrived in Florence in 1484, on the day and at the very hour when Ficino's edition of Plato was being published, he immediately suggested that Ficino translate Plotinus. Cosimo had hoped that Ficino would take on this author after Plato, and Pico's suggestion struck him as the voice of Cosimo speaking from the grave. The third book of what he would call his *Liber de Vita* began as a commentary on a section of Plotinus' *Enneads* called *De Favore Coelitus Hauriendo*. Ficino completed this commentary on July 10th, 1489 and called it *De Vita Coelitus Comparanda*. On August 7th, 1489 he read a treatise by Arnaldo della Villanova on how to retard old age. The book was poorly written, Ficino says in a letter to Pico the next day, and difficult to understand. He decided to write his own book on this subject, which he finished on August 29th, 1489. He seems to have written one chapter a day, a "chapter" meaning simply the sum of his writing for that day. In writing this book, he says in another letter to Pico, he was not thinking so much about how to retard the onset of his own old age, but merely how to hold onto what he had left! He called this book the *De Vita Producenda*. Then he decided to combine the two, along with a piece he had written in 1480, called *De Cura Valetudinis Eorum Qui Incumbunt Studio Litterarum* (*On caring for the health of those who are preoccupied with the study of letters.*) This book was originally written as an attempt to counsel men of letters concerning the plague epidemic then sweeping Florence. He revised much of this earlier book, calling the new version *De Studiosorum Sanitate Tuenda*. He called all three books his *Liber De Vita*, though he refers to it by other titles, including *De Vita Triplici*, or simply *De Vita*.

Book Three proved the most controversial. Even as Ficino was writing it, he seems to have recognized the quarrels that would arise from a discussion of images, the power of the planets over human will, and the legitimacy of ancient magic and astrology. The reader will easily detect Ficino's exasperation, his elaborate disclaimers, his reluctance to admit that he is doing anything but describing what others said. We are not often so poignantly reminded of what an evangelical police state the Renaissance could be.

We must remember too that only two years before, Pico della Mirandola had brashly run off to Rome proclaiming nine hundred theses (mostly silly) that he was defying anyone to challenge. Ficino had encouraged him in this, but then Ficino seems to have encouraged everyone in everything, and if it meant in this case taking the side of his impetuous young friend against the merciless sobrieties of Old Man Rome, then all the more fun. The audience of bishops and professors was not impressed, and Pico was charged with heresy by Pope Innocent VIII. Many of these theses were simply Ficino's ideas undigested—except for where Pico was pushing his own lately acquired knowledge of Hebrew and claiming words of magic only worked in Hebrew, the original divine language. The whole episode left a bad taste in Rome's mouth for those privileged upstarts at Careggi. Furthermore, Pico's book *Heptaplus*, a Cabbalist interpretation of creation, appeared on March 9, 1489 only a few months before the books Ficino was now writing. The Pope let it be known that he objected to this book by Pico, too. Pico of course later renounced all astrology and magic, and coming under the influence of Savonarola said it was an aberration of his youth. But in his letters, Pico claims it was Ficino himself who suggested he write against astrology, that no one was more against astrology than Ficino, and that when he and Ficino joked at Careggi, the most frequent butt of their jokes, when not priests, was the gullibility of astrologers. In all of this, however, as Lynn Thorndike was the first to point out, Pico seems to have misunderstood the depth of Ficino's commitment to the astrological and magical. A hopeless literalist (he was an Aristotelian when he first met Ficino), Pico took everything literally, leading to his needless troubles at Rome, his imperceptive writing against astrology, and his eventual vulnerability to the self-indulgent pieties of Savonarola. Though Pico was a necessary and valuable soldier in Ficino's many-sided war on the medieval mind (and Thorndike may be too hard on him because on the losing side) it is no wonder, with Pico behind him, that Ficino was prepared for a hostile reception for his *Book of Life*.

And hostile reception is what he got. He had no sooner finished the book when it was attacked by various clerical enemies as a work of demonic magic and necromancy. Ficino was reported to the Pope, the same Innocent VIII who had dealt with Pico. On September 15, 1489 Ficino wrote a letter to his friends the "three Peters," Nero, Guicciardini, and Soderini, outlining the strategy they were to use in defending him, declaring that his magic was not demonic but natural. In this letter we see clearly the bemused attitude Ficino maintained throughout the crisis. The recipients of the letter were from three of the most powerful families in Florence; but in addition to other duties they are assigned the job, jokingly, of rallying Ficino's more famous friends Landino, Poliziano, and Pico. When Ficino tells them to "rouse that Hercules" Poliziano (who had no use for astrology), we must remember that this poet, a *'uomo delicato'* as the Italians say, was as far from a Hercules as could be imagined. And when Ficino tells them to beg Pico, "our Phoebus," to fire his arrows and kill the monster Pytho "emerging once again from his swamp," saying that once Pico starts shooting "he will kill the whole poisonous pack with one shot," we must remember that just the opposite was the case: the monster had chastened Pico after the Rome episode and again on the *Heptaplus* publication. If anything, Pico was a lousy shot. As for Landino, "our Amphion," one can imagine this 65-year-old Professor of Oratory and Poetics using his lyre as a field mortar.

Ficino had reason to be scared given his situation with the book, but he never lost his humor or (unlike Pico) his perspective. He knew exactly what to do and whom to see to come out on top, an imaginative gift we may attribute to the flexibility of his polytheism and an ability to avoid literalist binds.

The letter to the "Three Peters," his *Apology*, was printed at the end of the first edition along with a letter to three other friends from the Academy, Canacci, Canigiani, and Corsini, whose names Ficino puns on as his *'canes'* (hunting-dogs) and *'cursores'* (chasers)—the pun is closer in Italian. Filippo Valori, who had paid for the publication of Ficino's Plato translations, now paid for the *Book of Life,* which was published on December 3, 1489. Copies were sent to friendly bishops and Cardinals in the hope that they would intercede for the author with the Pope. Ficino wrote to Antonio Calderini on May 27th, 1490 begging him to give a copy to the great humanist, Ermolao Barbaro. "Whoever reads my book," he wrote to Calderini, "with a sane, undisturbed mind, will clearly see that I wrote it with sincerity, with a pious mind, and with a reverence for religion." It was Ermolao Barbaro who finally convinced the Pope that the book should not be banned. Not until June of 1490, however, was Ficino out of the soup. He then proceeded to his full translation and commentary on Plotinus, which was published in May of 1492 (a month too late for his patron, Lorenzo).

What, we may ask, was the significance of the *Book of Life* for Ficino and for his friends? He tells us in the dedicatory letters to

Lorenzo de Medici, Filippo Valori, and the King of Hungary, that he hopes they will study the book and thus lead long and healthy lives—Lorenzo had a large nose but no sense of smell at all, and is possibly in Ficino's mind when he writes so much here about smell and spirit, and he may also have been in mind because he was seriously ill with gout a great deal of the time. He died at 43.

Ficino was himself 56 in 1489, and as he tells us in the text, he considered himself an old man (though he would not die for another decade, in 1499). He had, of course, studied medicine, and he had observed his father at work. His mother was in her eighties, the recipient of much attention and advice from her busy son about her health. No doubt some of his advice to her on diet is in these pages. But the spring of much of Ficino's composition here must have been his own experience with depression. A life-long melancholiac, born under that ominous sign of Saturn, he had developed a unique and remarkable therapy for himself and his fellow melancholiacs of the Academy (they all thought of themselves as Saturnians) based on a polytheistic imaginative ordering of psychological moods and feelings. Melancholy, he thought, was a natural condition of the soul in the body, and the scholar-philosopher was particularly prone to it. Ficino is far more cosmologically complicated about this than the Christian position canonized by Augustine ("Our hearts are restless, O Lord, until they rest in Thee.") For the neo-Platonist, the soul does not want to be in the body, and melancholy is its cry for escape. Ficino is thus the source of this widespread idea in the Renaissance, as Panofsky and Saxl have shown in their study of Renaissance art, *Saturn and Melancholy*. But while the standard medieval view of this melancholy often led to a denial of the body and cloistered asceticism as the answer to the soul-sufferer's dilemma, Ficino's "therapy" enlarged on the idea of the psyche as the home of many divinities, a whole heaven within us, as he often liked to say. Those plagued by Saturn's dry and depressing influence must turn to Jove for help, letting a little "Joviality" into their lives to balance or 'temper' the Saturnian tendency to somber extremes and dry philosophical binges. They must let a little of Phoebus Apollo in too, by associating with

'Solar' people (blonds! he advises). Saturnians must get out of their dark, gloomy laboratories and take walks in radiant gardens. There can be no denying the claims of sex either, for Venus must have her place if we are not to be but sterile subjects of Saturn's kingdom of mean old men. Indeed, Ficino's sometimes startling language and lively discussion of sex may offend some readers who forget that he writes in a time when Italy was much more at ease on this subject than it would be in the next century, when under Spanish influence women put on, in mourning, those ghostly black dresses some wear to this day. In addition to Venus, planets like Mars, Mercury, and the Moon make their demands, too, on the Ficinian psyche.

His purpose, however, is more than simply the relief of melancholy through a juggling of astral images. Though these Gods are planets, which ancient astrologers and more recent Arabians had studied for their influence on human behavior, Ficino is not a literalist. It is more important, he says, to recognize the impact these Gods have on our imagination than any fatalist impact they may have on our lives. For Ficino is cobbling ancient astrological lore into a psychological system. His real concern is the soul and how to live with it. He recognized that while we can do much to expand and 'temper' (one of his favorite words) the psychological influxes of the Gods in our lives, in the end we must be ready to endure them. They do not come without 'gifts' however, even Saturn. (Once during a particularly severe experience of depression, Ficino's friend Cavalcanti told him to stop moaning, and reminded him—to Ficino's own amusement—that Saturn, for all his attendant melancholy, had deepened Ficino's work.)

By imagining life as governed by planetary Gods, each one presiding over certain foods, flowers, animals, metals, and modes of behavior, Ficino lifts the world and human life from the categorical deadness of his Aristotelian contemporaries, and profoundly ensouls it. Suddenly, everything is reborn, everything comes alive with a numinous meaning larger than man. Suddenly, the world is seen as a garden of gifts that the Gods have bestowed upon us. Suddenly, we see *renaissance*.

But it is not a renaissance of the soul alone, as Michelangelo, living with the Medici and frequently present at Careggi, would remind us. Soon to sculpt the magnificent David, he understood Ficino's almost unprecedented sense of the importance of body. (In a letter to Pico, Ficino once suggested that they imitate Prometheus and together compound a man, with (ironically) the handsome Pico as its soul and Ficino, who had a hunched back, as its body.

While he followed the ancient system of the four humors, he imagines this too under the planetary and psychological influence of Gods. Though Galen was Ficino's source here, the doctrine of the four humors was part of the so-called "Hippocratic Collection" and first appears in the tract called *On the Nature of Man,* which Aristotle attributed to Polybus, the son in law of Hippocrates.

Disease in antiquity was usually seen as an imbalance of the humors, which have a natural tendency to equilibrium but occasionally go out of whack. Ficino shared this view, paying special attention to the humor of black bile or melancholia, and how to avoid its running to excess. The humors or fluids coursing through the body are blood, phlegm (*pituita*), black bile (*melancholia*), and yellow bile (*cholea*). Ficino got not only his theory of the humors from Galen, but his theory of the natural, animal, and vital spirits as well. In addition to air, these three kinds of spirit enliven the body. The natural spirit arises in the liver, where it enters the veins as blood. Part of this enters the right ventricle, passes slowly into the left ventricle as dark blood, joins with air brought in from the lungs and becomes the higher vital spirit, the principle of arterial blood. This arterial blood then passes throughout the body, part of it going to the base of the brain, where it becomes the animal spirit which is distributed by the nerves.

To see a divine influence on these humors and spirits was not original with Ficino. Ancient Greek medicine, from Hippocrates to Galen, saw the Gods as related to diseases as well as healing. There is a remarkable sentence in the *Sacred Disease,* a tract of the Hippocratic Collection, which illustrates this. "No need to put this disease in a special class as more divine than others," it says breezily, "for they're all divine and they're all human."

Where Ficino is original, however, is in his vast and careful conceptualization of all this physiology and psychology under an imaginary polytheism. For the first time the astrological lore of antiquity, the soul discourses of the neo-Platonists, Greek, Roman, Arab, and Italian medical and dietary treatises, herbals and alchemical practices, all are brought to bear on the prevalent psychological constitution of an imaginative, depressed friar who lived in the splendor of Europe's greatest family.

Here is a psychology, then, truly worthy of the age of humanism, though that Renaissance catchword, especially today, seems mired in our secular misconceptions about man as the measure of all things. For Ficino Gods are the measure, man but the recipient of their gifts. So that while there is deep depression here (from Saturn), there is also great joy (from Venus and Jove).

In a letter to his friend Matteo d'Arezzo, Ficino looked back with affection a year after the publication of the *Book of Life* and remembered how he wrote it "in the summertime, among the flowers," in the field at Careggi. Adding to this affection, perhaps, as the reader will see, was no small amount of wine (from Dionysus), and considerable humor (from Jove, Venus, and Mercury). Ficino is described by his first biographer, Corsi, as melancholy but "always humorous and festive in public," his conversation always "full of witticisms, jokes, and laughter."

Ficino's reputation in the history of philosophy has too long been based only on his seminal translations of Plato and their impact on the Renaissance. Most studies of Ficino, like Kristeller's, have valued his Platonic side to the virtual neglect of the Hermetic. The first man to translate the Hermetic texts into Latin, amplifying these ideas through the rest of his work, Ficino vastly enriched the 'occult' tradition of his day (though it was not, of course, all that 'occult' in his day). Florence had long been a center of magic, and astrology was as serious and as controversial a subject to the educated man of the Renaissance as 'psychology' has become today.

Thanks to the brilliant work of Frances Yates and D. P. Walker, this side of Ficino is now becoming better known, though one still finds in odd sources like the *Columbia Encyclopedia* an outrageously brief and uninformed sketch of Ficino's work that for too long has been the typical Anglo-American view ("He translated Plato into Italian [1482] and his version is still regarded as the best in Italian. His importance lies in this work, as his other writings are unreliable and unoriginal.") The negative result is such capsule assessments as John Addington Symonds' comment that Ficino's was "an unintelligent eclecticism." This view, and the prejudices of other nineteenth century British aesthetes, seems on the wane.

In recent years, James Hillman's writings have illuminated the internalized polytheism that is behind Ficino's (and Hillman's own) psychology of soul. Hillman shows Ficino's work to be a psychology of great subtlety and range. While Ficino always claimed there was a whole heaven of stars and planetary Gods within us, it has taken the attentions of a twentieth century archetypal psychologist to recover the significance of this. Hillman's reading of Ficino is fresh air on a subject staled by literalist presuppositions and Germanic systematizing. Hillman's work at least rescues Ficino from the Anglo-Germans and returns him to Italy— in one paper he reminds Italian psychologists that Ficino is a precursor.

Tom Moore's forthcoming book, *The Planets Within*, is a further analysis of Ficino's astral psychology. Centering on the third of the *Book of Life* trilogy, it is the first full-scale exploration of this work, and should do much to open this side of Ficino's reputation to a wider audience than the specialized academic ones.

Through such psychological approaches as these, we can begin to see how the *Book of Life* was the sort of thing the Medici heard when they turned to their resident archetypal (Ficino's word) therapist for help. One might ask, then, how good was the advice?

Considering some of the substances Ficino recommends for ingestion, it was atrocious. Cosimo, Piero, Giuliano di Cosimo, and Lorenzo de Medici spent years of their lives laid up with gout, and no wonder, if they ate some of these things. Worse, the author of a book called *How To Live A Long Life* must have been given pause confronted with the deaths of so many of his friends at early ages—in addition to Lorenzo, Pico died at 31, and Poliziano at 40.

Perhaps the Food and Drug Administration should attach a

warning label to this book, should a reader be found to try some of Ficino's formulas. This one from William Turner, the sixteenth century English herbalist who wrote a book on *theriaca* (Ficino's all-time favorite treacle cure-all, based on a formula of Galen), might be apt:

> Although both Galen and Aetius hath given sufficient warning unto all men and women, at what times, in what ages, complexions, and in what diseases these medicines may be hurtful or wholesome to the receivers of it, yet marking the great dull grossness of many Englishmen that cannot understand what is plainly spoken, and the foolish hardiness of some others that care not for sufficient warning, but will boldly become murderers of themselves by misusing of God's creatures, not using them by the advice of Almighty God's servants and officers the learned physicians, but out of time and out of measure take them in, without all discretion, following only their own advice or else the counsel of some doting old gooddame, or some craking Cramer, or prating runagate pedlar, I cannot think myself sufficiently discharged, except I give warning to all men and women that will use these medicines, that they take them not in rashly and unadvisedly, without the advice and counsel of a learned physician who may tell them whether they be agreeable for their natures and complexions and diseases or no.

But Ficino would have been the first to admit that it was the imaginative process involved in such medicines that was the secret of health, and to this extent his advice was very good indeed. To this extent, furthermore, his reputation has been underrated and ignored, perhaps because it has been for so long in the hands of philosophy departments and art historians. For those of us who now read his imaginative side (Hermetic, astrological, occult, magical, daemonic, astral, alchemical—words almost generative of the modern imagination) he is the supreme polytheist of the human psyche. Read from the soul's perspective, Ficino is not only the man who set the philosophical course for much of the Italian Renaissance, but its great psychologist as well. He may be the first psychologist of the modern world.

A LIST OF WORKS CITED IN THE INTRODUCTION

Allen, Michael J. B., *Marsilio Ficino: The Philebus Commentary* (Berkeley, 1975).

Columbia Encyclopedia, ed. William Bridgwater and Elizabeth J. Sherwood, 2nd ed. (New York, 1950).

Corsi, Giovanni, *Commentarius de platonicae philosophies apud Italos instauratione sive Marsili Ficini vita* (1506), ed. Bandini (Pisa, 1772).

Ficino, Marsilio, *Opera Omnia* (Basel, 1576).

> *Note:* Carol Kaske's translation of *TBL* appeared too late for consideration in the Translator's Introduction.

Hillman, James, *Revisioning Psychology* (New York, 1975).

_____, "Plotino, Ficino, and Vico as Precursors of Archetypal Psychology," in *Loose Ends* (Spring Publications, 1975).

Hippocrates, *Oeuvres Complètes d'Hippocrates*, trans. E. Littré, vol. I–X (Paris, 1839–61).

Jayne, Sears, *John Colet and Marsilio Ficino* (Oxford, 1963).

_____, *Marsilio Ficino's Commentary On Plato's Symposium*, Univ. of Missouri Studies, XIX (1944).

Kristeller, Paul O., *The Philosophy of Marsilio Ficino* (New York, 1943).

Moore, Tom, *The Planets Within* (forthcoming).

Panofsky, Erwin, Fritz Saxl and Raymond Klibansky, *Saturn and Melancholy*, (London, 1964).

Pico della Mirandola, Giovanni, *Opera Omnia* (Basel, 1601).

_____, *Oration On The Dignity Of Man*, trans. A. R. Caponigri (South Bend, 1956).

Plotinus, trans. A. H. Armstrong (Cambridge, Mass., 1966).

Symonds, John Addington, *The Renaissance In Italy: the revival of learning* (London, 1877).

Thorndike, Lynn, *A History of Magic and Experimental Science*, vols. III–IV (New York, 1934).

della Torre, Arnaldo, *Storia dell'Acadèmia Platonica di Firenze* (Florence, 1902).

Turner, William, *A Book of Wines*, ed. Sanford V. Larkey (New York, 1941).

MARSILII FICINI

Florentini Medici atque Philosophi,

celeberrimi, de Studioforum fanitate tuenda, fiue eorum
qui literis operam nauant, bona ualetudi-
ne conferuanda.

LIBER I.

De nouem Studioforum ducibus.　Cap. I.

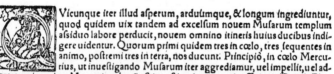

Vicunque iter illud afperum, ardulmque, & longum ingrediuntur,
quod quidem uix tandem ad excelfum nouem Mufarum templum
afsiduo labore perducit, nouem omnino itineris huius ducibus indi-
gere uidentur. Quorum primi quidem tres in cœlo, tres fequentes in
animo, poftremi tres in terra, nos ducunt. Principio, in cœlo Mercurius, ut inueftigando Mufarum iter aggrediamur, uel impellit, uel ad-
hortatur: liquidem Mercurio tributũ eft inueftigationis omnis officium. Deinde Phœ
bus ipfe, & quærentes animos, & res quæfitas fplendore uberrimo fic illuftrat, ut per-
fpicuè quod quærebatur, à nobis inueniatur. Accedit gratiofiffima Venus, Gratiarum
mater, atque almis omnino lætisq; radijs fuis rem omnem adeò condit, & ornat, ut quic-
quid & inftigante Mercurio quæfitum fuit, & monftrante Phœbo idm erat inuentum,
mirifica quadam & falutari uenuftate Veneris circumfufum, delectet femper, & profit.
Sequuntur tres itineris huius duces in animo, uidelicet uoluntas ardens, & ftabilis, acumen ingenij, memoria tenax. Tres in terra poftremi funt, prudentiffimus paterfamiliâs,
probatiffimus præceptor, medicus peritiffimus. Abfque his nouem ducibus nemo ad
ipfum nouem Mufarum templum peruenire uel potuit, uel poterit unquam. Cæteros
quidem duces ab initio nobis præcipuè Deus omnipotens naturâque tribuerunt, tres
uerò poftremos noftra adhibet diligentia. Sed præcepta officiâque, quæ ad patremfa-
miliâs, & quæ ad præceptorem circa literarum ftudia pertinent, antiqui plures, fapien-
tesq; tractauerunt, præcipuè Plato nofter, & fæpe alias, & in libris de Republica, ac de
Legibus diligentiffimè. Deinde Ariftoteles in Politicis, Plutarchus quoque & Quinti-
lianus egregiè. Solus autem literarum ftudiofis hactenus deeft medicus aliquis, qui
manum euntibus porrigat, falutaribusq; confilijs atque medicinis adiuuet eos, quos neque cœlum, neque animus, neque paterfamiliâs præceptorue deftituit. Ego igitur for-
tem eorum laboriofifsimam mifertus, qui difficilè Mineruæ minuentis neruos, iter a-
gunt, primus tanquam medicus debilibus & ualetudinarijs adfum, fed utinam facultate
tam integra, quàm propitia uoluntate. Surgite iam adolefcentes, Deo duce alacres. Surgite iuuenes, atq; uiri, quos ardentius Mineruæ ftudium nimium eneruat. Accedite li-
benter ad medicum, qui uobis ad inftituti ueftri perfectionem, monftrante Deo, atque
fauente, confilia remediaq; falutaria largitur.

Quàm diligens habenda cura fit cerebri, cordis, ftomachi & fpiritus.
Cap. II.

PRincipio quantam curfores crurium, athletæ brachiorũ, Mufici uocis curam ha
bere folent; tantam faltem literarũ ftudiofos cerebri & cordis, iecinorisq; & fto-
machi oportet habere rationem, imo uerò tantò maiorè, quantò & membra hæc
præftantiora, q̃ illa funt, & ij frequentius, atq; ad potiora his membris, q̃ illi il-
lis utuntur. Præter ea folers quilibet artifex inftrumenta fua diligentifsimè curat, peni-
cillos pictor, malleos incudesq; faber ærarius, miles equos & arma, uenator canes & a-
ues, citharã citharœdus, & fua quifq; fimiliter, Soli uerò Mufarũ facerdotes, foli fummi

boni

DEDICATORY LETTER FOR *THE BOOK OF LIFE* BY MARSILIO FICINO, FLORENTINE DOCTOR AND PHILOSOPHER, TO THE MAGNIFICENT LORENZO MEDICI, GUARDIAN OF HIS COUNTRY

Poets sing of Bacchus as the greatest master, the high priest, the twice-born. Perhaps they mean that it is necessary for the future priest, once he is initiated, to be reborn, or that he now seems reborn after becoming totally drunk with the God in his mind. Or perhaps, in a more humble sense, once a sprig produces the wine of Bacchus on the vine, like Semele, its clusters ripe under the sun, the lightning reproduces the wine in its barrel, like the foetus in Jove's thigh.

But we must not speak of the sacred mysteries here, where our intention is to help with physical strength those who are weak. This must not be done in a heavy, serious style, but free and joyful, once we have become aroused—I do not know how—by father Bacchus. And I really mean that I do not know how: maybe medicine is more prudently done under Apollo, the first of doctors, rather than under Bacchus. Yet, if it would not be a vain omen, perhaps a little Bacchus should be in our mouths right now! For Bacchus heals, perhaps even more healthfully, with some of his nourishing wine and his happy carefreeness, than Apollo does with his herbs and charms.

In whatever sense you take this to be true, the leader of these priests, Bacchus, is said to have had two mothers. Melchisidech, however, the high priest, barely had one mother, and barely even had one father. I, the least of priests, have had two fathers: the medical Doctor Ficino, and the Medici's Cosimo. From one I was born, from the other reborn. One commended me to Galen, first as a doctor, then as a Platonist; the other, however, consecrated me to the divine Plato. Both of them destined Marsilio for a doctor's life: Galen was a doctor of bodies, while Plato was the doctor of souls.

I have done the healing medicine of souls for a long time now, under Plato, interpreting all his books and composing, with endless pleasure, eighteen books on the immortality of souls, satisfying thus my Medici father. Wondering what I could then do for my medical father, I decided to compose a book on caring for the health of men of letters.

Men of letters will of course not just want to be in good health, but to live long too. So I have written another book for them as well, on how to live long. These books will be different, of course, in their medicines and remedies. In addition to these books on a healthy and a long life, I have added a book on how to make your life agree with the heavens, so that out of the living body of the world itself life might be made to flourish more in our own bodies, growing like limbs on the world vine.

Most generous Lorenzo, I hope you will ignore the fact that while I would be a doctor in these books of medicine, I am not a good poet. For Apollo, after all, is the founder of medicine, and the master of poets, and he bestows his life on us not so much through herbs as through his lyre and songs. Even Venus produces, for the astrologers, music and medicine.

But here I am, advising students and ordinary citizens alike to be more careful of life and at the same time I neglect the health of my books, always letting them be separated from themselves. So now, for the first time, I join them into one body. With their limbs joined in one form, may life now come to them.

This physical work, however, as if it were my body, cannot have life, unless it be my own. Its life, indeed, hangs from my soul. But this, for a long time now, lives with you, great Lorenzo, my patron, in that part of your vast buildings where, together with Plato's, our work on the immortality of the soul is kept, dedicated to your name. Yet my soul, even in this blessed place, where your land itself gives life, is nonetheless, as the theologians say, restless, while this physical work receives, as it were, its own body.

Accept, then, great Lorenzo, after my books on the soul, these, too, on the body, and with the same breath, breathe on these as you did those in the past. For thus this body, under your spirit, might live through its soul, and my soul, now with its body, might rest on your hearth.

BOOK ONE

*On Caring for the Health of Students or Those
Who Work in Letters, Taking Care of Their Good
Health,* by Marsilio Ficino, Florentine Doctor
and Philosopher

Chapter 1

The Nine Guides of Scholars

Whoever begins that bitter, arduous and long journey which leads with assiduous labor to the highest temple of the nine Muses, finds he needs nine guides for the journey. The first of these are the three in heaven who lead us, then the three in the soul, and finally the three on earth.

In heaven, Mercury either compels us or exhorts us, making us begin the journey by inquiring about the Muses. Mercury is in charge of all inquiry.

Then Apollo lights up with a rich splendor both the souls that seek and the things that are sought, so that we find whatever we seek carefully.

Then comes most gracious Venus, mother of the Muses. With her nourishing and happy rays she constructs everything and decorates it so that whatever had been sought at Mercury's instigation, and whatever had been found with Apollo's showing it, is now surrounded with her marvelous and salutary pleasure. Venus always makes one love it and enjoy it.

Then there are the three guides of the journey in the soul: an ardent and stable will, acumen of the mind, and a tenacious memory.

Finally, the three on earth: a father who is prudent, a teacher who is excellent, and a doctor who is brilliant.

Without these nine guides, no one has ever been able to come to the temple of the nine Muses, and no one ever will. From the beginning, almighty God and nature assign some of them to us, and the three last ones our own diligence pursues. But the teachings and duties which pertain to our father, and those that pertain to our teacher in the study of letters, have been discussed by many ancients and sages, especially by our dear Plato, in the *Republic* and in the *Laws,* as well as by Aristotle in his *Politics,* and by Plutarch and Quintilian.

The only guide lacking for the study of letters is some doctor who would reach out his hand and with healthful advice and medicines help those students, who lack neither heaven nor soul, neither father nor teacher. That is why, pitying this terrible state of affairs for those who make the journey while Minerva threatens their nerves, I come as a doctor for those in poor health, and I hope my ability will be as good as my will means well.

So rise up, you young people, you men and boys whom the hard study of Minerva has just about worn out. Come freely now to your doctor here, who only wants to make your studies perfect, and with God's help and wisdom offers you his advice and remedies for health.

Chapter 2

How diligently one must take care of the brain, the heart, the stomach, and the spirit

Runners take care of their legs, athletes take care of their arms, musicians take care of their voices. Those who study and write ought to be at least that much concerned about their brains, and their hearts, their livers and their stomachs. They should even be more concerned, since these parts are more important, and more often used. A skilled craftsman takes great care of his instruments, a painter his brushes, a sculptor of bronzes his hammer and chisel, a soldier his horse and weapons, a hunter his dogs and birds, a lyre-player his lyre, and so on.

Only the priests of the Muses, only the greatest hunters of good and truth, are so negligent and so unfortunate that they seem to neglect totally that instrument with which they are able to measure and comprehend the universe. The instrument is the spirit itself, which doctors define as some vapor of the blood, pure, subtle, warm, and clear. From the warmth of the heart, where it is produced from a thinner blood, it flows to the brain, and there the spirit works hard for the functioning of the interior, rather than exterior, senses. That is why the blood serves the spirit, the spirit serves the senses, and the senses, finally, serve reason.

The blood, however, is affected by a natural power, which thrives in the liver and stomach. The thinnest part of the blood flows into the fountain of the heart, where a vital power flourishes. The spirits of the mind are created there, and, as I shall show, there the ramparts of Minerva rise. In these, an animal force, that is for feeling and moving, dominates. That is why contemplation is so much more than an obedience of the senses.

The senses are as the spirit, and the spirit is as the blood, and those three powers which we have called the natural, the vital, and the animal, are such that it is from these, through these, and in these, that spirits are conceived, born, and nourished.

Chapter 3

Scholars are subject to phlegm and black bile

Not only should men of letters be very diligent in caring for their limbs, and powers, and spirit, but, as if they were sailing past Scylla and Charybdis, they should be particularly careful to avoid phlegm and black bile. To the extent that these are busy in the rest of the body, you will be that much slower in the brain and mind. This is why the pituita, which the Greeks call phlegm, and black bile, which the Greeks call melancholia, have come into existence.

Indeed, phlegm often blocks the intelligence and suffocates it, if it abounds or burns too much. Black bile vexes us with too much care or much silliness, and disturbs the soul and judgment. It does this so much that it would not be wrong to say that scholars would be very healthy indeed if it were not for that bothersome phlegm, and they would be the happiest and wisest people of all if it were not for black bile trouble, driving them to sadness or to silliness.

5

Chapter 4

The reasons why scholars are melancholiacs, and how they get that way

There are three major reasons why scholars become melancholiacs. The first is heaven-caused, the second is natural, and the third is human.

It is heaven-caused because Mercury, who invites us to begin our studies, and Saturn, who works them out and has us stick to them and make discoveries, are said by the Astronomers to be cold and dry. If Mercury is really all that cold, he is usually extremely dry, because of his nearness to the sun, and this dry condition doctors trace to melancholy. Mercury and Saturn give this condition to students of letters, and to their followers, and they increase it daily.

The natural cause seems to be that because the pursuit of knowledge is so difficult it is necessary for the soul to remove itself from external things to internal things, as if moving from the circumference to the center. While one is looking at this center of man (of which more later), it is necessary to remain very still, to gather oneself at the center, away from the circumference. To be fixed at the center is very much like being at the center of the earth itself, which resembles black bile.

Thus black bile rigorously provokes the soul so that it might gather itself into one piece, stay in one piece, and be contemplated. This drives the student to the center of each thing, like the center of the world, and moves him to understand the highest things, since it is in accord with Saturn, the highest of planets. Contemplation itself, on the other hand, with a kind of rigorous gathering up, almost a seizing, contracts one's nature like black bile.

The human cause is through ourselves. Because with Sagittarius the mind often violently dries up and a great part of its moisture is consumed (which is nourishment of its natural warmth), much of its warmth is also extinguished. The condition of the brain then turns dry and cold, which is why this quality is called earthly and melancholy.

Furthermore, because of the frequent movement involved in thinking, the spirit also is continually broken by such movement. The spirit thus broken, it is necessary to repair it with some thinner blood. Since the thinner and clearer parts of the blood are usually consumed, however, the remaining blood by necessity runs dense, dry, and black.

It all comes down to this, that with the mind and heart bent on contemplation, the stomach and the liver fail. Then, especially if you are eating rich or hard foods poorly cooked, the blood becomes cold, thick, and black. Finally, with an excessive swiftness of the limbs, and with neither the remaining stuff nor the hard glutinous stuff being separated, dusky vapors are exhaled. All these make for a melancholy spirit, a sad and fearful soul. Since these darknesses are much more inside than outside, they seize the soul with sadness and wear it out.

Of all scholars, those devoted to the study of philosophy are most bothered by black bile, because their minds get separated from their bodies and from bodily things. They become preoccupied with incorporeal things, because their work is so much more difficult and the mind requires an even stronger will. To the extent that they join the mind to bodiless truth, they are forced to separate it from the body. Body for these people never returns except as a half-soul and a melancholy one.

This is in fact what our dear Plato meant in the *Timaeus,* when he said that the soul, in frequent and intense contemplation of the divine, grows on such nourishment and becomes so powerful that it departs the body, and its body, left behind, seems to dissolve. It is as if it abandoned its bodily nature, fleeing sometimes with great agitation, and sometimes with none at all.

Chapter 5

Why thinkers get melancholy; which ones do and which ones do not

So far it is enough to have shown that the priests of the Muses get melancholy either from the very beginning or as they study, because of either heavenly, natural, or human causes. Aristotle confirms this in his book of *Problems.* For all men, he says, who are distinguished in some faculty, are melancholiacs. Plato points this out, too, in his book on *Knowledge,* saying thinkers are often very disturbed and upset. Democritus, too, says that nobody can become a great thinker who cannot become enraged. Our dear Plato, in the *Phaedrus,* seems to agree with this, too, saying that poetic doors are beaten on in vain without rage.

If, by chance, one wants to see this divine rage, nothing can beat the melancholiacs for showing it, at least according to the Natural Philosophers.

The reasons suggested by us, and by Democritus, Plato, and Aristotle, too, why nobody is more melancholy than thinkers, seem more divine than human. Yet Democritus, Plato, and Aristotle pursue this dubiously, I think, unsatisfactorily explaining the reason for so great a thing. One must dare then (with God's light) to track down the causes.

Melancholy, that is, black bile, is something double: some of it is called natural by doctors, but another part touches on burning. This natural type is nothing other than a part of the blood getting thicker and dryer. The burning type is divided, however, into four kinds: for it is produced by a combustion of either natural melancholy, pure blood, bile, or phlegm.

When the burning kind occurs, it is harmful to judgment and wisdom, for when this humor rises and burns, it makes you upset and angry, what the Greeks call 'Mania,' what we call madness. But even when it is extinguished, and its subtler and clearer parts broken, and all that is left is a foul soot, it makes you dull and stupid. This is why they call the melancholy disposition madness and insanity.

Only that black bile, therefore, which we have called natural, is conducive to judgment and wisdom. But not always! For if it comes alone, it is too black, darkening the spirit with a thick mass, scaring the soul, and thus blocking thought. If it is mixed with simple phlegm, which is cold blood that has compacted around the heart, it brings about a slowness with a kind of thick coldness, and a torpor. When this kind of melancholy makes you cold, it makes you extremely cold, because it is the nature of this stuff to be very dense. In this state, nothing is hoped for, everything frightens you, and you would hate to see even heaven itself. If the black bile, either simple or mixed, grows putrid, it brings on Fourth Day Fever, tumors of the spleen, and many things of this kind. Where it abounds too much, or if it comes alone, or if it is joined with phlegm, it makes the spirits thicker and colder, it afflicts the soul with continual weariness, it weakens the focus of the mind, and the blood does not flow easily around the heart.

It is best, however, for black bile not to be so small that blood, bile, and spirit touch each other as if out of control. That is when you get unstable thought and a slippery memory. Nor should there be so much black bile that we seem asleep, burdened with too much weight, and as if we needed a kick. So it is necessary for black bile to be simply the thinnest that its nature allows. For if it has been thinned greatly, according to its own nature, much of it will be free from noxious material, so that the bile will at least seem balanced.

Let black bile abound then, but very thinly. Let it not be lacking in a humor of thinner phlegm flowing around it, nor let it dry up further and come out very hard. It should not, however, be mixed altogether with phlegm, especially not colder phlegm, or more phlegm than bile, lest it turn cold. It should be a mixture of bile and blood so that one body is produced from the three, composed of an equal two parts to a double portion of blood. Where there are eight parts blood, and two parts bile, two portions again of black bile will occur. It will be inflamed a little by these two parts of black bile, and inflamed, it may shine, but they will not burn unless some material is harder (because kept too long), and then it burns and upsets you terribly.

When it becomes cold, black bile becomes cold to the depths. It is like iron, in that when it gets very cold, it will be cold to its core, though when, on the contrary, it inclines to heat, it will heat to its core.

It should not seem so surprising that black bile is so easily inflamed, and once inflamed, burns so terribly. If we imagine it to be like plaster, we see that when water is boiled out, it immediately burns up. Melancholy has a power just as extreme. It is stable when in a certain unity and of a fixed nature. This is the situation when extremity does not reach to the other humors. When greatly heated up, it moves to great boldness, even ferocity, and when it gets very cold, it moves to extremes of fear and cowardice.

There are middle stages between cold and heat, various stages of incompleteness, where it produces various effects, not unlike what happens with wine, especially with strong wine. Wine can make some drinkers drunk, or some just a little loosened up—wine has different effects on people.

It is good, therefore, to keep black bile in moderation. But even when it is moderated, and mixed with blood and bile, and its condition is as thin as its nature allows, its dry nature is easily inflamed because it is so solid and tough. Once inflamed, it burns a long time. Because it is very strong when combined with this tough dryness, it burns terribly. Like scrapwood, if you ignite it, it burns long, hot, and bright. From this long and terrible heat, a great blaze and a terrible and long-lasting commotion occur. Remember what Heraclitus said: Dry light = the wisest soul.

Chapter 6

By what arrangement black bile affects thinkers

Someone might ask, what is that body of humor like that you said was drawn together from these three humors? It is of such a color that we think we are looking at gold, but it tends sometimes to purple. When its natural heat is sufficient, and it causes a disturbance of either the body or the soul, it is nothing other than a burning, reddish, gold, with a mixture of purple when it heats and lights up. Just like a rainbow, it draws various colors from the heart being on fire.

Someone might also ask, by what arrangement does this humor lead to thought? Certainly the spirits are created from this humor, and the first of these are subtle, like that burning water they call Aqua Vita, or Aqua Vitis, 'Water of Life' or 'Water of the Vine,' which is pressed from the thicker part of the wine and distilled with fire. These spirits, compressed by the narrow passage of black bile, and much hotter because of their unity, are especially thinned out. Because they have been squeezed through such tight passages, they break out as more subtle. They are likewise hotter, and, for the same reason, clearer. Thirdly, they are spirits ready for action because of their extremely violent motion. Fourthly, since they flow out yoked to a humor that is solid and stable, they give a kind of long-lasting stability to our actions.

Our soul so strenuously, and with such obedience, tracks this passage, that it presses on in its studies for long periods of time. Whatever it shall have investigated, it finds easily, it sees clearly, it judges sincerely, and it retains its lessons. Add to this what we have said before, that with this instrument, or with this incite-ment—which agrees, as it were, with the center of the world, and which gathers the soul in its own center—the soul always seeks the center of all things, and penetrates to the core. It is in agreement with Mercury and with Saturn above, the latter being the highest of all the planets and the one which draws the student to the highest things.

Philosophers attest to this, especially since the soul, from such external movements, and separated from its own body, and so near the Gods, is made an instrument of the Gods. This is how, with divine influxes, and filled from on high with oracles, the soul al-ways ponders new and unaccustomed things, and even predicts the future. Not only do Democritus and Plato agree on this, but even Aristotle does, in his book of *Problems,* and Avicenna, in his books.

To what purpose, then, is all this stuff about the humor of black bile? It is so that we will remember this: we must seek and nourish as much black bile, even bright bile, as is best, and we must avoid as much black bile, as we have said, as works against itself. This is such a hard matter, this bile business, that Serapio has even said that its force is stirred up by an evil demon, and the wise Avicenna has not denied it.

Chapter 7

The five principal enemies of students: phlegm, black bile, coitus, over-eating, and sleeping late

We have digressed now a long way from our starting-point, where we were talking about how long the road is which leads to truth and wisdom. It is filled with heavy labors on land and sea. Whoever, therefore, goes on this journey, as some poet might say, will often be threatened on land and sea. For either he sails on a sea that is continually choppy with waves, tossed between Scylla and Charybdis, the two humors of phlegm and harmful melancholy, or he goes by land, and three monsters hurl themselves at him there.

The first monster is sent by Venus, the second by Bacchus and Ceres, and the third is sent nightly by Hecate. Apollo has to be summoned from the air, and Neptune from the sea, and Hercules from the land, to help. Apollo, with his spear, has to shoot these monsters that are so inimical to Minerva. Neptune has to rule over them with his trident. Hercules has to strike and wound them with his staff.

The first of these monsters is the coitus of Venus, for even if it is only a little excessive, it suddenly exhausts the spirits. It weakens the brain and attacks the stomach and the heart, troubles which could not possibly be more adverse to thought. After all, why did Hippocrates declare that coitus was like epilepsy? Because it overthrows the brain, which is sacred, and hurts it as much. As Avicenna, in his book, *On Animals,* has said: If someone should draw seed to flow in coitus beyond what is natural, it is more harmful than if he would bleed himself forty times, a harm, the ancients say, which neither the Muses nor the daughters of Minerva (virgins all) would want.

Plato has this to say on the subject: When Venus threatens the Muses if they do not worship at her rites, she threatens to arm her son against them. The Muses then reply: "Oh Venus, threaten Mars with such things—your little Cupid does not fly among us!"

For nature has put no sense more apart from the intellect than the sense of touch.

The second monster is over-consumption of wine and food. If there is either too much wine, or if it is too warm and strong, the head itself will fill up with bad humors and vapors. I will skip how drunkenness makes you unhealthy. But too much food takes away with its cooking all the force of nature, especially what is in the stomach. The stomach becomes as incapacitated, then, as the head. Thus, poorly prepared food, with its many thick vapors and humors, dulls the focus of the mind. This can happen even if food is prepared well. As Galen says, the soul that is suffocated with fat and blood cannot look upon something heavenly.

The third monster keeps you awake, after dinner and for much of the night, so that you want to sleep after sunrise. Because so many students fail in this, and are deceived by it, and because it is so harmful to thought, I want to go into this a little more. I suggest there are seven principal reasons for the problem. The first reason comes from heaven, the second from the elements, the third from the humors, the fourth from the order of things, the fifth from the nature of the stomach, the sixth from the spirits, and the seventh is drawn from fantasy.

To begin, there are three planets, which we have mentioned before, that are extremely favorable to contemplation and eloquence: the Sun, Venus, and Mercury. Moving together with equal steps, they leave us when night is coming on, and only when the day begins do they rise and revisit us. After the Sun's passage into the twelfth region of heaven, which is marked by astronomers as the darkness of a prison, they are suddenly gone. Thus, those people who study at night when these planets leave us, or who get up in the daytime after sunrise, when these planets are entering into the prison-house of darkness, lose out. On the other hand, those people who at sunrise are there seeking, rising to contemplate and to write when these planets also rise—only these people think with sharpness, only they can write and compose their work eloquently.

The second reason, as it were from the elements, is this: with the Sun rising, the air is moved, it is thinned and clear. When it sets, it is the opposite. The blood, however, and the spirit, flowing with the movement and quality of the air, follow it, driven by necessity, or, as it were, by nature.

The third reason, which is caused by the humors, is this: at dawn the blood is moved, and rules. Thinned by this motion, it heats up and clears. The spirits actually follow and imitate the blood. With night approaching, either melancholy, thicker and colder, or phlegm, dominates, and spirits that are without doubt the most inept for thinking return.

The fourth reason, which comes from the order of things, is this: the day is for waking, the night is for sleep. When the Sun approaches our hemisphere, or passes over it, he opens a passage of the body with his rays, and from the center to the circumference he dilates the humors and spirits, stirring us to action and waking us up. On the other hand, when he leaves, all things are narrowed, which in the natural order of things invites sleep, especially after the third or fourth part of the night. Whoever, therefore, sleeps late in the morning, when the Sun and the world is stirring him, will be awake for much of the night, when nature wants to sleep and to rest from her labors. He will be fighting against himself, and without doubt against the universal order of things when he is distracted and disturbed by these contrary motions. While he is being moved by the universe to outer things, he is moving himself to inner things. And the contrary: when he is drawn by the universe to inner things, he is trying to draw himself to outer things. Therefore, with perverse order and contrary motions, the whole body, and then the spirit and thought, collapse.

The fifth reason is in the nature of the stomach. The stomach, by a long-lasting action of the day's air, is dilated with its pores open, and with its spirits escaping, as it were, it is greatly weakened. Therefore, with night departing, it draws a new abundance of spirits, with which it is nourished. If someone at this time begins long and difficult contemplations, the stomach has to strive to draw these spirits back to the head. They are distracted, and can neither satisfy the stomach nor the head. It is especially harmful if, after dinner, working by lamplight, we spend much time and attention on our studies. For at that time much of the spirits are working on digesting our food, and the stomach is in need of much of its heat. These spirits are diverted to the head by late-night study, which is why they are not sufficient then for brain or stomach. In addition, the head, because of such movement, is filled with the thicker vapors of food, and the food that is in the stomach is abandoned by heat and spirit. It becomes hard and rots, whence it fills the head up again, and hurts it.

One must rise in the morning hours so that each part of the body might purge all the excrement that was retained in sleep. So it is the worst thing to do to break up what is cooking inside the stomach by burning the candle at nighttime study, and then, sleeping late in the morning, to force yourself to hold back for a long time the expulsion of this excrement. All the doctors agree that this is very harmful to thought and to the body. Those who use night for day, against nature, and conversely, those who use day for night, are really like owls—they unwittingly imitate owls—their eyes, as it were, in darkness under the Sun. The sharpness of their minds, under the splendor of truth, is therefore in darkness too.

The sixth reason, why sleeping late affects the spirits, is shown in the same way: the spirits, especially the most subtle kind, are broken down by daily fatigue. At night, therefore, only a few thick ones remain, but these are useless for the study of letters, so that their thought, supported by weak wings, is unable to fly— these people are like owls and bats! On the other hand, after sleep, the spirits are refreshed in the morning, and the limbs are so strengthened that they least need support from spirits. Many subtle spirits are then present which work for the brain, and which are able to do their duties expeditiously, busily nourishing and regulating the limbs.

Finally, the seventh reason, which is produced by the nature of fantasy. Fantasy, or imagination, or cogitation, or whatever other name it is called, also argues against staying up late: for in wakefulness it is distracted and disturbed by many long and contrary images, cogitations, and cares. This distraction and disturbance is very bad for someone who follows contemplation, or who seeks a tranquil and serene inner mind. Only with quiet nights is that agitation sedated and pacified. Night always comes on with the mind disturbed, but always departs with it calmed, so that we might bring a tranquil mind to our studies. Whoever tries to do such things with a mind too agitated, is like the man who suffers from vertigo and thinks everything is turning around (as Plato says), when it is he who is turning around.

See also Aristotle's *Economics,* where it says that it helps to get up before dawn. He says it brings health to the body and is very productive for the study of philosophy. But this must be so undertaken that, with a quick and modest meal, we avoid most diligently morning indigestion.

Remember, too, that the sacred high priest, David, the trumpet of almighty God, never spoke in the evening, but always in the morning, rising at dawn to sing God psalms on his lyre. We should all get up at this hour at least in our mind, and soon in our body, too, if it is at all possible.

Chapter 8

What is the most opportune hour for beginning studies, and how they should be continued

From what we have discussed in the previous pages, it is now sufficiently clear that we should begin our studies either immediately at sunrise, or even an hour or two—at the most—before sunrise. But before you get out of bed, first rub your whole body all over, gently, with your hands. Then rub your head with your nails—but even more lightly! This is what Hippocrates advises us to do. For with this friction, he says, if it is strong, you harden the body; if light, you soften it; if a lot, you diminish the body; if a little, you increase it.

When you have got out of bed, do not rush right in on your reading or meditation, but for at least half an hour go off and get cleaned up. Then diligently enter your meditation, which you should prolong for about an hour, depending on your strength. Then, put off a little whatever you are thinking about, and in the meantime comb your hair diligently and moderately with an ivory comb, drawing it forty times from the front to the neck. Then rub the neck with a rough cloth, returning only then back to meditating, for two hours or so, or at least for an hour of study.

Studies are never able to be done except with little intermissions, up to the noon hour. But then, in the afternoon, unless you pause for lunch, studies should be done with only a brief intermission, for around two hours at a clip.

The Sun is powerful around sunrise, but it is also powerful at mid-day. In that region of the sky which immediately follows the middle, which astronomers call the ninth part, the house of wisdom, the Sun rejoices the most. All the poets say Apollo is the leader of the Muses and the sciences, so these hours are very powerful if something lofty is to be contemplated. If the Muses are sought, they are sought in these same hours with Apollo as their leader. The remaining hours of the afternoon seem best suited for reading over old material rather than for thinking about new stuff.

We must always remember, however, at whatever the hour, that at least once we must stop whatever the mind is thinking. For the spirits break down because of such constant thinking, and if you never pause, you will be slow.

While you are working with the soul, keep the body quiet. Fatigue of the body is bad, fatigue of the soul is worse, but worst of all is fatigue of both, with opposite motions distracting a man and destroying his life. Let meditation walk no further than pleasure, and even a little behind.

Chapter 9

Rules for avoiding phlegm

It would seem to be our duty to go over briefly those things which we said were harmful to men of letters, and to discuss their remedies in each case. Therefore, lest phlegm increase too much, one should practice emptying the stomach twice a day—never, however, straining at it lest the sharp spirits be destroyed. Excrement must be diligently purged from all the passages. Wash thoroughly all the dirt from your body, especially the head. Then, using a moisturizer, wipe dry with deep rubbing.

Avoid too much cold food, and even moist food, lest black bile become a problem. Avoid anything fatty, poisonous, sticky, oily, or glutinous, or things which easily decompose. If the stomach is cold by nature, or because of age, you should put aside this kind of food altogether, or lighten it with a glass of water. It is necessary that eating be moderate, but even more moderate must be your drinking.

The room you live in should be high up, far from heavy mists and air, the humidity driven out of it either by fire or incense. Cold must be kept away from the head, and especially from the neck and the feet, for it is very harmful to thought. A small amount of aromatic spices is useful on colder dishes. Dishes spiced with nutmeg, cinnamon, saffron, and ginger, served on an empty stomach in the morning, are especially good for the senses and for memory.

Chapter 10

Why black bile must be avoided

Black bile, which we have been attacking throughout the above pages, is made worse by the following: a thick, turbid wine, especially black wine, hard food, dry food, salted food, bitter, sharp, or stale food, burned food, roasted or fried food, rabbit and beef, old cheese, pickled fish, beans, especially fava beans, lentils, cole slaw, cabbage, mustard, radishes, garlic, onions, leeks, blackberries, carrots, and whatever else warms you up or cools you off or tires you out. And everything black: anger, fear, misery, sorrow, haste, solitude, and whatever offends the sight, smell, or hearing, especially darkness. Above all, too much drying out of the body, either from too much lack of sleep, nervous fear or worry, or frequent coitus, or too many hot things, or dryness from either immoderate purging and urinating, or from laborious exercise, fasting, thirst, heat, or cold, dry air.

In fact, when black bile is always very dry and cold, you must absolutely resist even mildly warm things and instead take moist things, foods well-boiled, which cook easily, and which bring about thin and very clear blood.

But meanwhile, to take care of the stomach and phlegm, just as for black bile problems, foods should be spiced with cinnamon, saffron, and cornflower. The seeds of pumpkins and cucumbers, and pine nuts with the shells washed away, are helpful for this. Also good are the meat of birds, chickens and hens, and suckling quadruped, and especially eggs, as well as the limbs of animals, the brains, and sweet apples, fruits, melons, damascene plums and the like, gourds properly cooked, moist but not viscous greens. I least recommend cherries, figs, and grapes.

I hate nausea and the feeling of satiety. Nothing, however, is more powerful against such a feeling than a light wine, clear, smooth, fragrant—it is the best thing beyond all else for producing clear spirits. Plato and Aristotle both liked to soften this humor with a little wine, and to sweeten and clarify it, either with water drenched in lupine, or heated with a hot iron. But as useful as it is for the spirits and for thought, remember, abuse of it is just as harmful!

Furthermore, it helps to put gold into the drink, or silver, especially heated silver, and their leaves, and to drink from a small gold or silver vessel, and to eat food from one. It is also useful if often on an empty stomach you swallow the juice of licorice, also the juice of red sweet apples or sweet oranges.

Pleasant smells help considerably, especially mild ones. It is good for cold to rule over those people who are inclined to heat, or for heat to dominate those inclined to cold. One must therefore be moderate with roses, violets, myrtle, camphor, cornflowers, and rosewater, which are cold. And the opposite with cinnamon, lemon, orange, India spice, mint, honey, saffron, aloe, amber, and musk, which are warm. Spring flowers are helpful, and the leaves of lemon, orange, fragrant apples, but above all, wine. The smells of these are good for you and open up the nostrils and move the chest and stomach. We do not, however, recommend many warm smells, or dry ones, if they are the only ones, and if they are continuous. Hyacinth may be held in the mouth, which exhilarates the soul terrifically! Vervain, that is, the clear forest kind, is good for food and for fragrance. The herb called ox-tongue, and borage, and honey, are good with water. Lettuce, endive, eggs, and almond-milk, ought to be most familiar items on your table. Escape from any air, too, if it boils you, or if it is freezing or misty, but air that is moderate and serene should be freely enjoyed.

Mercurius, Pythagoras, and Plato claim that a dissonant soul, or a sad one, is helped by strumming a lyre and by constant singing and melodious playing. David, that holy poet, freed Saul from un-healthiness with his psaltery and psalms. I, too (if it is permitted the lowest to appose the highest things), have often found out at home how much the sweetness of the lyre and song avail against the bitterness of black bile.

I recommend the frequent sight of shining water, the sight of green or red colors, the use of gardens or woods, walks and rivers. Take strolls through beautiful meadows, go horse-back riding, trav-el in carriages, and go sailing. Above all, I recommend easy occu-pations, diverse employments that are not a bother, and the con-stant companionship of gracious men.

Chapter 11

Taking care of the stomach

Obviously, we must take great care of the stomach, lest satiety lead to nausea and indigestion, and offend the head. Food should be taken moderately twice a day, lightly flavored with cinnamon, mace, or nutmeg. Always, however, let dry food exceed in weight soft food, unless, of course, you are trying to avoid the dryness of black bile. If you can do it comfortably, let food wait until you are hungry. Let drink wait until you are thirsty. Let greed for either one be no part of your table. Keep loathing and fullness far away.

You must abstain from all those things which, on account of their excessive moistness, strong oiliness, or fatty material, weaken the stomach by loosening it. Even cold or very hot foods must be avoided, or those cooked badly because of their hardness. Long after you have left the table, such foods bring back an unpleasant taste to the palate, or inflate you, or fill the head with vapors. Avoid things which easily decompose in the stomach or outside it.

We in no way recommend sweet tastes or bitter ones if they are the only ones. Instead, we prefer the sweet to be tempered with the sharp, and the bitter with the dry. Mastic-gum, dry mint, fresh salvia, eggs, quince in sugar, chicory, rose, coral, capers, and vinegar, are the stomach's best friends. Try also red apples, their taste a blend of tart and sweet, and anything else that is moderately tart, even a little on the astringent side, which doctors call styptic, or things that are a little sharp, tangy, or aromatic. Balsam, however, beats everything.

Drink red wine rather than white, even a little bitter in taste, but lacking neither in warmth nor proper distilling. It will best be drunk with a little unmixed pure wine. Always, however, the more liquid foods should be consumed before the harder foods. After the food, it is good to eat coriander, quince, red apple, medlar, dry peaches and the like.

It is important to chew thoroughly before swallowing anything. If the stomach needs further help, use mastic-gum, rose, mint, or coral.

Be careful that for two or three hours after eating you do not take up difficult thought or serious reading. Perhaps even four hours of inactivity will be necessary if the food or drink were very rich, or the food very hard. It is bad to stretch the stomach with food or drink, but it is worse to think about difficult stuff with your stomach so stretched.

Nor should you sleep after the noon meal, unless pressed by the greatest necessity, and even then do not do it until you have been awake for two more hours. After the evening meal, however, one hour seems sufficient for staying up. Coitus is bad for the stomach, especially if you have just been stuffed, or if you are lying down hungry. The stomach dislikes haste but loves exercise, except when it is full of food. Immediately after you eat food, go take a little walk, and then sit down.

Chapter 12

Things which especially nourish the limbs and spirit

Our work must be done in such a way that we need nothing from a doctor's office for either the stomach, the heart, the brain, the spirits, thought, or strength; or anything to hold off attacks of phlegm, excrescences of black bile, or the threat of nausea.

All doctors agree, without objection, that nothing is better than theriaca for taking good care of each of the parts of the body and their powers, their spirits and thought. We should use at first half a dram of this remedy, or at least a third of a dram, twice a week, autumn and winter, but in summer and spring only once a week. If the weather is cold or humid, and you like to take it with a little clear wine, I approve. For warm and dry weather, especially if it only seems warmer because of your nature or age, take it with two or three twelfths of rosewater, on an empty stomach, six or seven hours before food. If you do not have any theriaca, use mithridatum. But when we take theriaca or mithridatum, we must abstain on that day from anything warm inside, and if it's spring or summer, cold stuff must be used.

As a substitute, all the doctors approve of aloe when correctly used, and lotus. Take two drams of chebulan balsam, one dram each of dark roses, red cornflower, emblic balsam, cinnamon, crocus-shell, fruit filaments, behen, and honey, and twelve drams of aloe carefully selected and washed. Make a pill out of these with some of your best wine, and take this at dawn once a week, in whatever size pleases you, of course. Take it in summer with rosewater, other times with wine.

On other days, however, when you take neither theriaca, nor these pills, use the following confection, morning and evening, two or three hours before food: take four drams of the best cinnamon, two drams of chebulan balsam, two drams of emblic balsam, half a dram of saffron and roses, two drams of red cornflower, one dram of coral, and as much of your whitest sugar-juice as is necessary. Pour the sugar-juice into equal portions of rosewater, citrus juice, or beet-juice, and cook until smooth. Then add a third of a dram of musk, and the same of amber. Finally, make solid bits, which are popularly called "morsels," and roll them in gold.

These three methods which we have described do the same thing, we have found. Each is a confection good for every part of the body, for its strengths and spirits. Each makes the senses and thought sharp, and memory strong. It is easy also with these pills to bring up or correct phlegm and bile, including black bile. Above all others, these three methods should be very familiar to you, whatever your age or nature.

Chapter 13

Remedies for restraining and for bringing up phlegm

If one is struggling bitterly against phlegm pouring out, we recommend a pill in the morning from the remedies of Galen, or one of those that Mesues called 'Elephanginas'—of course, only as much and as often as shall be appropriate. Even for those people whose condition is stronger we recommend that remedies and pills be mixed with an equal portion of hiera and agaric fungus, taken with honey rosewater, vinegar-honey, and fennel-water. This syrup is good for dissolving phlegm even before you take any pills at all, but especially good after you take them.

If, along with phlegm, other humors are churning up, we would purge appropriately with rhubarb pills (Mesues), or pills which later authors call the 'Without Which.' We dislike any sudden, violent purging and emission inside; for it weakens the stomach and the heart, exhausts many spirits, breaks up the humors, and darkens the spirits with fumes and the humors with furrows.

Chapter 14

A remedy for catarrh and runny noses, a common ailment of students

When the head is stuffed because of all this phlegm, we would recommend, at the hour of sleep, some of the following pills. We like, especially at this hour, but at other times too, to use incense, for it works wonderfully to help these flowings, all the senses, and memory, too. Back aways we advised nutmeg and theriaca to be taken orally. Maiorana, which they now call marjoram, is also good for the nostrils, when it is either mixed with water or moistened. After eating food, we urge you to take some coriander and quince-juice.

Chapter 15

Headaches

If the head hurts from being weighed down with a cold humor, we like, beyond all other remedies we have named, the one they call plirisarcoticon, or diamber, or diacora, taken orally. Chew mastic-gum often. Furthermore, rub the face, the temples, and the neck with a solution of marjoram, fennel, and oil from the leaves of rue, perfectly dissolved in rosewater.

Chapter 16

Remedies for foggy vision

When the eyes smoke up, although not reddening or offering any other sign of heat, make an eye-salve from fennel water, marjoram, swallow-wort, rue stuck with saffron, and antimonium. The water for this must be pressed through a thick cloth. Do not apply anything to your eyes until you have purged them with pills of Lux. But if, when they smoke up, the eyes redden, too, immediately purge them with pills composed of smoke-of-the-earth. Then an eye-salve made of rosewater and sugar is good. Sometimes it helps to add eggwhite or milk to this. At any rate, the daily use of fennel protects vision and sharpens it.

It often helps to take fennel seed in the mouth, even to eat the leaves. Triphera minor, which has been described by Mesues, is excellent. Good, too, is balsam taken daily on an empty stomach, and with this some bread from sugar and fennel that has been ground into a powder. This is also good for thought and for a productive life.

The use of euphrasia is a singular protection for the eyes. In all headaches or smokiness of the eyes, the vapors must be diverted back with rubbing or with an eye-cup. If heat is part of the cause, and it abounds in the blood, we would put leeches on the neck and shoulders.

Chapter 17

Restoring the sense of taste

Students of letters have stomachs that often lose all sense of taste. If it is phlegm that kills it, which is shown by an acid taste in the mouth, or a lot of very gluey saliva, do the following: after you have applied the medicines for the stomach that we have told you about above, use aromatic rosewater mixed with sugar, and honey with cinnamon, either alone or mixed with ginger, or mint syrup, but above all with theriaca. If, however, there is an abundance of bile, which is often shown by a bitter mouth, then after purging with aloe, just as we have said, do the following: take rhubarb, or triple cornflower, or vinegar sugar, composed of sugar, white vinegar, and sharp red apple wine, with peaches or pears mixed in or in a syrup, as Mesues advises. Or use our own special formula for this, which is very healthy for the taste: take four parts rosewater sugar, two parts blackberry juice, the same amount of sweet wine, two parts, a half part chebulan balsam, the same amount of emblic balsam, and a half dram each of red palm and red coral. Pour it all into citrus juice or lemon juice, either two or three parts. If the stomach is weak and cold, add two drams of cinnamon. These must be taken two hours before eating.

Sweet wine always removes nausea from each humor, and capers with vinegar can be used for this, too. On an empty stomach, a drink of white vinegar and rosewater is good for nausea, if two portions of sugar are mixed with it. Use mint and absinthe, too. Also, mint either mixed with vinegar, or diluted in an acidy red apple juice, and watered down.

Chapter 18

The most careful remedy for black bile

Now really we have been dealing with lighter matters, so let us return again to something which is most dangerous, that is, black bile. When it abounds and rages, it weakens the whole body, especially the spirit, which is the instrument of thought, and thought itself, and judgment. Let the first rule for curing it, as Galen taught, be this: do not strain to bring forth black bile suddenly, lest part of it turn more liquid and thin, and the remainder stay very thick and dry. Little by little, let it be softened, broken into pieces, and brought forth.

Second, while your head and your whole body is being kept moist for strength with foods that are moist, and with baths that are sweet and moderate, and even with fingernail rubdowns, remember this caution: do not let catarrh irritate you, or let the stomach be destroyed, or the liver, or the passages of the body be blocked.

The third thing is this, and it is especially necessary so that the head gets taken care of and strengthened with the right things: some things must be taken inside the chest and nostrils, and some things must be taken outside. Those things which are pleasant should be seriously looked at, listened to, smelled, and contemplated. Those things which are not pleasant should be kept far away.

Chapter 19

Best method for making a syrup for melancholiacs

Many people have created many things for this humor. I will now offer three kinds of remedies from the many possibilities that exist, the three best and safest of all, used first by the ancients, then proven by more contemporary people, and now adapted by us for our own use. First, the composition of the best syrup; second, the most recommended pills; third, the safest medicines that melt in the mouth. If you correctly stick to these remedies, your melancholy humor will be softened, broken down into pieces, and dissolved. Your spirits will be sharpened and made bright, your thought will be nourished, and your memory strengthened.

Here is the syrup: take borage, ox-tongue, the flowers of each, honey, some Hair-of-Venus, endive, violets, oak-berry, oak fern, thyme, a handful of each, twenty damascene plums, ten fragrant fruits, one part passula, one half part licorice, cinnamon, red cornflower, citrus pulp, three drams of each, and a half dram of saffron. Cook everything in water, except the thyme and aromatic herbs, until a third is boiled down. Then cook in sugar and thyme, and have the concoction pressed through a sieve. Finally, the aromatic stuff, like cinnamon and saffron, is poured in. Three parts of this syrup are to be drunk at dawn, at the same time taking two or three parts of ox-tongue water, and at least two or more of the following pills, as fits each person. One must make a pact, as it were, to move the stomach a little each day.

Chapter 20

Pills for softening bad humors, and for purging them

As for pills, there are two types, one for delicate people, and one for stronger people. The first can be called golden or magic, made in part by imitation of the maguses, in part by our own invention, composed under the influence of Jove or Venus. These pills will remove your troubles with phlegm, bile, and black bile.

They strengthen each limb, sharpening and brightening the spirits. They dilate such spirits, because when constricted they produce sadness, but when dilated and in light they rejoice. They stabilize such spirits, too, because too much extension makes them vanish.

Take, therefore, twelve grains of gold, especially gold leaf, if it is pure, incense, myrrh, saffron, aloe wood, cinnamon, citrus pulp, honey, pure red silk, mint, white behen, red behen, a half dram of each, red roses, red cornflower, red coral, all three balsams (emblic, chebulan, Indian), one dram of each, the same of well-washed aloe, all of this coming to about a pound. Make the pills with the best wine you have.

The following pills are a little stronger for dissolving melancholy, although still the least violent: take peonies, myrrh, Arabic vine, honey, incense, saffron, all three of the balsams, one dram of each, fungus balls, oak fern, thyme, senna, well-prepared lapis lazuli, Armenian lapis made in the same way, three drams of each, two parts aloe, and mix the pills with a perfect wine. The heats in this formula are cold, so if heats appear to dominate with the melancholy, a third more must be added to the formula.

These pills, which are useful for students of letters, I have made up following Greek, Latin, and Arabic. I did not want to mix in anything stronger than these, like hellebore, which was used by that fanatic, Carneades. For men of letters, or for those even a little stronger, nothing is worse than violence, so I would advise such people to ignore all India pills, lapis lazuli, or Armenian lapis, and what they call leraglodion.

If you want a simpler formula, such as the one I use with my familiars: take one part aloe, emblic and chebulan balsam, two drams each, two drams of mastic-gum, two also of rose, especially red rose, and make the pills with wine.

With all these pills which I have recommended, either the former or the latter kind, remember: no one should ever use the sun with these or he will dry out too much, which is the worst thing in melancholy. On the contrary, in that case take the syrup, which we have given above following Mesues and Gentile da Foligno. Or take the formula with one part of light and fragrant wine, or two parts, or three parts, whatever you think you need. Or take it with a water of honey, passula, and licorice. Or if heat then dominates, take it with violet-wine and rosewater.

At any rate, I advise men of letters, who are prone to black bile, to use this purge at least twice a year, say spring and autumn, for fifteen continuous days, or twenty, using pills and the syrup. Anyone who is a little less prone to this sickness will find it enough if he just takes the first pills or the last pills of the year once a week, using violet-wine, as we have said, in summer, and regular wine the rest of the time.

Chapter 21

Remedies using liquid medicines

It is important to remember that in cases where there is great danger threatening from drying oneself out, but it is nonetheless necessary to purge, one must discontinue the pills and use instead the syrup, or a similar concoction made of ox-tongue water. Pour into it, meanwhile, some diasenna, or diacatholicon, or one part Persian triphera, or at least a half part. But if your body is stronger, or tighter, and your stomach gets constipated, add one or two drams of melt-in-the-mouth hamech. Also useful for this is a confection of wild cinnamon. Vegetable-juice is even more useful.

These do not work for every type of melancholy, but they are especially good for the kind that is created by burning. If, however, your melancholy is just natural, some of these are still good for it, especially if a double portion of oak-fern is added to the syrup, or a triple portion, and likewise licorice, saffron, and passula. The same if you add two parts honey-rosewater to the medicine. The syrup should be taken as often as we prescribed above. But the medicine must be used with this three times in twenty days.

If no melancholy humor appears, but there is a melancholy complexion, like a cold and dry quality of the limbs, forget about the stomach and abandon any blood-letting, and only do the other things which we said, or which we will say, especially those things which pertain to moderately heating the body and greatly moistening it. Do those things which pertain to the spirits, as much as possible brightening them and nourishing each part.

Where the black bile humor overflows, we would not dampen the body so much, we would not dampen this humor, but we would break up the stomach, with our usual caution, never to do it violently. As Plato in the *Timaeus* warns us, a long disease like melancholy must not be irritated by medicines that are too strong and by drugs that are harmful.

Chapter 22

Rules for letting blood

Some people are very eager to let blood, but they are detested by wise doctors. For blood is the measure of black bile, the kindling of spirit, the treasure of life. Only where blood seems to be in abundance, or where there is profuse laughter, boldness, and much confidence, or a red color and a swelling of the veins, should you let the blood of men of letters.

When it must be done, then from the veins on the left arm, with a wide incision, take four parts in the morning and evening. Then, after a few days—at least seven but at the very most fourteen—let out three or four more parts of blood. Irritate the hemorrhoids first with a hard rubbing, then apply leeches, which they call Bloodsuckers. Both of these procedures can be used on stronger types. For weaker types, if necessity demands it, just irritate the hemorrhoids, as we have said.

But do not purge the belly with medicines, nor let blood, unless you have first lightened it with big, soft syringes. Let this be a general rule for the melancholy nature when work is to be done on it, that, if it is appropriate, the lower stomach must always be lubricated and purged with frequent enemas of this kind.

Chapter 23

On melt-in-the-mouths and confections

The following are melt-in-the-mouths. I recommend the ones that Rhasis called 'exhilarating,' and those which Avicenna presented in his book on the powers of the heart. But even more, I recommend the one Mesues prescribed: take raw purple silk, fresh-smelling, one pound's worth, mix it with the juice of sweet and pleasantly smelling fruits, and mix this with the juice of ox-tongue and rosewater, one pound of each. After twenty-four hours, cook it all up smoothly, until the water reddens. Then extract the silk and squeeze it diligently. Pour in immediately a hundred and fifty drams of your whitest sugar, and cook it again, until it thickens like honey. Remove it from the fire, and while it is still warm, pour in six drams of carefully cut up raw amber, and let the amber turn to liquid. Finally, add this powder: take raw aloe wood and cinnamon, six even drams of each, thirteen drams of lapis lazuli, properly washed, some unio-pearl, that is, white margarita, two drams, one dram of true gold, and a half dram of select musk. Take one or two drams of this with wine, morning and evening, three or four hours before food. This is my favorite above all others.

But I also recommend the sweet diamusk of Mesues, and the composition of gems, taken with rosewater. I would also recommend what was so astonishingly put together by that great philosopher, Pietro d'Abano, except that he himself became frightened from the immoderate use of it and from an excessive dilation and exhilaration of the spirits. That is why I think the two formulas given above are the safest, and each person's measure of them should be made according to the time, the age, and the nature of the person, as to how sweetly each formula should be mixed. These are nourishing and strengthening.

Furthermore, if you want something good for firming up the spirit and thought, as well as for sharpening and brightening them: take in a sugar two parts cooked ox-tongue, with the flowers, one part the pulp of citrus fruit mixed with sugar, two parts chebulan balsam, one dram of your best cinnamon, cornflower, red coral, cut-up raw purple silk, saffron, pearl, a half dram of each, gold, silver, a third part of a dram of each, amber, musk, two grains of each. Pour it all into a citrus juice, or lemon, cooked with sugar.

The following is another formula, perhaps even healthier, certainly more pleasing: take four parts sweet almonds, pine nuts (of course washed for a whole day), cucumber seeds, four parts, hard sugar, called Candum, that is to say, white sugar, four parts, and another sugar, your whitest kind, one pound and a half. Pour all this into rosewater, with lemon and citrus, in which you have extinguished burning gold and silver, and cook it up smoothly. Finally, add cinnamon, red behen, red cornflower, and coral, one part of each, the most shining pearls, saffron, raw silk (purple) minutely rubbed, a half dram of each, gold, silver, twelve grains of each, hyacinth, emerald, sapphire, carbuncle, a third part of a dram of each. If you do not have any gold, silver, amber, musk, or precious stones, these formulas still do a lot of good without them.

The three I have selected are the best. I took one from Mesues, and two are my own. For most people who will be using them, the above should be sufficient.

But if someone wants something simpler, appropriate for everyone: take a perfectly ripe citrus fruit, cut the whole thing up, cook it with a lot of sugar and a lot of rose-juice, mix in a little cinnamon and some saffron, or aromatic rosewater, sugar rosewater, ox-tongue rosewater, two parts of each, and mix it with diamusk. Even if these two are not all that simple, they will nevertheless be had easily enough. And if you are afraid of heat, add plums and violet-sugar.

Chapter 24

A remedy for wasteful sleeplessness

It often happens to melancholiacs, especially to those who are men of letters, that their brains become dried out, and they become weak from long nights of sleeplessness. Because there is nothing

that increases black bile trouble more than prolonged sleeplessness, one must take great pains to find help for this problem. These
people should eat lettuce after some of their meals, together with a
little bread and a little saffron. They should drink pure wine after
the lettuce, and they should not stay up working beyond that hour.
When they go to bed, they should take this formula: take two parts
white poppy-seed, one part lettuce seed, balsam, and saffron, a half
dram of each, and six parts sugar. Dissolve and cook it all in
poppy-juice. Eat two drams of this stuff, and at the same time drink
some poppy-juice or wine.

   You can also smear on your face and temples an oil of violets,
and if you do not have any, use camphor; the same with milk and
oil of almond, and violet water. Move the nostrils with the fragrance of saffron and camphor, and with clippings from sweet fruit
trees. Go very easy on vinegar, but use a lot of rosewater.

   Smooth your bed with the leaves of cool plants. Delight your
ears with pleasant songs and sounds. You can dampen your head a
lot with a little bath in some water in which perhaps you have
cooked the fruits of poppies, lettuce, purslain, mallows, roses,
vines, willow, and the leaves of reeds, adding camomile. Having
sweetened your bathwater with all these things, get your whole
body wet with it, including arms and legs.

   Furthermore, it is especially good to drink milk mixed with
sugar, on an empty stomach, of course, if the stomach will tolerate
it. This dampening business works wonderfully for melancholiacs,
even for those who get enough sleep. Remember that almond milk
should be very familiar to your table.

Chapter 25

Remedy for a dull memory and forgetfulness

It sometimes happens that students, either because they read and
write with their heads so seriously bent, or because they become
stiff too quickly, get a thick and cold phlegm, and melancholy
seizes them and weighs down their heads, making them dull and

forgetful. Their heads must be freed from this burden with the following remedies, in addition to the other good things for phlegm that we have described elsewhere. If they did not suffice, take recourse in Indian and cocchea pills, and hieralogodion. Diacoloquin is very good, or Archigenes, or Andromache, or Theodotion, or the pills of Judea which Mesues describes in his chapter on headaches.

If your condition or age is colder, and heat does not present a problem, after purging use the formula called anacardina, which Mesues goes over in the chapter on Forgetfulness, following the opinion of his son, Zachary. Give, at most, one dram in the morning, but let whoever takes it abstain until the next day from anger, coitus, drunkenness, labor, or anything warm. These are very strong against dullness and forgetfulness.

But if you prefer more familiar things, take a compound of ginger mixed with a little incense, which is great for the senses and for memory, especially when you add some of these: sweet anacardum, sweet chebulam, vinegar, caper, amber, and musk. Even diamber is good, as well as sarcoticon, and diacora: but these must be kept in the mouth a long time, and even poured into the nostrils and the ears. The odor of incense, marjoram, fennel, nutmeg, rue, and India spice are good, too. Remember, however, that theriaca must never be postponed or neglected for any of these remedies that we have been prescribing.

Finally, for dullness and forgetfulness, smear the following unguent on the temples and neck: take one part oil of elderberry, two parts oil of behen, a half part euphorbia, the same amount of castor, and rub the arms, legs, and neck strenuously. If a cupping-glass is effective, apply that to the neck. Afterwards, you will have to cover the top of your head with marjoram, incense, and nutmeg, and thus warm it and comfort it.

Chapter 26

We should be guardians of our spirits

Men who seek truth ought to take care of their bodily spirits with as much diligence as doctors, for neglecting these spirits creates impediments to the search for truth, and one's service in the cause of truth then becomes inept. Yet they must even more diligently take care of their non-bodily spirit, that is, the intellect itself, founded on moral discipline, where alone that truth which is incorporeal is grasped. It is not all right just to take care of the body, which is only the servant of the soul, and neglect the soul, which is the king and master of the body.

There is a saying of the maguses, and of Plato, that the entire body so hangs from the soul that unless the soul is well the body cannot be well. This is why the founder of medicine, Apollo, decided that Socrates was the wisest of men and not Hippocrates, though Hippocrates was born from Apollo's own lineage. As much as Hippocrates studied the health of the body, Socrates studied the health of the soul, although what both of these men tried to do only Christ brought about.

Let us try to take care of our mind with the excellent habits taught by Socrates, so that we might more easily and with a serene mind pursue the light and truth sought by our natural instinct.

And how much more appropriate, even, must it be for us to venerate that divine truth that is in holy religion? The mind has not been created for anything else but for the seeking and grasping of this, that our eyes might look at the light of the sun.

As our dear Plato says, no sight is ever visible at all unless something from on high is visible in it, that is, some splendor of the sun itself. The human intellect never apprehends anything intelligible unless there is something intelligible in it from on high, the light of God always and forever present for us. A light, I say, which illumines every man who comes into this world. A light which David sings of: In your light we shall see light.

When someone purges his eyes and looks at that light, he suddenly finds its splendor pouring in, shining grandly with the colors and figures of things. It is the same when through moral discipline the mind is first purged from all the disturbances of the body, and directed by a religious and most ardent love to divine truth, that is, to God himself. Suddenly, as the divine Plato says, a divine truth flows into the mind, and happily explains true reasons, which are contained in it, and in which all things exist. It surrounds the mind with as much light as the joy that it pours so happily into the will.

The End of Book I

How To Prolong Your Life

The Second Book by Marsilio Ficino, Florentine,
Beginning With A Letter To Filippo Valori

A lthough our dear Plato lives in his Genius and will live, in my opinion, as long as the world itself lives, my own Genius always forces me nonetheless to look at the life of Plato before all else, after divine worship. To this purpose now, for a long time, the House of Medici has helped us more than anyone. And you help too, in the same project, my Valori, great friend of the Medici and scholar of the Platonic glory and discipline.

How I wish always that there be life for Plato. How I wish there be life for the Medici, and for Valori, too. That is why I urge you, and beg you, my Valori, that just as hard as you always concentrate on the works of Platonic glory, you might read and heed with the same diligence these rules of mine on how to live a long life. Doing this, and living a long time, you and the magnanimous Lorenzo Medici will be able to show your favor even longer toward the Platonic discipline as it is now rising afresh.

BOOK TWO

How To Prolong Your Life
by Marsilio Ficino, Florentine,
Distinguished Doctor and Philosopher

Chapter 1

*For the perfecting of our knowledge, a long life is necessary: the
care that must be taken*

For the perfecting of our art and knowledge, it is not so much a
docility of thought or a firmness of memory as it is insight from
prudent judgment that leads us on. But because it rests on ambiguous and differing conjectures, judgment is difficult and to confirm
it one has to experiment. But experiment, too, is deceptive on
account of the difficulty involved in judgment itself, and on account of the fleeting brevity of time for suitable experiments. For
these reasons we conclude that Hippocrates was right in saying that
art is long and that we are unable to pursue it unless we have a
long life.

Long life is not only a matter of what the Fates have put in
store for us from the beginning, but something our diligence takes
care of as well. The astrologers admit this, too, when they talk
about Selections and Images, and it is confirmed by the diligent
care of doctors and by experience itself.

By taking precautions, not only do men who are strong by
nature often attain a long life, but even those who are sick do so. It
is no surprise that a certain Herodicus, one of the sickest of all the
men of letters of his time, as Plato and Aristotle tell us, lived
almost a hundred years because he took precautions! Plutarch tells
us, too, of many other cases where the body was weak but long life
was attained through diligence alone.

I will pass over for the present how many weak people I
myself have known, who by the gift of prudence lived years longer
than people much stronger than they.

It would not be useless, then, nor vain, after the book I wrote on *Taking Care of the Health of Students,* to offer some further rules that would lead to a long life for those who love thought and knowledge.

But I really do not want to communicate these ideas to dullards who say they are "on journeys," or to those who are simply lazy. For why should I care if such people live a long time, when they do not really *live* at all? As if I should feed drones, instead of worker bees! And I do not care to divulge my ideas to those men who have become wrecks through the destructive indulgence of pleasures, who stupidly prefer some daily little pleasure to a long life. Nor do I care to explain my stuff to the immoral and the evil people out there, whose life is the death of every good thing. I write instead for men who are prudent and temperate, for men of intelligence who are useful either privately or publicly to the human race.

Chapter 2

Our vital heat is nourished by a humor, excess of which becomes corruption and dissolution

Life is like a light in that it consists of natural heat. The nourishment of this heat is an airy humor, fat and almost an oil. If by chance, therefore, this humor should be deficient, or flow backward, or be polluted, the natural heat is immediately weakened, and then extinguished. If its heat is weakened by a defect in the humor, and is lost, this weakness makes death approach. If, on the other hand, life is overwhelmed by an excess of this humor, or by a defect, life perishes through suffocation. The suffocation of this humor comes through an overflow or through putrefaction, especially by an excrescence or putrefaction of phlegm, so that it is no misnomer to say of phlegm that it covets your life. Rules are necessary, then, for prolonging life, and for avoiding this weakening, this suffocation and putrefaction.

In my opinion, the humors work evenly. For if humors and subtle spirits can cure a warmer, or dryer man, and one whose passages have been opened, they attack weakness even more. If, however, for the opposite reason, they treat an affected body, they help relieve the suffocation. In either case they are very zealous, if there is decline in one place or at one time.

But when one is offering advice to thinkers and students, each rule is equally necessary, and each must likewise be observed, because those people who are warm and sharp thinkers, and for whom the movement of the imagination is strong, seem to be threatened by weakness, weariness of the body, indigestion, and suffocation. Never do doctors work more strenuously, therefore, than when they work on caring for such men.

Although the whole argument of the previous book was concerned with prolonging life too, nonetheless there would seem to be need now for a particular study of such problems as these, a cure, in other words, that I will try, briefly, to explain, as far as I am able.

Chapter 3

How heat and humor are moderated, and the advice of Minerva

When we talk about that fatty oil which is so necessary for a fiery vigor, Minerva, the inventor of this vital oil, and of the olive, laughs at us—as if she were being born from the head of Jove—because while we look at the quantity of her gift, this oil, we do not see its quality. Laughing then, she says, "To you I have given abundantly of this oil, not only enough to keep your flame burning, but I have even filled your lamp with it, without a drop of the dregs."

This is what she says. But we offend her because we no longer hear her words or value the lamp. We must become acquainted with this lamp, then, and make its oil continually furnish flame, that is, make ourselves diligent so that we do not suddenly put the lamp out with an overflow, or scatter its fluid. But these two things I think we have touched on enough in the preceding pages.

There are still two other matters for us, on one of which we seem to have lightly touched already, but on the other hardly at all. They both concern Minerva, who never used to laugh, but who has laughed at us. Why?

First, we should realize that the flame, though small, has a great appetite, and the lamp would burn longer if we adjusted the wick on the flame so that it does not gulp the oil, but only sips it. In every diet, therefore, we must take care lest, especially in youth, we become too weak from having the fire inside devoured by its own nature. It would be enough if we restrain the humor from inundation and ward off the penetrating cold. We should realize that a lamp is quickly extinguished when it does not burn on quality oil, but, so to speak, on the dregs. For shortly after fungi start growing on the dregs, they put the light out.

So let us receive this nourishing oil from Minerva, an oil that is very airy, pure, and tough, with a native strength and firmness. What we get from taking a little of it is that not only are we made equal to it, but made like it. To be like it does not mean that we become airy and fat, but free from dregs inside, that is, from the, junk congested out of earth and murky water. If this congestion and junk are to be avoided, we must flee from foods of this kind, and from lethargy, indigestion, and filth.

In the meantime, let us worship Minerva with such moderation that she will improve our heads—she was herself born from one—and not threaten our nerves and stomach.

Chapter 4

The causes of the drying out of the natural humor, and of a strange abundance. And how necessary it is for life to make your digestion perfect

These dry out the natural humor quickly: a richer flow of blood, a violent breaking up of the stomach, lubrication of the stomach for long periods of time, profuse sweating, a wide opening of the body passages, coitus done to the point of weakness, a panting thirst, a tortured hunger, excessive sleeplessness, the use of hot things, the use of dry things, a laborious movement of either the soul or the body, anxiety, anger, sorrow, very dry and very burning air, especially heat from a fire, a very dry, violent, or prolonged wind. The opposite of all these increases the humor.

Drunkenness frequently does both. For, when drunk, we dry out the humor with too much warmth, and then we suffocate it.

Nothing, however, is more harmful than indigestion. When food is not digested, the humor does not get irrigated, and then the rotting food remains, and overflows, burying the natural heat. This is why Avicenna said that the blood gets spoiled when digestion itself gets spoiled and, following Galen, why he called digestion the root of life. It is a good idea, then, to keep in mind this almost singular rule of Galen's: take care of digestion before anything else. The greatest rule of all, for health anyway, would seem to be this, that food does no good unless you digest it.

From the causes I have listed, just as from their opposites, you can see that a very harmful humor is flowing when undigested stuff flows into the limbs. Foods that are less fancy are less trouble, at least if they are well digested. We must therefore diligently avoid such a serious thing as indigestion, which is the cause of laxness and of suffocation, by taking only the quantity of food and drink that is appropriate for us. The same goes for the quality of our food: simple preparation, chewing it well, fasting, restraining hunger. If it should be necessary, it helps even to have an exterior application to the stomach, and to take certain kinds of internal styptics after dinner.

Let us be very cautious that drink does not exceed food, nor that food be very liquid or very hard, nor that either be too cold, nor that there be too many different kinds of food, nor that we pile one raw food on top of another. These are all terrible for digestion.

Let us be most cautious of all that we do not have coitus immediately after eating, or too often take an unnecessary post-luncheon nap, or stay up all night, or take on any kind of wrong labor of the soul or of the body, or do anything else that would impede digestion.

What I call digestion is not only the first stage, which is in the stomach, but the second too, which is in the liver, and the third, which is in the veins, and finally the fourth, which is done in the limbs. When there is a long interval in which they are empty, or impeded, food is not supplied to the humor.

Just as digestion is necessary for life, so also is the purging of excrements. It is necessary even to cleanse dirt from the skin. The motion of the body must be as continuous, as moderate, and as various, as if it were the motion of the heavenly bodies themselves, and of air, fire, and water, all in the service of digestion and the need for sleep.

Avoid fatigue and avoid laxness. Let us get ourselves out from the shadow of dullness and decay. Let us live under the open sky, under the light. That is something that my father, the distinguished Doctor Ficino, always used to say. To do this, happily, he had to get away from urban business and at a very early age get his body accustomed to various rustic exercises and the like. Meanwhile, he maintained that just as with food, it was necessary to make life varied, too. That is what that prudent man always used to tell me. After all, those who at every age live with splendid curiosity often live less safely. Those who did little as adolescents to accustom themselves to their bodies at least can do it now as adults, trying it little by little and cautiously.

Chapter 5

The blood and humor appropriate to life ought to be airy,
moderate in quality, medium in substance, and tough

All the Greeks say in their rules for a long life that it is necessary that we nourish ourselves with euchymes. Euchymes are what they call health food, which brings good nourishment, that is to say, good blood. By good blood we mean blood that is not cold, dry, or turbulent, but warm, moist, and clear. Warm does not mean sharp heat. Moist does not mean the humor is watery. Clear does not mean extremely thin. For a very burning blood first sharpens the natural heat, then dries out the humor, and the heat it brings to the humor dissolves and scatters it. A very moist blood, one very much like water, destroys the natural heat and the natural humor, or weakens it, or forces it to liquefy under the heat, or smothers the heat with humidity.

All told, if some portion of the natural humor is drawn from watery blood, it easily putrefies, then flows out quickly and dissolves. This happens because those who eat softer fruits and vegetables (unless this is unusual for them, or they are taking them as medicine to soften the stomach) fill up their veins with a lot of raw juice with its harmful putrefaction inside. To prevent this from happening, it is safer to take food that either gets digested or at least is mixed with bread.

Let the blood, therefore, be neither fiery nor watery, but airy. Do not let it be like a thick kind of air, nor let it be inclined to water. Nor should it be like the thinnest kind of air or it will easily turn combust, but make of it a medium substance in which a middle sort of air holds most dominance.

Let other elements be present which are appropriate to the rule of air. Do not let its substance be extremely thin, lest it generate an unstable humor, and a volatile spirit, and be prone to dissolution. Do not let it be extremely thick, or it will be of least service to thought, and will barely be able to change itself into the natural humor and spirit, obstructing the passages and giving cause for suffocation.

The spirit which is thus created is not very thick in its density, and is itself little fitted for life. It suffocates the natural heat as if it were a thick smoke overpowering a flame and extinguishing it. (I will pass over the fact that it is so dark it makes one sad, and makes life worse.)

It seems to me helpful for a long life, then, if the blood and its substance are airy, not thick; if they contain some glutinous and tough humor; if their thinness is almost like olive oil; and if the humor is fat and thin at the same time, like an eel, and its oil drawn like turpentine. So choose your foods carefully, and everything else which makes this kind of blood and humor. For such blood and humor is like the oil to a flame, a food for its vital heat, having both subtlety and firmness.

Rhasis had a rule for preserving youth, that things should be eaten that draw blood to the breast and nourish the heart itself. Avicenna agreed, saying we should studiously avoid a watery and slippery blood.

A difference in individual bodies, however, must be noted. Where the body is very thick, one must use every remedy to make the blood thinner, for it is very seldom at its right thickness. Where the body is of medium size, it is likewise safest to go the middle route. We must never try to uproot the natural condition of the body, lest we uproot life itself.

With the above it is good to remember: where we fear a thinness of the blood and a stomach that is not strong by nature, we must proceed only with very tiny steps to a thicker blood. We must try to nourish a delicate man with thicker foods, nourishing his stomach, and seeing to his sleep. Exercise must be increased for the powers of his body, lessened for his spirit, which it often harms.

But if one consumes excessively oily, hard, or cold foods, at least use coral, cornflower, roses, coriander, balsam, quince, and quince juice, rose sugar and other styptics to make the blood and the humor strong. Also excellent for people who cannot digest the oily limbs of the larger animals is a juice made from the pistachio nut and the licorice root, with sweet almonds added, and the oil of these, and quince-seed, sesame oil, with a very white sugar, and rosewater. There are, also, the entrails and testicles of roosters, goats, tortoises, and snails.

We would not take white wine but red, making sure it was styptic and bitterish, and tempering it with iron-water or mastic-gum. We would soothe the skin with an oil of mastic and quince, and avoid in the meantime anything that would make the blood thin or boiling, unless, perhaps, we added some saffron or cinnamon to tougher foods so that they would be more easily digested and carried through the narrow body passages to the limbs already digested. For it is difficult with weak stomachs to get viscous foods, or harder foods, into the third and fourth digestion, unless they are helped there by these other items, and provoked by the soothing massage I just described. When you do this, by the way, make your hands soft, remembering to wet them with a little sweet-smelling wine in which you have cooked camomile, myrrh, and roses.

Chapter 6

A rule for ordinary eating and drinking and the quality of food

But let us put aside for now our concern for the most obtuse or the thinnest of bodies, and take up instead the ordinary business of living for people with ordinary or medium physical condition.

Beware lest for any reason the body passages be opened or obstructed as above described. For then there will be injury and weakness, and danger of putrefaction or suffocation.

Even though I am not for the strictest observance of the following rule—something Hippocrates, too, condemned—I would nonetheless urge you not to relax your hold on the reins to the point of licentiousness. Take sparingly vegetables and the wetter fruits, even more sparingly of milk and fish, and anything with honey. Be most sparing of all with mushrooms, taken with aromatics or with pear seeds. Likewise, a pure drink of water: take sparingly.

Wetter foods, or fatter foods, mix with aromatics and bitters. Otherwise, a lot of foreign and putrid humor will be carried to the limbs, and even if these are necessary to help the natural humor, remember that they are prone to rot. It is just like a watery wine, quickly clouded and easily soured. This leads to paleness, early graying, and senile wrinkles.

If you eat meat every day, even if with an equal amount of bread, it leads to quick putrefaction. Thus Porphyry, on the authority of the ancient Pythagoreans, detested all food from animals. Did not men live long lives before the Flood because they did not eat animals? Still, doctors do not forbid the use of meat, only the abuse of it.

Flee from the harm caused by moist putrefaction, damp and fat foods that make the memory old quickly. That is what Hippocrates says, and the matter speaks for itself.

46

Again, take the dryest foods only moderately, or at least loosen them up with a drink. It is safe to take a middle route here. Nevertheless, Avicenna preferred the dryer kind of food to the soft, to avoid aging.

Be extremely wary of food that is too cold or too hot. Go for warm and moist. If the air is sweltering, spare your humor hot food; if freezing, give your humor some heat. Be moderate in any case. Let heat and humor contain something glutinous and styptic, so that the humor, having irrigated the limbs, might stick to them more strongly and last longer under heat.

Eat wheat: bread is a good source of it. Also, red styptic wine, and wine slightly sweet. In third place we would put pine nuts, and things like them in heat-value and toughness. In fourth, meats that are not as moist or loose as suckling pigs and sheep. Nonetheless, the ancient doctors, like Galen, strongly recommend the meat and blood of pigs, on account of a certain similarity to our own bodies. Pork is best, therefore, for rustic and robust bodies—bodies given much exercise—especially if it is boiled for four days with Indian spice, a coriander preparation, and a little salt. Pig's blood is perhaps useful if cooked with sugar and stirred until it all becomes liquid.

But to return to our ranking of these: moist meats are not recommended, as we said, nor hard and dry ones like old rabbit and beef, but a middle kind of meat—like rooster, hen, capon, peacock, pheasant, partridge, perhaps even doves, especially the domestic kind. Also good are goats, young calves, yearling sheep, and even boar. I would not ignore suckling kids, or fresh goat cheese. But I would pass over small birds, for the frequent use of subtle foods only makes the stomach less tolerant of heavier foods, and you only get the steam, as it were, or the humor escaping from these.

I would not pass over the eggs of chickens, if the yolk is eaten with the white. The yolk alone is a food for delicate stomachs, for Avicenna recommended no food more for the thinning of the blood and the dissolving of the spirit around the heart than the yolk of chicken eggs, partridge, or pheasant. Do not be afraid of eating goose raised on spelt or shining water, and after you kill it cook the meat in a salt and coriander-vinegar preparation, marinating it for seven days before you eat it. Likewise for deer, if your stomach is extremely strong. It seems probable that animals that live a long life confer long life, even if their meat is young. Other meats should be roasted first, then boiled.

See to it that there is twice as much food as drink; twice as much bread, and one-and-a-half as much eggs, three times as much meat, four times as much fish, vegetables and moist fruits, as the amount of your drink. Do not begin the meal with drink, nor let the drink be richer than the meal. Always let something styptic, in place of drink, or with only a little drink, follow the meal.

Where condition, age, place, or time happens to be warm or dry, you must also lean to the opposite conditions. When they happen to be cold or damp, likewise lean to the opposites. Where moderate, stay moderate.

Adding a little exercise for the body, and ceasing exercise for the soul, when we eat the harder foods, is necessary if you want a long life. Eat twice a day, nine hours apart, and sparingly each time, more sparingly at dinner. Exercise twice a day after you have digested, until you first begin to sweat. Sleeping at night, because it is always necessary, is always good, but sleeping by day, unless absolutely necessary, is never good.

Chapter 7

Avoiding foods that rot quickly, which wine and which wheat to select, and why putrefaction and looseness must be avoided

The animals we take care of must be fed on clean and select foods before we eat them. These and all others should be selected from high and fragrant pastures. On this subject one should always keep in mind the rule of Arnaldo the Philosopher: the animals, vegetables, fruit, produce, and wine must be chosen, as we said, from high, fragrant regions, where temperate winds blow, where the pleasant rays of the Sun shine, where no waters are stagnant, where no dungpiles lie, but where there is a natural moisture, and where things that grow last a long time unspoiled.

It should be our habit to eat things that are grown only in such places, things which are little inclined to rot, things which nourish our humor for a long time before they do rot. We should not expect to live a long time where the fruits of the earth are not themselves unspoiled for long periods of time, and where the people who live there are not long-lived, too.

Differences in places and customs, of course, are seen in the fact that what is poison to a Persian is good for the heart in Egypt. Hellebore is eaten without question in Anticyra, though it is poison elsewhere.

Aristotle chose for his house a high spot facing east and the mid-day sun, where the air was thin and neither damp nor cold. Plato, too, said old age was to be found in the highest, temperate regions.

The worst thing is manured fields, or waters drawn stagnant from such fields. Everything raised in them is quickly subject to decay. This is why I must denounce those people who attack the wise Hesiod because on the subject of farming he neglects to mention dungpiles. He was prudent in advising health rather than fertilizer! He thought it was enough for a field to be productive if it was ploughed seasonally, and left with the leaves of beans and lupine.

But if we are forced to cultivate damper and fouler regions, and to take foods from them that last only shortly, it is as if we are taking care of a patient like doctors in a plague. In which case, let us do what it says in the book on plague: let us use warm and pleasant odors. Let us wash often with properly made aloe. It is made properly when it has been washed in rosewater or the juice of roses, or if it is mixed with fresh, ground-up roses. Then balsam is added to it, and mastic-gum, and maybe rose. This medicine is beyond question miraculous for keeping *mens sana in corpore sano.* Let us exercise our bodies, too, and make fires to keep warm when we have to.

Let us sweeten our meals with the following powder: take a fourth part emblic balsam, a half of cornflower, a whole part cinnamon, and an eighth of saffron. With this powder and with other sharp substances, we should be able to inhibit such things as the rotting of food and its putrefaction.

We must remember, however, that many more people die from putrefaction and suffocation than from looseness, and we must take special pains to resist these. Where the opposite occurs, use aromatic spices, and dry odors and the like, oil being a good temporary retardant for putrefaction, or for injury from the cold. Use a bath of water and oil for looseness brought on by work or warm temperatures.

Likewise, rinse the mouth often with water, holding in the mouth some licorice-juice, or crystal sugar. Wash the hands and face with a lot of rosewater, and with a little rose-vinegar, and use perfumes of this kind. Every seven hours refresh yourself with a little food, resting the body and the soul, and avoid heat.

We should be very concerned about the quality of the wheat and wine which we consume so assiduously. These should be such that they last for more than a year and even for a whole three years, if we really hope to get an incorruptible nourishment from them. Make sure your wine, whether it is white or red, is clear, smooth, styptic, fragrant, and not watery—unless you find a wine that is strong and at the same time light and durable, because that is the rarest kind. Even better, as the philosopher Isaac said, wine should be cooked by the Sun, washed by the winds, and tempered with water from a pure fountain a short time before we drink it, so that it will be perfectly mixed. He warns us, however, to flee from watery wine, or weak or bitter wine, because it quickly turns to acid in the veins and limbs, or rots in other ways.

Since watery wine is prone to putrefaction, its conserved substance may be cooked, and this at least would make it useful, because it will not create a corruptible humor. Otherwise, it is not recommended. Its sharpness, however, must be tempered in good water. The kind of wine we have recommended, Isaac says, is like a great theriaca, according to the ancients: it warms someone who has a cold disposition, it cools off a warm one, it moistens a dry one, it dries out a damp one, and (as Galen said) it refreshes the natural humor, nourishes its heat, and balances both.

It is even more necessary for wine to be mixed in this way for the young rather than the old, and least of all for the old who are cold. For a cold and hard old age (as Plato said) is warmed and softened by wine the way iron is by fire, or water by lupine.

As to what we have said wine does, and the way it smooths over different problems, realize that even licorice does, too, but more weakly. Even an oil of rose does this, but only on the outside.

So let all these be familiar to you. Have no doubt that something temperate in quality and powerful in strength can temper other things, as cold, for example, can freeze other things. They have this temperament through Jove,, who made these things healthful. But this must be discussed elsewhere.

Chapter 8

Diet and nourishment is the medicine of the aged

Those who have had seven times seven years, and are rounding fifty, know that Venus signifies the young, and Saturn the old, and, as the astronomers say, these stars are the most inimical. With Saturn, the old finally escape from the Venusy stuff that takes away so much of the life of youths. Venus is not concerned with those who are already born but with those who are about to be born. She even dries up the flowers themselves once they have produced seed.

Old people should realize that the night air and cold weather are deadly for them. They should be careful to get food which will produce a lot of blood and a lot of spirit, such as fresh lamb, and wine a little on the sweet side and very fragrant. Lamb is especially good for the heart's blood and wine especially good for the spirit. Diet for such people should contain the most select meats, with everything cooked thoroughly, increasing the warmth and moisture of the food.

They should vigorously refresh their spirit with fragrances, especially wines. They should avoid staying up late, fasting or thirst, avoid labor of body and soul, and avoid solitude and sadness. They should find music again, if by chance they ever abandoned it, and they should never abandon it again. They should recall the games and habits which they once played in childhood, so far as it is fitting.

But it is difficult, as I have said, to rejuvenate the body unless you have first become a child again in the mind. Therefore, at every age, it is overwhelmingly important for life that we retain something of our childhood, and that we always pursue a variety of amusements. Long and profuse laughter, on the other hand, should be kept to a minimum, for it dilates the spirit too much toward the external parts.

But let us return to the aged. If they feel cold, they should take warm and aromatic poultices, and likewise damp ones. They should remember that the child-poultice of Avicenna, once made by David, is not just for children but for older people, too. This poultice is marvelous for the aged: the inside of some fresh warm bread, mixed with mallow wine and mint powder, applied to the stomach, and sometimes just applied to the nose for the smell. With just the use of bread-innards like this, Democritus, when he was dying, was able to keep up his spirit, which was trying to leave him.

In addition, old people should get light massages or, when taking baths, work the nourishment of their food to the extremities of their bodies.

More than anything else they should always have pine nuts handy, washed of course. The ancient doctors recommended this nourishment as the best thing for old people. For it is warm, moist, and fat, and it smoothes away all roughness. Likewise (which is incredible), while it increases the natural humor it meanwhile dries up the overflow, purging any putrid stuff out of the humor. Some people propose that old people eat one dram of these nuts daily after meals. I would propose an additional dram for old people with weak stomachs. They should be golden pine nuts, fresh, and warm.

I would mix up a melt-in-the-mouth this way: take four parts sweet washed almonds, the same amount of pine nuts, two parts pistachios, one part cucumber seeds, one part assorted washed nuts. Chop it all up, and cook with white sugar, to which you have added one dram of freshly made ginger, a half part of saffron, a third part of musk, and the same amount of amber, sugar, honey water, that is, the citrusy kind. Pour in some roses, including a lot of gold leaves.

If old people use this every day, they will get a stronger and a longer life. They can take this at the dinner table, and many hours before dinner. It would be good, however, for them to drink some sweet white wine with this concoction.

In warmer seasons, a rose-sugar, with gold leaves, and mixed with balsam, provides life for old people. No one would deny that theriaca is good for persons who are humid, or in humid times. But enough has been said on this in the previous book.

No one will deny that old people will also find good the root of elecampane, and behen root, both white and red, especially when fresh, the former for its nourishment, the latter for their aroma, and anything else that is warm, moist, aromatic, styptic, and fat.

Old people should certainly be familiar with licorice juice. They say, after all, that licorice is similar to the heat of the human body, and similar to its humor, and helps various diseases that old people get. Almond-milk and starchy food should always be handy, as well as sugar and eggs.

Rhasis has a concoction made of triphera from Indian balsam and emblic balsam. A concoction made of Indian balsam and sugar not only proves good for old age but even for slowing it down. Avicenna praises greater and lesser triphera of balsam, as well as a concoction of iron filings, and even one of gold filings. It is good to take balsam every day, especially chebulan balsam prepared correctly, for the different ailments of old age.

Chapter 9

On the nature of aromatics and cordials that are necessary, and some more on the nourishment of old people

Keep in mind that balsam contains many virtues. First, it miracu-

53

lously dries out excess humor, which means that it prevents graying. Second, it gathers the natural humor and protects it from
corruption and inflammation, which means that it leads to a long
life. Third, it has a styptic and aromatic power, which collects the
power and the natural animal spirit, nourishing and strengthening
them. One might think that balsam was the Tree of Life in Paradise!

Others that work in a similar way are gold and silver, coral,
spode, and precious stones, although instead of an aromatic power
they offer the faculty of brightening. We commented earlier, remember, on how good aromatics were for life, when with a certain
aromatic vigor they are moist as well, and warm, and have a thick
pliancy, and are added to the diet in the form of the roots of red
and white behen, especially fresh ones. At least they are good,
when, with a certain subtle, fragrant, sharp power, they have a
dense substance and a styptic property.

Those cold cordials whose composition contains balsam or
amber seem to be the best of all. A second choice would be rose-
juice and citrus seeds. A third choice would be cornflower, coriander, myrrh, and the like.

For warm cordials, use setwall, aloe wood, citrus pulp, Indian
spice, nutmeg, mace, frankincense, mastic, wolfsbane, and even
sage. They say that amber and musk have a styptic power. Ginger,
on the other hand, because of its moistness, especially when fresh,
is good for old people. But this and Indian spice, on account of
their strong heat, must be taken cautiously. Setwall must be taken
cautiously, too, though it is like theriaca, and has a similar styptic
and thick nature, and is very liked by old people.

Amber, whose heat is almost tempered, may be taken quite
safely. Because of its thickness and its styptic ability, it has an
excellent strengthening power for the limbs and spirits. If a water
is made from it, it is good for washing the skin, restoring the fourth
digestion, and expelling any diseases in that region.

Aromatics which have a subtle substance, like cinnamon and
saffron, must be mixed with cold and harder cordials. For if the
aromatics are too warm and subtle, and are taken by themselves,

54

they excite the natural heat too much, and dissolve the humor. It is necessary first to digest the colder and moister foods, then the harder cordials that go to the heart.

You should not ignore the fact that the humor that is necessary for life has its home in the heart, and in its veins and arteries, as Isaac taught so perceptively, and as Avicenna, too, has agreed. This humor is frequently irrigated and nourished by the natural humor of the other limbs. So one must be careful lest the humor of any limb somehow dry up, and even more careful that the humor of the heart area not be threatened.

For nourishment, poultices, or cordials to pass easily through the narrow passages of the heart, mix in some saffron. For them to stay there, take balsam. If you do both, however, take, with the warm stuff, musk and amber; with the cold stuff, roses and myrrh.

Remember, sweet fennel is useful for old people, too. It spreads nourishment through the limbs like milk, and increases the natural humor. Dioscorides said that snakes shed their old age every year through the use of fennel. We recommend sage, too, because it gently warms and strengthens the power of nature, and thus holds off paralysis. We recommend, also, the moderate use of ginger, because it has thickness with warmth.

Chapter 10

On gold, and foods containing gold, and on the reviving of old people

Everyone praises gold above everything else, as if it were the most temperate of all things, and the safest from corruption. Perhaps because of its splendor, it is consecrated to the Sun, and on account of its temperateness, to Jove. It can marvelously temper the natural heat with the humor, and keep the humors from corruption, and it can fill the limbs and spirits with a Solar and a Jovial power.

Yet it is necessary to thin and to make penetrable the thickest substance of gold. For cordials know how to refresh the power of the heart only when nature does not have to work very hard in drawing them in. So that nature does not become weary, gold should be made very thin, or be supported with very thin stuff.

They say it is best if gold is made drinkable without anything else mixed in. If this is not possible, most people prefer to take it ground up and formed into leaves. Gold is made drinkable this way: take borage flowers, ox-tongue, honey, the kind we call citra-ria herb, and when the Moon is in Leo or Aries, or Sagittarius, and looking at the Sun, or Jupiter, cook it with white sugar, rosewater, and carefully pour in three gold leaves. Take it on an empty stom-ach with a little gold wine, or with water distilled from steaming a capon, or with a rose julep, in which you have previously ground up some gold leaf. Finally, extinguish the burning gold in water from the purest source, and grind up the leaves of gold. Temper the gold wine with this water, and with this drink eat some fresh lamb.

You will easily keep the humor in all the strength of the body if you will have conserved it in its roots. Therefore, take the heart, liver, stomach, testicles, and brain of roosters, pullets, and capons, cook them in a little water and a touch of salt. When cooked, grind up all the meat and all the juice, adding some sugar and some fresh lamb, and make a little gold pizza out of it, with cinnamon and saffron. Eat this at least once, when you are hungry, every four days, and if it is all you eat, have a drink of clear wine, too.

Chapter 11

On the use of milk and human blood for the life of old people

Often after the seventieth year, and sometimes after the sixty-third year, the human tree little by little weakens as the humor dries up. Then this human tree must be irrigated with a human and youthful fluid to revive it. You should therefore select a clean girl, one who is beautiful, cheerful, and calm, and, being ravishingly hungry yourself, and with the Moon rising, proceed to suck her milk. Immediately thereafter, eat a little powder of sweet fennel made with sugar. Sugar does not coagulate or putrefy milk in the stomach, and fennel, which is both thin and a friend of milk, will dilate and spread into the limbs.

Good doctors try, with human blood distilled in fire, to restore those whom old age has eaten away. What is wrong with our giving this drink of blood if it will restore people who are almost half-dead with age? It is a common and an ancient opinion that certain old women who were fortune-tellers (which we call witches) used to suck the blood of infants and become rejuvenated from it.

Why not then have our own old people—who have no other hope—suck the blood of an adolescent—of a willing adolescent, I mean, who is clean, happy, temperate, and whose blood is excellent but perhaps a little excessive? They could suck it the way leeches do, an ounce or two from a vein on the left arm barely opened. Afterward, they should take an equal amount of sugar and wine, and they should do the sucking while hungry and thirsty and with the Moon rising.

If they cannot digest this blood raw, cook it up beforehand with some sugar, or distill it into some moderately warm water, mixed with sugar, and then have them drink it. It is sometimes helpful to nourish the stomach by drinking pig's blood that has been taken flowing from a pig's vein with a sponge that has been dampened with warm wine and brought immediately, still warm, into the stomach.

Galen and Serapio say that the bite of a rabid dog is cured by drinking the blood of a dog. The reason for this, however, is not easy to find. I myself spent two days researching this, and I have come to the opinion that the saliva of a rabid dog is poisonous and gets inserted into a man where his foot got bit, little by little rising through the veins to the heart the way poison does, unless something is done in the meantime to draw it out. If, therefore, in the meantime, one is given another dog's blood to drink, that raw blood for many hours swims around in the stomach, which finally ejects it from below as a foreign substance. But meanwhile that dog blood draws away to the stomach the rabid saliva which had penetrated the outer limbs and which was heading for the heart. For in dog blood there is a power to draw dog saliva, and in saliva, on the other hand, there is a similar power to follow blood. With the poison, therefore, kept away from the heart, and the blood that has been drunk now swimming around in the stomach, the poison is drawn down with the blood through the lower extremities, and the man is left unharmed.

Why mention all this? First, because in a matter so occult as this, I would like to help explain the cause of something very puzzling, and second, so that I might advise you that blood can indeed be drunk, and even healthfully, and that there is a power in human blood which draws itself to other human blood and joins it mutually. So, you should have no doubt that young blood, drunk by an old person, can be drawn into the veins and limbs, and there do a lot of good.

Chapter 12

The diet, housing, and conversation of old people

It helps if the very old remember not to weaken nature by tiring it with too much food, or dividing it with too much diversity of foods. This is a vice that brings old age even in youth. The old should therefore divide their meals so that there is not so much food all at once, and instead eat more often, with an interval allowed for digestion. For often, after the stomach itself has digested but the liver has not quite digested, they take more food, and divide nature, and tire it, leading to constant weariness, and hastening an early old age.

Old people in winter should be like sheep seeking open sky. In summer they should be like birds seeking pleasant places, visiting streams, and dwelling among green and fragrant plants. For these living and breathing things work to increase the spirit of man.

Let them escape to places that bees like, let them be with bees and take honey in winter. Honey is the best friend old people have, unless they are afraid of burning bile. Fresh cheese is their friend, too, and dates, figs, eggs, capers, sweet apples, jujubes, hyssop,

coral, and betony, but above all, pistachios. Pine nuts are especially good, too, as we have said. These are much more nutritious
if they are kept in warm water for about twelve hours before eating.
For then they will not bother the stomach.

Finally, while the old eat these things, they should dwell
among the vines, or the pine trees, or the olive trees, or at least
inhale the vapor and odor of the pine. They should rub the body
often with a wine or an oil of pine gum and pine-tears. These trees
are in all probability endowed with a long life, especially those that
stay green in winter, and their shade, the vapor of their new fruit,
and the use of their wood, or whatever, will bring you a long life,
too.

As far as long-lived animals are concerned, we have discussed
them before. But you can obtain the same effect if you live among
people who are healthy and friendly and of a similar nature to
yours, especially if these people are a little younger than you. As
for whether the frequent conversation of young people is really
good for slowing down old age—that is something you will have to
ask the virtuous Socrates about.

Chapter 13

*The help that old people get from the Planets in caring for their
limbs*

You troubled old people, you should consult Apollo instead, who
declared Socrates the wisest of Greeks. Consult Jupiter above, and
Venus. Phoebus himself, the discoverer of the art of medicine, will
give you nutmeg for the care of your stomach. Jupiter and Phoebus, together, will give you mastic-gum and mint. Venus will give
you coral. For the care of the head, Phoebus will give you peonies,
incense, marjoram, and, together with Saturn, myrrh. Jupiter will
give you spikenard and mace. Venus will give you sweet fennel and
myrtle.

For taking care of the heart, you will receive from Phoebus
something citrusy, as well as saffron, aloe wood, incense, amber,

musk, wolfsbane, Indian spice, citrus pulp, and cinnamon. From Jupiter, the lily, ox-tongue, clover, and mint, and red and white behen roots. From Venus alone, myrtle, cornflower, and roses, and, together with Saturn, coriander. Mix these carefully.

For the stomach, make quince oil into a wax plaster. For the head, pour spices into an oil and rub the neck, temples, and face. For the heart, take some gold wine and rosewater and apply these around the heart area.

For the liver, it is necessary above all to make blood, and I do not know how we can get around that. Phoebus will always help you here with agrimony and balsam. Jupiter will help with pistachios and eggs, and Venus with liver, endive, spode, and chicory.

For the care of the spleen, your Saturn, together with Jupiter, will give you capers, scolopendrion, and tamarisk. For the bladder, Jupiter and Venus cure you with pine, licorice, starch, cucumber seeds, mallow, marshmallows, vegetable juice, and cheese.

Saturn is feared by many, but you old people should not run from him. He may be a stranger to the young, but he is your household servant. Let him help make your whole body thrive, and let him strengthen you, by receiving things from him when he rules over you.

Receive a gift from Phoebus, too: the meat of a roast goose, rubbed with a little goose grease. Grind it up carefully, mix with chebulan balsam and Indian honey, amber, musk, and saffron. And have faith, this stuff is a real medicine for life! With this you will say that God has answered your prayers! You will realize that the things he has created, especially the heavenly things, are absolutely miraculous for increasing and preserving the power of life.

Chapter 14

The conversation of old people should be under Venus in a green meadow

But I want to call you old people away from these heavier Gods and, little by little, get you back to Venus through gardens and meadows. I summon all of you to nourishing Venus, not for her to play with you, but for her to make jokes with you.

The first thing she does, I tell you, is she sets up this joke-oracle, for you and for me (I am old too): "I am the one who gave you life through the pleasure and movement of my son (in case you did not know). I, therefore, shall be the one who, with a certain pleasure and movement now—though not necessarily the same kind—will save your life for you. Liber, the planter of the vine, the propagator of life, will save you, too, with some of his liberty. Liber himself always detests slaves, and offers his wine with its long life only to free men. Once my life and mind were under the reign of Saturn, and Liber gave me mint to help diminish Saturn's power, and I take it daily. For you, however, mint is even better, it is great for your mind and your life. Gather up the laughter in my gardens and do not bother with the figs. When you go there to pick violets, imagine that you are picking lilies, and when you are picking lilies, imagine that you are taking the crocus. Jupiter himself planted the lily, which he took from Phoebus in the shape of a crocus. I took the lily from Jupiter and transformed it into the violets which you see here. Let the Morning Star be a rose for you, and the Evening Star your myrtle."

After Venus gives us this oracle for our contemplation, she sends nature, with its green things, to bloom everywhere, not just to make us alive, but younger, giving us our healthy humor back, and making us overflow with a lively spirit. The frequent smell, and sight, and use of these, and living among them, pour a youthful spirit into us.

While we are strolling through all this greenery, we might ask the reason why the color green is a sight that helps us more than any other, and why it delights us so wholesomely. We find that the sight of nature is bright, a friend of light, though it is fickle and easily dissolves away. While it spreads itself all around through this friendly light, too much light nonetheless forces it to be snatched back and to be dissolved by a strong scattering of itself. It is by nature afraid of darkness, its enemy, and it flees from darkness by retracting its rays into a narrow focus. It chooses to be expressed through its friend, light, so that it can be spread around through its friend and not dissipated. Yet wherever there is more darkness or blackness than light, it does not spread out, its rays are not spread out to be seen by anyone. Where, on the other hand, there is more splendid color than black, it spreads itself wide, drawing off the harmful stuff by a certain pleasure.

This is why the color green, more than anything else, tempering the black with the bright, is foremost, just as water keeps away something from the rays of the eyes, without offending them, dispersing it farther and farther away. Things that are hard and rough likewise break these rays, and things that are very thin open an approach by their dissolving. But whatever contains some kind of solidity, and a smooth evenness, like mirrored bodies, does not break the rays, and does not let them be dispersed far. Besides these, things that are tender and soft, like water, and things green, sweeten the liquid rays of the eyes with their softness.

Sight is a ray that is naturally lifted up by a certain water in our eyes, and it seeks a tempered light in the water, a light that to a certain extent resists it. Thus water delights us, and we take pleasure in mirrors, and enjoy everything green. In green things the light of the Sun located there has the humor of Spring and a subtle water filled with a certain hidden light. Therefore, the color green, when it is thinned, is broken down into a saffron or crocus color.

So what? you may ask. Well, so that we might know that the frequent use of green, a use that supposedly refreshes the spirit, re-makes the animal spirit, because green is foremost for the animal spirit. We should remember that if the color green, because it is the middle step in colors, and the most temperate, is so good for the animal spirit, its temperate qualities are even more useful for providing the natural and vital spirit in nature, as well as much else in life.

Nothing in the world is more temperate than heaven, nothing under heaven is more temperate than the human body, and nothing in the body is more temperate than the spirit. Therefore, through temperate things, the life that is remaining in the spirit is refreshed. The spirit, through temperate things, conforms to the heavens.

Finally, the temperateness of green, which gathers and spreads the animal spirit, even brightening it and greatly helping it, can also be found in cordials that we make out of aromatics and subtle and strong things. These cordials will extend the spirit or even brighten it. They are made with saffron, cinnamon, with aromatics that are mixed with styptics, or mixed with balsam and the like.

Do not neglect those things which, without any aromatic sharpness, do both—they dilate a little and they gather together a little. They brighten you up considerably, and in addition to those we already named that do this, there is gold, silver, spode, coral, amber, silk, and precious stones, among which hyacinth comes greatly recommended for its Jovial properties when it is held in the mouth.

Since these beautiful and almost heavenly things cannot come into existence under the earth without some high help from heaven, it is probable that they contain wonderful heavenly powers. The composition of this stuff, which evenly gathers the spirit by dilating and brightening it, so delights someone inside and refreshes him that it is as if a greenness has come over his eyes. It keeps him, even if he is an old man, for the longest time in a kind of natural state of greenness, as if he were a laurel tree, an olive or a pine, still green in winter. It does this even more when it does it inside, and especially if its composition abounds in an aromatic fragrance and allures you with its flavor.

Just as the body is composed of four humors out of its thicker parts, and takes on a fifth form, so the spirit is constituted from the most subtle portions of these same humors and has a fifth form that is naturally very temperate and lucid, and thus heavenly. It must be preserved in this same form to be subtle and yet strong, as we have said. It must be altogether lucid, but, at the same time, somehow solid. It must be carefully nourished by fragrant, strong, and lucid things, if we want to preserve life, which flourishes in the spirit, and if we want to claim our heavenly gifts.

Having now contemplated these matters by order of Venus, I think we can say that we have been listening to Venus herself.

Chapter 15

The personification of Mercury, and his advice to old people about pleasure, smells, songs, and medicines

It was as if Venus herself had been telling this story to old people, and telling it so beautifully, at least up to this point. She would have continued her story even more lengthily, perhaps, had not Mercury, the founder of speech, interrupted her with the following words.

"What is it with you old folks that you are always with that girl, Venus? Why are you always trying to reason with Venus? Don't you and I have stuff to talk about, too? Isn't reason something that belongs only to you and me? Listen to me now, then, with the same attention you paid Venus, and with a lot more attention, please, than she paid you!

"You know that there are five senses: sight, hearing, smell, taste, and touch. Now you will learn that there are five reasons for these. For your soul is filled daily through your five senses, and it perceives the reasons for these. Five such reasons exist, all so that things might be judged. Just as there are five of these so-called senses, or, so to speak, reasons, the tenor of life is disposed around sense and reason in five steps.

"That's why we say there are five ages. Your first age is when you are totally under the control of the senses. The second, when you are allured more by the senses than by reason. The third, when you alternate, more or less equally, between being led about by the senses or by reason. The fourth, when you are led more by reason than by the senses. And the fifth, when you are ruled entirely by reason. The first and second ages are, therefore, as it were, subject to Venus—if it pleases Venus to dare say this about her—and the remaining ages belong to me, Mercury.

"I, therefore, am addressing those of you who are in the remaining ages, not so much for myself but for Diana, whom you see here on my left. For while she has no tongue, I have two, and by her own rule, whose tongue I have, I shall speak.

"The one pleasure that Venus gives you is certainly harmful. It is a pleasure that would harm you, though it helps those who come after you, emptying you little by little as if through a widening pipe, and filling someone else with your colors. She is creating someone else and leaving you like the skin of an old cicada to lie exhausted now on the ground, while she goes looking in the meantime for a still younger cicada.

"Don't you see, Venus is producing out of your material something fresh and alive, something endowed with your senses. She then snatches away, I tell you, your youth and life and these same senses right out of your body, all for the pleasure of another body that she is working on.

"Well, having warned you about the quality of this material that rules in the fourth digestive region, I advise you now to help your human vine with foods cooked well for the fourth digestive region. Take whole fresh eggs, drinking them with sugar, a little saffron, and human milk, or cow's milk, or goat's milk, with a little honey. These two are even more healthful when they are burning from their natural heat. But if you want another egg after this, especially if you have a weak stomach, make sure it is cooked lightly.

"If we may return to Venus for a moment: if you have ever seen Venus you saw her as young, dolled-up in finery and makeup as if she were a prostitute. She who is always new always wants the new, and she hates the old. She destroys what she has made of the old in order to make new all over again. Again, if I may say so, she is like a prostitute who is not content with one man but loves everybody, and, if I can speak dialectically here, she promiscuously favors the species rather than the individual.

"She doesn't just knock you out with a touch—oh no, she

deceives you daily with the taste, too, and those who are deceived by her she then destroys. For while there are moderate flavors that you can taste in things, made pleasant by some moderate tempering, these are what Diana gives you, along with some gift from Apollo or Jove. The insidious Venus, however, fabricates her enticements through marvelous flavors which slowly destroy your life as if you were secretly caught on a hook.

"Why, therefore, do you attack Mars? Why attack Saturn? Mars hurts you rarely, and only in public! And Saturn, too, at least shows you his face is your enemy, and only hurts you slowly, and never denies anybody the time for remedies.

"Only Venus comes on openly as your friend, and is secretly your enemy. You should be attacking her if you're going to be attacking any of the Gods. Arm yourself with the shield of Athena against her many ambushes, and teach your eyes to be like the eyes of Argus. Block your ears to her sweet promises as if they were the lethal songs of the Sirens. Receive from me this flower of carefulness, which you can use to avoid the poisons of this Circe.

"She promises you her deadly pleasures, and promises more than she ever delivers them, but they are only two. I, on the other hand, with the help of my father and brother, promise you five, and I deliver five, pure, permanent, and healthy ones. The lowest is in smell; the highest in hearing; the most sublime is in sight; the most eminent in imagination; the most superior and divine is in reason. Venus offers you more pleasure in touching and in tasting, through which she frequently does grievous harm to your life. On the other hand, the more you find my kind of pleasure in smell, hearing, and sight, even in imagination and sometimes in reason, the longer will you make the thread of your life.

"Yet just as I warn you to beware the crafty Venus' delights of touching and tasting, I must tell you to beware, also, Saturn, with too much of his busy and secret delight in the contemplative mind, for he frequently devours his own sons in this. He seizes them with the enticements of his more sublime contemplations, and knows that he is in the meantime cutting them off from the earth with a kind of scythe if they are lingering too long there. He often kills the earthly life of these unwary people.

"In this, at least, he is a little easier than Venus, because Venus, when she takes your life away, gives it to someone else and does not give you anything in exchange. Saturn, however, separates you from your earthly life, from which he is himself separated, but returns you to heavenly and eternal life.

"Venus and Saturn, though, would seem to be alike in this, that while one rejoices in Aquarius, the other reigns in Libra, so that both he and she trouble and harm men with the desire of creating, and all for the sake of posterity. Venus fertilizes the body, and stimulates fertility. Saturn presses the mind, pregnant by his seed, to give birth. You should therefore remember this proverb: do not be too busy in anything, and restrain your pleasure with the reins of prudence, for both of these Gods give birth.

"Saturn wounds much more grievously and quickly those whom he first hits with weariness, torpor, sadness, cares, and superstition, than those whom he raises above the powers of the body to the highest occupations of mortal man. I advise you, then, to be on guard, as Jupiter taught Pythagoras and Plato to be, taking care of human life through an equal proportion of soul and body, feeding each with its own foods and exercises, and understanding both equally. If someone, especially by his education, makes himself much stronger in one thing than in another, he is doing no small damage to his life. Therefore, the man who selects from the art of doctors the things that are good for both the soul and body together, has done his life the most good. Among these are wine, mint, balsam, musk, amber, fresh ginger, incense, aloe, hyacinth, and precious stones, and herbs of this sort, and whatever else doctors come up with that can be applied to both equally.

"But, to interrupt these rather long digressions, realize that I, too, have come here as a doctor. If you have taken the flavors from things no longer living, the odors from dry aromatics, things with no life left in them, and you thought these were very useful to life, why should you hesitate to take the odors from plants with their roots still growing on them, still living, things that have wonderfully accumulated powers for life?

"Furthermore, if the vapors exhaled from vegetable life are terrific for your life, how useful would you say songs are? How useful those in the air to the airy spirit, those that are harmonious to the harmonious spirit, songs that are warm and lively to the lively spirit, and how useful are songs full of feeling and conceived in reason to the sensitive and rational spirit? I present you, therefore, with this lyre that I have invented, and the Apollonian song you will make with it, the solace of all your labors, is a pledge I give to you of a long life.

"For just as things most temperate in their quality, together with aromatic things, at first temper the humors among themselves, and then temper the natural spirit with itself, so also odors of this kind temper the vital spirit, and their harmonies, in turn, temper the animal spirit. Thus, when you put your faith in the lyre and its sounds, the tones that are tempered in your voice likewise temper your inner spirit.

"And lest I, myself, seem more selfish than Venus, who, without Bacchus, becomes cold, receive through me this nectar from the same Father Bacchus. Those among you who become cold, or in cold seasons, should take twice in every seven days two parts vernacea wine, or sweet mallow wine, with one part bread, three hours before eating. Or take one dram of the thinnest water distilled from wine, with a half part of rose julep. Even rub the skin with this liquid, and it can be very comfortably taken in the nose, too.

"I would like to say that I brought you ambrosia, too, after this nectar, so here is a medicine from Jove on high; take four parts chebulan balsam, three of rose sugar, and one part ginger (in winter, but only a half-part in summer). Cook these three up smoothly with emblic honey and decorate with seven leaves of gold. Take a morsel of this four hours before lunch, on an empty stomach. Take it every day for at least a whole year, that your youth might be rejuvenated like the proverbial eagle's."

Let us pretend this speech was really said by Mercury.

Chapter 16

Confirmation of the things discussed previously, and rules for avoiding coitus and prolonged thought

The astrologers say that Venus and Saturn are enemies of each other. Nonetheless, in heaven, where all things are moved by love, where there is no fault, there can be no hatred. When they say enemies, therefore, we must interpret this as meaning that they differ in their effect.

Let us put aside for now the other aspects of this. Imagine Saturn now as in our center, giving pleasure, and Venus at the circumference, giving pleasure. Pleasure is really a kind of food for the spirits. So, from opposite sides, Venus and Saturn chase after the flight of our spirit. She lures us to external things through her pleasure, while he, meanwhile, through his pleasures, calls us back to the innermost things. So they distract and dissipate the spirit if they both move at the same time.

This is why there is nothing more harmful to the business of being contemplative or curious than Venereal activity, and nothing more contrary to Venereal activity than careful contemplation. The man who contemplates the physical world, and the religious contemplative, are in the same company, as well as anyone who is preoccupied with his business and bothered by heavy cares. Here, again, if we want to ease and console someone who is seized by Saturnian business or by too much contemplation, someone pressed down with cares, we do so in vain and we even hurt them when we try to do this through sexual acts, sexual games, and sexual jokes, trying, as it were, to help them through remedies far distant from their problems.

Likewise, if someone is really destroyed by Venereal activity, wrecked by sexual games and sexual jokes, and we want to straighten him out, we do not really help him through the severity of Saturn. The best rule is: a little bit of Phoebus and Jove, who are midway between Saturn and Venus, to call people back to the middle who have declined toward one or the other. For this we must be like doctors.

Just as a fire can be extinguished in two violent ways, blown out by the wind, or smothered with ashes, so the spirit either gets blown out by the Venereal, or we suffocate it slowly with Saturn, and break it and put it out.

The spirit, flying to the outermost places, frequently returns empty or a stranger to its life. When it is then driven to the innermost places, it makes the limbs less equipped for life there, too. Quickly, then, Venus brings old age to our inside parts, and Saturn brings it to our outside parts. Venus, in particular, is good at this because of her old habit of weakening our body and making it languish. But Saturn, too, is powerful, when from whatever duty, care, or labor in contemplation, he weakens the powers of mind and body. When this happens, it does not matter if someone is born for contemplation or born for pleasure, nor does it matter how strong a person is by nature in either one of these callings. For nature is often but an adjunct of pleasure, and easy.

A man, therefore, should know which way he is, and be his own self-regulator. A man should be his own doctor. Let those who plan to live in a state of constant coitus consult somebody else!

In the previous book I advised more exercise for men of thought, and a diet to be used by everyone for all kinds of remedies, by which the limbs, the spirit, the senses, the mind, and memory, might all be strengthened. I said that breaks should be taken during thinking sessions, and that thinkers should not wait until fatigue comes on from contemplation, especially when they are already gray-haired. Some people, however, turn gray not so much by a weakness of nature—young men growing gray hair—as by a sickness of the mind, or by some preceding sickness of the body, and some simply get it from their parents, who had passed it on.

Chapter 17

Medicines for old people, and some more on their housing and diet

The rule of the Chaldaeans for recovering youth perhaps should be recommended, too: foreign humors imbibed into the body must gradually be cleaned out of it, using competent medicines on the inside, and rubdowns and forced sweating on the outside. In the meantime, the body should be filled, little by little, with healthy and long-lasting foods.

Some suggest pills made from vipers, or even from hellebore, to flush out all the humors, including the old and rotten ones. Once they have cleaned out and restored the humor to health with health foods, they claim, they have restored youth. Some are more cautious: they have hens eat the hellebore, and then they eat the hens. But this kind of regimen, in my opinion, is dangerous, and should be tried only in youth rather than in old age, unless perhaps we are trying for that youth promised by Medea to old Pelias. For, as Hippocrates observed, youths who take medicines rather than purges quickly age.

Where diet does not suffice, however, you are safe to use enemas, vegetable-grain laxatives, or well-washed aloe. If your stomach is even more constipated, a vegetable-grain laxative taken with the juice of a capon and some balsam has a lot of power. If less constipated, here is a laxative that you will find handy not only in youth but even when you are old: take one part washed aloe, two drams emblic balsam, the same of chebulan balsam, two parts of purple roses, the same of mastic-gum, and make pills out of this with some mallow-wine. Make this when the Moon is happily in place and enjoying the sight of favorable Jupiter, especially if the Moon or Jupiter are in their fixed houses. These are tremendous pills for giving a long life. You can even use a rhubarb in this, mixed with the aloe, half and half. As often as it is necessary, take one to three pills every morning, or one to five pills with a little wine. If you are afraid of phlegm, you can take very comfortably in these pills a third part of an agaric pill, together with two-thirds aloe, omitting the rhubarb.

But I have found the first of these pill formulas, for many years now, to be safe for every age. Here is another one: take one part each of emblic balsam, belliric, Indian, and chebulan balsam, two parts cinnamon, one part wolfsbane with purple roses, two parts red cornflower, one dram saffron, a third of a dram of musk, and the same of amber. Mix in white sugar with citrus juice and rosewater, cook it, and roll into gold balls. You take this four hours before lunch, and we have found it useful for strengthening one's powers and for brightening and strengthening the spirit.

It will be especially effective if, a little before you take it, you drink some gold wine. It is often good to pour rosewater and gold wine on warm bread with a little cinnamon on top, mixed with a rich sugar. It is good, too, to take two of these pills with almond milk and a little bread, for such mixtures bring a Jovial nature.

Furthermore, even though we have explained it before, or at least noticed it, all city people must be diligently careful of the following: heat, cold (either the kind of cold that comes after heat or the nocturnal kind), mists, winds (either the kind that blow off swamps or the kind that break out in confined places), and places where either the air moves very violently or is not moved at all. Avoid housing that is humid, foetid, sad, or torpid.

Be diligent followers of Mercury, most diligent of all when you are old. First thing in the morning, after you have lightly massaged your whole body, moisturize it against the discomforts of the air and fatigue with a warm oil or with a slightly bitter wine, in which you have have poured myrrh, rose, and myrtle. Keep sage in your mouth often, for it is very nice to the nerves and the teeth. If, because of a lack of teeth, you are like a baby, and have to eat foods that are only liquid, beware of the softest kind. Take milk and wine sparingly.

Fire is a kind of medicine, insofar as it expels cold and sustains one's heat, but it is a glutton insofar as it likes to dry out the natural humor. The Chaldaeans find the Sun, of course, delightful, and a kind of food, but they avoid it when their noses are running, and they avoid too much of its heat. They enjoy the easy movements of the body, working up as much heat as is necessary for these. But they hate great trials of the body, and even more, great trials of the soul, no less than prolonged thirst or hunger or sleeplessness.

Chapter 18

Nourishing the spirit and preserving life through odors

We read of people in certain warm climates, especially in places which are fragrant with odors, who are thin of body and weak of stomach and seem to be nourished by odors alone. Perhaps this is because the nature of the place itself drives the juices of its herbs and fruits into many odors, and then these break down the humors of human bodies into spirit. Each of these, odor and spirit, is like vapor, and is nourished in the same way, so it is no surprise that spirit and spiritual man take nourishment from odors. Nourishment through odors or poultices, no matter what it is, is necessary for the old and the thin, as a way of compensating for their weakness with more solid or more real food.

Some people, of course, like to argue about whether the spirit can be nourished by odors. I am of the opinion, however, that one can be nourished by these alone, when food, which is thick, gets thinned out into vapors with digestion, and the spirit itself, which we have already said was a vapor, takes its nourishment from this. That is why wine which is full of fragrance suddenly refreshes the spirit, which other things hardly do at all.

We call an odor the vapor into which cooked food has finally been transformed, both because an odor is everywhere a vapor, and because this vapor, drawn inside through foods, will hardly give the spirit any nourishment unless its odor is pleasing to the spirit. This is why we agree with our dear Avicenna, who said that the body is nourished with a certain sweetness, the spirit with a certain (to use his word) 'aromatic.'

Thickness of the body does not help in being strong, unless it is through a thick quality, the kind that seems to be in sweetness. Thinness of the spirit can be helped with nothing but a kind of smoke, or vapor, in which 'aromaticness' itself flourishes. By aromatic we mean a quality that is fragrant and sharp, and to a certain degree styptic.

Because the liver is in charge of the food that goes to the body through the blood, the liver is increased with sweetness. The heart, however, because it both creates spirit and generates food for the spirit, rightfully desires aromatics. It helps, nevertheless, to supply aromatics to the heart for pleasantness, and to mix sweet, pleasant things with aromatics for the liver, but to avoid, in the meantime, excessive sweetness or pleasantness.

What more can I say? Galen himself followed Hippocrates in thinking that the spirit was nourished not only by odors but even by air. Not by simple air, of course, but rather air that was properly mixed. And, if you can believe it, it is our opinion that nothing— neither food nor delight in anything—is more necessary to life than the air that is appropriate for us.

For air is easily and always affected by the qualities of the lower and the heavenly bodies, and it is surrounded by an immense (so to speak) amplitude, with its perpetual motion penetrating us everywhere. It brings us its qualities miraculously, especially its spiritual quality, and its vital quality, flourishing in the heart, into whose innermost recesses it busily flows. Then, suddenly, it goes on to affect the spirit, and through the vital spirit (whose material and origin is animal spirit), it affects likewise the animal spirit.

The quality of air is of great importance for thinking people, those who work so hard because of this spirit. Therefore, pleasure in odors, in pure luminous air, and in music, pertains to none other than these spirits. These three are considered poultices for the animal spirit.

The right air is extremely powerful for life. Indeed, those born in the eighth month in Egypt live a long time, and some of the temperate regions in Greece are very healthy because of the air, as Aristotle says, and Avicenna confirms.

Just as the body is composed of various things and is nourished by various foods (though not by too many different ones), so the spirit is likewise composed of, and enjoys, and is nourished by, a certain variety of air. The spirit must be daily refreshed by this kind of variety. For air and odor seem almost like spirits. Alexander and Nicolas, the Peripatetics, concur with Galen that the vital and animal spirit is so nourished, first by odor, then by air, because each is mixed and similar, and each is drawn in to penetrate the heart area. Here, they scatter through the arteries, to be cooked and to be tempered, for life. When each one is thus cooked, it again nourishes the spirit, so they say, especially the animal spirit.

They even say that breathed air is not only good for cooking off heat, but for nourishing, too. Animals breathe very cold air.

They say that a very thick air is like the natural spirit, as if it were more body-like: it breathes subtle, pure, and clear, for the vital spirit, but most of all for the animal spirit. Nor should it seem surprising that the spirit that is so thin should be nourished by thin things. After all, many little fish are nourished on shining water, and basil lives in water—grows, flowers, and is fragrant. I will not even bother to mention those elements that salamanders and chameleons live on.

Let us get back to our subject. What concerns us is the kind of air we breathe and the kind of odors we draw in. For such is the spirit that goes into us. The soul invigorates us through life only as much as the spirit keeps a harmony with the soul. The spirit in us lives first and foremost, and lives almost alone. Does it not sometimes happen, in an accident, that life, the senses, and movement suddenly leave the limbs as if the spirit had gone and hid in the depths of the heart? But often these forces will immediately return to the limbs through massage and odors that make the spirit return, as if life resided in this spirit in a volatile way rather than in the humors or limbs. Otherwise, because of the thick tenacity of the limbs, life would come and go much more slowly in them.

Whoever, therefore, desires to produce life in his body should cultivate the spirit first, increase it with foods that increase the blood, keep it temperate and clear, see that it always gets good air, nourish it daily with pleasant odors, and delight it with sounds and songs. But beware of odors that are too hot, flee from those that are too cold, and go for the temperate ones, tempering the cold with the warm, and the dry with the moist. Realize that every odor is the most subtle part of the body and therefore contains some heat, and that when they are separated from things which they nourish, odors drive us to nourishment. They do this the way aromatic fruits do, and things that are like fruits, or even more, fresh warm bread, roast meats, wine, or anything else with a flavor that terrifically pleases. They are the source of much quick nourishment, or an occasion for nourishment of the body, because the odor has become spirit itself.

I would like to remind you again that Democritus, when he was almost dead, held onto his spirit for four days only on the smell of warm bread, and he would have held on even longer if he had wanted to. He did this to humor his friends.

There are those who say that the odor of honey could have done this, too, but I think if honey is used for this it should be made into liquid with a white wine and then poured over hot bread. The odor of honey should not be scorned. For honey is the flower of flowers, and it nourishes in no small way with its sweetness, and by its quality it protects things from putrefaction. If one knew how to eat this food so that it would not fill up the body passages with too much of its sweetness, nor draw out an excess of bile with all that heat, it would certainly be a help in getting long life. At least use this condiment, then, on cold and hot things.

But I must get you back to odors again: whenever you are afraid that the spirit will suffocate or be too compressed because of frequent sadness and torpor, you will love being surrounded by odors. Where you fear your spirits will fly away through exhalation, take in the odors that are infused with your food.

If you want to wear some odor on the outside, like a shield, apply it to your left side. See how suddenly the source precipitates itself up and down with odors? See how quickly the spirit flies to the mouth and the nostrils, allured by a pleasant odor?

When the spirit is either thin or very flighty, and easily dissipated, as in pusillanimity or weakness of the body, or many other things, allure it back with odors not so much on the outside as the inside; feed it; retain it.

Go for the odor of wine beyond all others, for it nourishes the spirit considerably, exhaling its odor from nature, nourishing the body quickly, and affecting the senses with pleasure. Wine of this kind is best when warm, moist, fragrant, and clear. Even sugar is

said to be like this, if it has an odor. Likewise cinnamon, wolfsbane, anise, and fennel, if a little sweetness is added to their sharpness.

But if nature does not provide a balanced formula, make one
yourself. As often as you fear distraction of the spirit, apply very
warm, sharp, and subtle things which manage to hold the flight of
the spirit a little, and stabilize it, things like saffron, India spice,
cinnamon, baked bread, rosewater, rose vinegar, rose, myrtle, violet, cornflower, coriander, quince fruit and citrus. I detest camphor, which hastens gray hair. I always like fresh mint, healthful
for the mind and totally safe for the spirit.

Remember that everything that is the opposite of poison is
good for life, not only through its taste but also its fragrance,
especially theriaca. We have described all these in our book against
plague, and we will describe them in the following book. Among
these—in case you have not noticed it—we include wine. For just
as hemlock is a poison to man, so wine is to hemlock, not exactly
in the same way, but a little after it has been drunk.

Lest I allure you here only with odors, I will give you also a
melt-in-the-mouth you can make, to be tasted every morning, one
that is really mellow for smell and taste and healthful for your life.
Take three parts chebulan balsam, one emblic, and one Indian, one
part bellirica, a half-part wolfsbane, two parts cinnamon, one dram
saffron, a third of a dram of amber, and the same amount of musk.
Grind it up carefully and take it with as much rose sugar as your
taste likes. Add enough red cornflower to give it color, and enough
emblic or chebulan honey to give form to this as a sucket. Add as
much gold leaf as we said before.

Since this multiple composition is very difficult, we have also
found a simple one that is excellent, made simply from chebulan,
sweet fennel, sugar, liquefied rosewater, taken first on an empty
stomach, and then again after dinner. You should remember, however, that mixed balsams are better when dried at least a whole day
in oil of sweet almond, or else pour butter from cows into them as
you mix.

Avicenna recommends a formula for you out of emblic and

Indian balsam with anacardine honey, cooked in butter; also che-bulan balsam with ginger and iron scalings, or even better, gold ones.

Pietro d'Abano recommends a formula from saffron, mace, and castor, in equal parts, ground up and mixed with wine. He guarantees that it will produce life even in people who are dying.

By the way, Ali the Astrologer, an excellent doctor, asserts that the use of triphera likewise brings about a longer life. Balsam is the base of all triphera, and it overpowers the triphera with certain subtle and soft things, especially when the balsam is dry enough to penetrate and not block the passages, nor dry out the stomach too much, or bind it. We use it best with wine, but only a little, lest it dilute it.

At any rate, this formula of Pietro's, which I just mentioned, if it is useful at all, is more useful for smelling, in my opinion, than for drinking.

Chapter 19

The medicine of the Magi for old people

The Magi, observers of stars, came with a star guiding them, to Christ, the guide of life. They brought him a precious treasure of life in their gold, incense, and myrrh, three gifts on behalf of the three lords of the planetary stars, dedicated to the Lord. Gold, indeed, is the most temperate of all things: it is the temperament of Jove. Incense, however, burning in its heat and fragrance, is from the Sun, Phoebus. Myrrh, strengthening the body, does its strengthening through Saturn, the strongest of all the planets.

Come, then, all you old folks, to the wise Magi, who bear their gifts to you for the prolonging of life. Come, you old people, suffer-ing so gravely from old age, and come, you other people, too, who are nearing old age and are scared of it. Take, I beg you, these vital gifts right away.

Take two parts incense, one part myrrh, and a half dram of gold leaf. Grind them all together, mix, pour into pills, with a little gold wine, and take this when Diana rejoices at the happy sight of Phoebus or Jove. Take a small portion of this treasure just after dawn, and pour it into a drink of thin wine, unless it is a hot day, in which case drink it with rosewater. If someone among you, however, is afraid of more heat, he should add balsam (either chebulan or emblic) in an equal weight to the incense, myrrh, and gold.

This will, beyond any doubt, protect your natural humor from putrefaction. It will keep the humor from breaking up. It will nourish the three spirits in you, the natural, the vital, and the animal, and it will strengthen and fortify them. It will make your senses flourish again, sharpen your mind, and strengthen your memory.

Chapter 20

On avoiding the dangers that threaten your life around the seventieth year

Since the astronomers have divided the single hours of the day according to single planets and likewise the seven days of the week, and declared that babies are under the offices of the planets in their womb months, why not do the same thing for the years? So that whatever infant is hiding in the stomach, Saturn rules over him in the first month, the Moon rules over him in the next, and so on in a continuing order, after he is born, with the Moon in charge in the first year, Mercury (if you want) in the second, Venus in the third, the Sun in the fourth, Mars in the fifth, Jupiter in the sixth, and Saturn in the seventh, and this same order repeated through life.

Therefore, in the seventh year of life there will occur a great changeover in the body, one that is extremely perilous, since Saturn is a stranger to us, and from him, then, on the highest tract, the governing of the planets returns to the Moon on the lowest. The Greek astronomers call these years climacteric, while we call them scalar, or grades, or decisive.

In diseases, too, the planets rule every day in this same order over the motion of the humor or nature, so that every seventh is for this reason called the Judiciary. The fourth is too, because it is in the middle of the seventh.

Therefore, if you want to prolong your life into old age, uninterrupted in any of these steps, every time you get to the end of a seven-year period, consult an astrologer carefully. Discover what decision threatens you, and then either find a doctor, or find temperance and prudence. With these remedies, the threats of the stars can be thwarted, as Ptolemy declared. He adds that the promises of the stars can be increased through virtue, the way a plougher of fields increases his land through his virtue.

Pietro d'Abano agrees, with many arguments and with the testimony of Aristotle, Galen, and Ali, that the exact natural end of life is not determined from the beginning to the end, but can be moved back and forth. He argues this first of all from the stars, and then from matter. He concludes from these authorities and reasons that a natural death can be altered, with the schemes of astrology, or the advice of doctors. But let us not weary ourselves going over these precepts.

Do not hesitate to ask your doctor what your natural diet should be, or your astrologer which star is favorable to life and when it will do good for you, and what the Moon does to it. Use what you learn for profit. Do not be embarrassed to consult sometimes even those people who look like they have pursued a prosperous old age through virtue rather than just luck.

Ptolemy and other professors of astronomy promise a long and prosperous life through the use of images made from certain stones and metals made under a certain star. We will have a lot to say about images and the other favors of the heavenly bodies in our commentary on Plotinus, a book which we think we will tack onto this one, just as we have tacked this one onto our book *On Caring for the Health of Men of Letters*.

The heavenly favor of a long youth—as long, in fact, as the poets always like to say, and as long as the doctors can make it—we have to seek from Phoebus and from Bacchus. Youth is only eternal for Phoebus and Bacchus, for long hair is appropriate on these Gods. Phoebus and Bacchus are always individual brothers, but they are very much the same. Phoebus is the soul of the sphere; the sphere is Bacchus. Phoebus is the whole circle of the sphere; Bacchus is that flaming ring within the circle. Phoebus is the nourishing light in this flaming globe; Bacchus represents the same healthful warmth from light. So they are always brothers and pals, always each other and the same.

Why? If the Sun in Spring is Phoebus, exciting the song of birds with his own song, tempering the seasons again with his lyre, Bacchus, founder of wine, is the same as the Sun in Autumn.

Father Liber, who loves hills, Bacchus, brings us three things for preserving our youth: he brings us open hills, and then the magnificent wine that is in these hills, and the the perpetual freedom from care that is in this wine.

Phoebus, too, Bacchus' brother, gives with an equal generosity three things: our daily light, the grasses that grow so fragrantly under this light, and in the shade of this light, his lyre and song.

With these rations and with these threads, Clotho prolongs the thread of life for us, and not just as a Fate. All the poets sing of three Fates. Though I am not a poet, I sing of three Fates, too: a prudent sparingness in all matters of food begins long life for us, a constant sparingness in treatments prolongs life, and a negligent sparingness in enjoying the heavens cultivates life.

Pythagoras, that temperate man, praised three things above all else, and we are praising these three right now: keeping temperance in emotions, keeping temperance in all foods, and keeping a temperate climate.

With such prudence of the humors, with God's help, you will keep far away the intemperateness which is the cause of early aging and an early death. If you choose to live each day of your life in this way, the author of life himself will help you to stay longer with the human race and with him whose inspiration makes the whole world live.

End of the Book *On Prolonging the Life of Scholars*

Epistolary Beginning to His Third Book,
On Making Your Life Agree With the Heavens,
by Marsilio Ficino, Florentine

To the Most Serene King of Hungary:

The ancient philosophers, most happy king, carefully scrutinized the powers and natures of the lower heavens, since they thought that a man knew nothing if he did not know himself. They seem to have brought all their scrutiny to bear on making their life, above all, agree with the heavens. They decided, in my opinion anyway, that the elements and what they are composed of would be known in vain, and the movements and influxes of the heavens would be pointless to observe, unless all this knowledge at some point was conducive to life and happiness.

This kind of contemplation, it seems, was useful for their daily lives. For Pythagoras, Democritus, Apollonius of Tyana, and whoever else studied this carefully, pursued the knowledge of such things in order to have good health and a long life. It was good for their future life, too, either through the glory they attained among those who came after them or through the glory they would enjoy with God in eternity. Out of the marvelous order of the whole world they discovered, as it were, its master, and they loved that discovery beyond all else.

Your magnanimity, your magnificence, your perpetual victory, promise future glory too, through all the centuries. Your divine clemency, your piety and justice, promise blessed life for you with God. The happy stars have decreed for you a prosperous life among mortals, and one satisfactorily long (as much as it has been permitted me to conjecture from certain indications).

What the stars have promised, however, they will prolong with an even greater abundance thanks to your diligence and the care that your doctors and astrologers will doubtless take. The learned astrologers and doctors all admit that this can be done with knowledge and prudence.

Among those books of Plotinus destined for the great Lorenzo Medici, I recently composed a commentary on the book of Plotinus that deals with how one draws down the favor of the heavens, one of many commentaries of mine on him. I have decided to select this one now, with Lorenzo himself approving, and dedicate it profoundly to your majesty.

I hope, indeed, that while I might advise you on your life and welfare, your life might itself come to be consulted both as the splendor of our time and of the human race. May what we have to say be of use to your health and the prosperity of your kingdom. It is for such *value* that I thought to send it. I beg you, therefore, most clement king, to embrace our Valori, too. May your nature, power, and authority be so strong that without you not even valor itself can prevail.

10th of July, 1489. Florence.

An Exhortation by Marsilio Ficino to the Reader

G ood health, honored guest! Good health to any of you who come to our doorstep hungry for health! I beg you, the guest who is hungry, to see how hospitable I am. For no sooner had you entered than I asked about your health. Anticipating your health, I bid you good health as soon as I saw you. When you entered here, unknown to me, I received you with great pleasure. If you follow my customs, I will give you the health promised (if God allows it).

You have happened upon a host who is friendly to everyone, and full of love toward you. If you bring a similar love, and if you have put aside all your hate, what vital medicines will you find here! For it was love and the pleasure of your parents that gave you life. Hatred and sorrow, on the other hand, destroy life. Any of you who is suffering from the sorrow of hate, then, there is no place here for you, no vital medicine left that will ever help you. Therefore, I am speaking to you not so much as a host, but as a friend.

The laboratory of your Marsilio is somewhat larger than just the space you see bounded here. For not only is it enclosed in the following book, but in the two preceding books, too. All of it is offered as a kind of medicine for the powers of life, so that your life will be healthy and long. It is based here and there on the work of doctors who are helpful on planetary matters. Our laboratory here, our antidotes, drugs, poultices, ointments and remedies, offer different things to different types of people. If you do not like some of these, just put them aside, lest you reject the rest because of a few.

If you do not approve of astronomical images, even those that have been found to be good for the health of mortals, remember that I, myself, do not so much approve of them as describe them. You can, with my permission, or even, if you prefer, with my recommendation, put such things aside. At least you should not neglect the medicines that have been strengthened with a little planetary help—or you will have neglected life itself. For I have found, through frequent and long experience, that these medicines, as well as other things made correctly by astrologers, are as different as wine is from water.

Even when I was an infant, born in the eighth month from conception, in Florence, in the month of October, early in the evening, when I was half-alive with Saturn in retrograde, only such diligence seemed to be what kept me alive. My life was almost returned to God. Such diligence kept me healthy for my first three years. Even if I must tell you more things like this, know that I speak the truth. I bring it up not to boast (which is something very wrong for a philosopher), but rather to exhort you.

But we have spoken to you enough now, advising some things, exhorting you to others. Now let us speak with Plotinus, whom you must consult very carefully.

Chapter 1

What the powers consist of, according to Plotinus, that draws the favor of the heavenly bodies, that is, the soul of the world, of the stars and of daemons; souls are easily allured by the proper forms of bodies

If there were only intellect and body in the world, but no soul, the intellect would not be drawn to the body (for it is altogether immobile, and lacks the affect of motion, as if it were the furthest possible distance from the body), nor would the body be drawn to the intellect, since it is ineffective and inept in itself for such motion, and very remote from the intellect. So if a soul, conforming to each, is placed between them, each one is easily attracted to the other.

We are easily moved by the soul, first and foremost because it is the first mobile thing, mobile from itself and of its own doing. This is because, as I have said, it contains in itself all the middles of things, and is thus nearest to each. It is connected to all things, in the middle of these things that are distant from each other, for they are not distant from it. It conforms to divine things, and to things fallen, and it verges on each with its affect, and is everywhere all the same.

The soul of the world, the *anima mundi,* divinely contains at least as many seminal reasons for things as there are ideas in the divine mind, and with these reasons it fabricates as many species in matter. Therefore, any species whatsoever answers through its own seminal reasons to its own idea, and can often easily receive through this something from that idea, whenever it is affected through it. Thus, whenever it degenerates from its own form, it can be formed again by this middle thing next to it, and through this middle thing it easily re-forms. You thus correctly use many of its things, whether an individual's or a species', things which are scattered but conforming nonetheless to an idea.

Soon you draw the singular function or gift from the idea into this material that has been so conveniently prepared, and you draw it, as it were, through the seminal reason of the soul. For it is not the intellect, itself, but the soul that does this.

No one, therefore, should think that in certain materials of the world there are numinous elements, separated, inside, from material, and that these elements get drawn out; but one should rather think of these as demons and gifts of the animate world and the living stars. No one, furthermore, should marvel that the soul can be, as it were, allured through material forms. If it can be allured to harmonious foods by these forms, it does so, and it always and freely dwells among them. There is nothing so deformed in the whole living world that it has no soul, no gift of soul contained in it. The congruities of these forms, therefore, to the reasons of the soul of the world, are what Zoroaster called the divine lures, and Synesius agreed, calling them magic charms.

One certainly should believe that all gifts are drawn out of the soul at a certain time and for their own material species, but for convenience the seminal species produce these gifts, with their seminal elements conforming. Thus, as a man, you pursue and claim your human gifts, and not those proper to fish or birds, who get their own. You pursue, however, things which pertain to a certain star or demon, going into the flow proper to this star or demon, the way wood when it is doused with sulfur bursts into flame. This happens not only through the rays, themselves, of the star and demon, but even through the *anima mundi,* itself, wherever it is present.

The reason of the star and demon flourishes in the *anima mundi,* in part so that the seminal will be generated, and in part so that the exemplary will be recognized and known. For the soul, according to the ancient Platonic philosophers, builds figures with its reasons beyond the stars in heaven, and some of these are such that it becomes something of this figure itself. It impresses its properties on all these things. In the stars, however, and in figures, parts, and properties, all species of lower things are contained, as well as their properties.

Altogether it has forty-eight figures, as it were the twelve in the zodiac plus thirty-six more. Thirty-six must be added to the number of images in the zodiac. In the same way, the number of grades or stages is three hundred and sixty. For in any grade there are many stars, with which images are made. These images, beyond those in the zodiac, are divided into many figures, according to the same number of grades. Certain habits and proportions in the universal images are then set in place, and these are also images. Such figures have their continuity from the rays of their stars, one after another, each with its own special property.

From these most carefully arranged forms hang the forms of lower things, as if they were arranged there. These heavenly bodies, as if they were disjunct among themselves, proceed to join by reasons of the soul. The mutable ones proceed from the stable ones. But these, to the extent that they do not comprehend themselves, are carried back to the forms in the mind, comprehending themselves in the animal part or in something more eminent. They are a multiplicity, but they are, as it were, reduced into the one that is simplest and good, like the heavenly figures at the pole.

But let us return to the soul. When the soul produces the special forms and powers of the lower bodies, it makes these through its own reasons, with the help of what is under the stars and heavenly forms. The singular gifts of individuals, which are often in some people much more marvelous than those that appear in the species itself, are shown through similar seminal reasons. They do this not so much with the help of heavenly forms and figures than with the location of the stars, the habit of their movements, and the aspects of the Planets. They are first shown among themselves and then in the more sublime stars.

Our soul, beyond the powers of the limbs, produces a power of life common everywhere in us, but especially in the heart, as if it were a fountain of fire nearest the soul. The *anima mundi* flourishes everywhere in the same way, but it especially unfolds its own power of life in the Sun. Thus, they locate the soul, both in us and in the world, as whole in any limb, and especially strong in the heart and in the Sun.

Yet always remember that just as the power of our soul adheres to the limbs through the spirit, so the power of the *anima mundi*, through the quintessence, which everywhere flourishes as if it were a spirit inside the worldly body, spreads out through all things that are under the *anima mundi*. It especially infuses its power into those which draw its spirit the most.

The fifth essence, however, can be taken inside more and more by us, if we know how to separate it from the other elements with which it is heavily mixed, or at least if we know how to use those things which abound in it. This is especially true for things in which it is purer, as in select wines and sugar, balsam and gold, precious stones, things which are pleasantly fragrant and things which shine, especially those that have a warm, moist, and clear quality in a subtle substance, which, besides wine, includes the whitest sugar, especially if you add gold to it, and the odor of cinnamon and roses.

Just as foods that we eat properly, though they are not alive in themselves, return us to the form of our life through our spirit, so also our bodies draw the most from worldly life when they are properly fitted to the spiritual and worldly body through worldly things and through our spirit. If you want food to take form for your brain or liver or stomach, you should eat, as much as you can, food such as brains, livers, and the stomachs of animals that are not far distant from human nature.

If you want your body and spirit to receive power from some limb of the world, for example from the Sun, learn which are the Solar things among metals and stones, even more among plants, but among the animal world most of all, especially among men. For there is no doubt that they confer on you similar qualities. These and more should be held forth and taken inside for their powers, especially on a day and in an hour of the Sun, with the Sun reigning in its figure in the sky. Solar things are all those things that are called Heliotrope—because they are turned to the Sun—for example, gold and the color of gold, chrysolite, carbuncle, myrrh, incense, musk, amber, balsam, golden honey, aromatic calamus, saffron, spikenard, cinnamon, wood aloe, and other aromatics, the Ram, the Hawk, the hen, the swan, the lion, the beetle, the crocodile, people who are golden-haired, curly-haired, sometimes baldheaded people, and the magnanimous.

Our bodies are able to be fitted to these in part through foods, in part through fragrant ointments, and in part just through habituation. They should be felt, frequently thought about, and even loved. One should very much seek out light.

If you worry about destroying your belly from a poultice of the liver, draw the faculty of the liver to the belly, first with massages, then with poultices that gather the liver, using chicory, endive, spode, agrimony, and liver salve. In the same way, lest your stomach be destroyed by Jove, move your body on the day and in an hour when Jove is reigning, and meanwhile use Jovial things, like silver, amethyst, topaz, coral, crystal, beryl, spode, sapphire, green and airy colors, wine, white sugar, honey, and thoughts and feelings that are very Jovial, too: constant ones, balanced ones, religious and law-abiding ones. Associate with men of this kind, sanguine and handsome, venerable and versatile.

Remember, against cold things, the first things to be taken are gold and wine, mint and saffron. The Jovial animals are the lamb and the peacock, the eagle and the calf. In the same way, the power of Venus is drawn by turtle-doves, pigeons, the white water-wagtail, and other things which modesty does not permit me to list.

Chapter 2

*On the harmony of the world, and on the nature of man
according to the stars; how one is attracted by a certain star*

Let no one have any doubt, we and all the things that are around us, with certain preparations, are able to lay claim to the heavenly bodies. For that is how the heavenly bodies are made. They rule strictly, and they have been prepared for this from the beginning.

In fact, the animal world in itself is more a wine than something animal, even if we are talking about the most perfect animal. Therefore, just as in us the principal quality and movement of one limb always pertains to the others, so the acts of the principal limbs of the world move everything, and the lower limbs easily give way to the direction of the higher. This is the reason why, when one limb is ready to act, another is inclined to give. So a little preparation applied by us to what is overhead is all that is needed to receive the gifts of the heavenly bodies.

One must fit himself earnestly to what is overhead, to which one is earnestly subject anyway. But before we consider any of this our property, we ought to consider the property of the human species. The Arab astrologers have decided that it is Solar. I guess this is true, when you consider the stature of man, erect and handsome, with his subtle humors, the clarity of his spirit, the perceptiveness of his imagination, and his zeal for truth and glory. But I would add that he has a Mercurial property too, because of the strenuous movement of his versatile mind. Because the human race is born naked, empty, in need of everything, it acquires for itself all those industries which belong to Mercury. I would add that man has a Jovial property too, because of the temperate complexion of his body and his laws. We receive life in the second month, when Jupiter dominates, and we are born in the ninth, when he again receives his domination.

The human species could therefore claim for itself even greater gifts from these three heavenly bodies if it would, from day to day, more and more, fit itself to the Solar, the Mercurial, and the Jovial.

What about the others? Saturn does not easily signify the quality and lot he shares with the human race, except for the man who is separated from others, either divinely or brutishly, blessed or pressed by extreme misery. Mars, the Moon, and Venus share the feelings and acts of man equally with the other animals.

Let us return then to the Sun, Jove, and Mercury. We have already described some Solar and Jovial things, and I do not know how we missed the Mercurial things, but these are a silver and lead alloy called Stannum, silver, especially quicksilver, silvery marcasite, Achates stone, Porphyritic glass, and what you get when you mix yellow with green, emerald and lacca. Clever and smart animals are Mercurial, and strong ones, like apes and dogs, as well as men who are eloquent, sharp, versatile, with oblong faces and with hands that are not fat.

The things which touch upon some planet ought to be learned and used, for example the hour and day, as we have said, in which the planet is reigning, if this can be done, and when it is in its house, or in the ascendant, or at least in its triplication, as well as its end, its corner in the sky, and its position in relation to the Sun, the Hours, and the Moon.

If someone asks some benefit from the Moon and Venus, he should observe them at similar times. We have described Venus' animals, and she also has horn, sapphire, lapis lazuli, yellow, red, and coral colored metals, all the beautiful and variously colored flowers, and the harmonious and pleasant fragrances and flavors. The Moon has things white, damp, and green, silver and crystal, pearls, and silvery marcasite.

Saturn has dominion through his stature and perseverance. To Mars, however, belong the movements of efficiency, from which we are sometimes forced to seek protection. From him and through his materials you scare, you paint, you make things of lead, and from him you also get dark stone, the magnet, brass, and sometimes gold and gold marcasite. We get to Mars through red fires, red metals, all sulfurous things, iron and bloodstone. Saturn has some of his material scattered in gold. This is why it is thought to have weight. But it is like the gold of the Sun, and is thus contained in all metals, just as the Sun is in all planets and stars.

If someone were to accuse Saturn and Mars of being harmful by nature, I would not believe it, for they, too, are to be used sometimes, the way doctors must sometimes use poisons, as Ptolemy in his *Centiloquio* says. When the power of Saturn is cautiously taken, it is useful, just as the things doctors use are useful for binding up and holding together. After all, they even use things to stupefy, like opium and mandrake. The same goes for Mars, with euphorbia and hellebore. The Pythagorean maguses seem to have been extremely cautious in this matter, when they would become frightened that their constant philosophizing was the tyranny of Saturn, so they would dress up in white garments, and each day sing songs and make music with Jovial and Apollonian things, and in this way they lived a long time under Saturn.

Remember that wherever we are easily and suddenly exposed to the planets through the feeling and exertion of the soul, and through the same quality of spirit, they are marking that same feeling and its exertion and quality. Very often, therefore, in human affairs we are subject to Saturn, through idleness, solitude, or strength, through Theology and more secret philosophy, through superstition, Magic, agriculture, and through sadness. We are subject to Jove through civil and ambitious business, through natural and common philosophy, and through civil religion and laws. We are subject to Mars through anger and struggles; to the Sun and to Mercury through the study of eloquence, skill in song, and the glory of truth; to Venus through happiness, music, and feasts; to the Moon through food from plants.

But keep the differences in mind. Look to the Sun for exercise of the mind that is public and spacious, but to Mercury for the kind that is private and artificially produced. Then again, music that is heavy is of Jove and the Sun, music that is light is of Venus, while a middle kind is of Mercury. The same thing applies to the fixed stars. Here is a general rule for the human species: the proper rule for somebody should be to explore those stars which promised some good at his birth, and to seek grace from them rather than from others. One should not seek the gift of a certain one which is really someone else's, but expect one's own, except of course for those many generous things that one gets from the Sun, the common leader of the heavens, and from Jove likewise, and likewise all the worldly things one gets from the soul and spirit of the world.

How one gets these from being animal, and even more so just from being animate, is explained by the Platonists, and not only by them but by the Arab astrologers, too. They agree that, from a certain application of our spirit to the spirit of the world through the art of natural philosophy and through affect, the celestial goods get thrust into our soul and body. This application goes through our spirit, which is in the middle of us, then gets strengthened by the spirit of the world, then through the rays of the stars happily working into our spirit, likewise with rays in nature, and finally it fits us to the heavens.

Chapter 3

Between the soul of the world and its manifest body, is its spirit, in whose power are four elements; how we are able to draw it in through our spirit

Actually, the worldly body, as it appears from its movement and generation, is everywhere alive, as the Indian philosophers say of it, because all over the place it generates living things out of itself. It lives through the soul which is everywhere present to it, and which is directly accommodated to it. Therefore, between the body of the world that is tractable, fallen in fact from part of it, and its soul, whose nature is too distant from its body, spirit is everywhere present.

It is the same as between the soul and body in us, when life is shared between a soul and its thicker body. For such spirit is necessarily sought as a kind of middle, in which the divine soul is present in a thicker body and bestows life on what is inside.

All of this body, however, is easily sensible to you, as if it

94

were fitted or accommodated to your senses. It is very thick, and it is a long way degenerated from its most divine soul. It is necessary, therefore, to support this higher body, as if it were not a body. Let us know, then, all living things, plants as well as animals, through which its spirit lives and generates. Among the elements, because it especially belongs to the air and weather, it very rapidly comes forth, and is perpetually moved as if it were alive.

But meanwhile, you may ask, if the elements and animate beings generate something like its kind of spirit, why do not stones and metals generate it too, since they lie between the elements and animate beings? Because the spirit in them is stuck to a thicker material. It is like a nursery-garden's power to generate, when you separate seeds and preserve correctly what you separate, as long as these are then applied to some material of the same kind; or the way naturalists, who use metals and make gold, will carefully separate the spirit from gold with a certain sublimation in fire. When such spirit is correctly extracted from gold or some other substance and kept, the Arab astrologers call it an Elixir.

But let us return to the spirit of the world, through which the world generates everything. Since through its own spirit it generates everything, we can call this heaven, and the fifth essence. Whoever this is in the body of the world, it is like what we are in our body. With this exception: that the soul of the world does not draw this out of the four elements as if they were its own humors (the way we draw ours), but on the contrary (to talk Platonically or Plotinically), it creates out of its own genital virtue or power (as you do out of your mind), and with this it produced the stars and the four elements. It is as if in the power of such a spirit was everything.

This is indeed a body that is extremely thin, almost no body at all, and almost, in fact, a soul. In the same way, it is almost no soul, and almost, in fact, a body. In its virtue or power there is the least amount of earthly nature, more, however, of watery nature, more, even, of airy nature, but most of all fiery and starry nature. According to the measures of these grades or steps, you get the same quantity of stars and elements.

Its power flourishes everywhere in everything as the nearest author and movement of all generation, from which comes the saying: the Spirit inside nourishes. It is all of its own power natural, bright, and warm, damp and enlivening gifts that come from it out of the higher gifts of the soul. Apollonius of Tyana drew much from this, as the Indian Hiarchas has testified, saying, "No one should marvel, O Apollonius, that you have pursued the science of divining, when you carry in your soul so much of the aether."

Chapter 4

How our spirit draws the spirit of the world through the rays of the Sun and Jove, and to what extent it can become Solar and Jovial

You must therefore learn how to bring this spirit into yourself. For in its midst you will carry back certain natural benefits, first of the worldly body, then of the soul, and then even of the stars and daemons. For its spirit is between the thick body of the world and the soul, and through it and in it are the stars and daemons.

Whether the body of the world and worldly things are near to the soul of the world (as Plotinus and Porphyry thought), or the worldly body and soul are, as it were, next to God, as I think, and perhaps Timaeus the Pythagorean thought, too, the world both lives and breathes, and it is possible for us to draw its spirit. It is actually drawn by man through his own spirit, conforming to it in its own nature, especially if it proceeds in a related way, that is, especially if it goes forth in a heavenly way. It goes forth in a heavenly way if it is purged of all filth, and of all the stuff that sticks to it that is unheavenly. I do not mean just the kind of filth that is in your viscera, for the spirit is often infected by the filth in your soul, on your skin, on your clothes, in your house, or in the air.

The spirit is made heavenly, as it were, if it makes discs or orbs of the orbicular motion of our body and soul; if at the sight and thought of light it glows; and if things that are like the heavens are used by it. By these I mean things which Avicenna, in his book

On the Powers of the Heart, says care for the spirit, and the things which I have recommended you use, in my book *On Caring for the Health of Men of Letters.*

First, obscuring vapors must be separated from this spirit, even with the use of purge medicines. Second, it should be illuminated with things of light. Third, it should be cultivated, so that it might be made fine and strengthened. Finally, our spirit would become heavenly, to the extent that reason dictates, if the rays and influxes of the Sun, ruling over the heavens, were strongly applied to it.

Thus, with this spirit in our midst, all the heavenly blessings will abound in our body and soul: I call them the *heavenly* blessings but really they are all contained in the Sun.

The Sun, however, when it is under Aries or Leo, and the Moon facing it, especially in Leo, confers in its Solar spirit a power that makes our own spirit flourish so much that it protects it against the poisons of an epidemic. This especially seems to happen in Babylon and in Egypt, and in regions facing Leo; for when the Sun is entering Leo, it calms an epidemic for the reason I just gave.

So be sure you organize your Solar stuff carefully. Start making use of Solar things, with this one caution, however: be careful to avoid getting dried out under its heat. The Solar spirit cannot easily come forth except in huge amounts. For amplitude belongs especially to the Sun. So take huge amounts of care when nourishing your heart with external and internal cordials, eating often and easily the more subtle and health-nourishing foods. Keep your movements here frequent and light, find suitable quiet, get air that is thin and serene and remote from heat and cold, and especially keep a happy disposition. It will not be Solar if it is not warm, subtle, and clear. You will make yourself subtle and clear if you avoid sadness and thick and dark things. Use things that are bright and cheerful, both inside and outside. Get plenty of light both day and night. Get rid of filth, dullness, and torpor. First and foremost, avoid darkness!

The spirit must be drawn forth out of the natural heat of the

Sun, so beware lest you bring on dryness in the third degree of heat. The heat, itself, from the Sun does not naturally dry you out—otherwise we would not call the Sun the Lord of Life and Generation and the Founder of All Increase. It hits with its drying rays only the hollow confines of dry matter. You will use and preserve in the spirit, therefore, the subtle humor with its heat, which is Solar and very Jovial, by using these things.

That is, of course, if you want to make your spirit Solar, for otherwise you might just lead it to the Martial rather than the Solar. Mars is, in fact, like the Sun in a few things and these are apparent, and not very good, and they are said to be even hostile.

Jove is most like the Sun in his many and excellent gifts, although these are more hidden than the Sun's, and we know that Jove is the friendliest one. That is what Ptolemy decided in his treatise on harmony. He said that Jove was in perfect harmony with the Sun, beyond any others, and Venus with the Moon.

All the astrologers attribute a universal benevolence to the Sun and Jove together, though the Sun is more effective in doing his stuff, and Jupiter works under the power of the Sun. In both of them heat flourishes and overtakes the humor. But in Jove it overtakes it moderately, in the Sun brilliantly, and in both beneficially. Since, therefore, they are so harmonious, you can easily put to use the Solar spirit alongside the Jovial one, and you can properly mix Solar things with Jovial things. It is especially good if you do these alternately, and use the spirit when Jupiter is facing the Sun in the third or sixth position, or at least when the Moon proceeds to face one after the other, especially when she proceeds from facing the Sun into a coitus with Jupiter. You are doing Solar things or Jovial things correctly when you observe the face of the Moon looking to the Sun or to Jove.

Once you get the hang of this, it will be easy for you. Realize that the sixth aspect is when two planets are separated by an interval of four signs. The third aspect is when they are separated by an interval of four signs. The conjunction or aspect of the Moon to the others is twelve steps further, and these are measured in the same way.

Chapter 5

The Three Graces are Jupiter, the Sun, and Venus, and Jupiter is the middle Grace between the other two, as well as the one best suited to us

You will find Jovial concoctions and cures, as well as Solar ones, in our book *How to Live Long,* and in our book *On Caring for the Health of Men of Letters.* In those books we have even mixed some of these together along with a lot of Venereal stuff. For we fear a drying out in students, which Venus stops.

This Venus is herself the best friend of Jupiter, just as Jupiter is to the Sun, as if they were three Graces, harmonious among themselves and joined to each other. From these Three Graces of heaven, and from stars of the same kind, the astrologers expect favors and carefully search for them. They think these are transmitted through Mercury and the Moon, as if they were messengers, the Moon being especially good for this when joined with Jupiter. They think she is happier when joined with Venus than if she were facing the sixth or third aspect. Nevertheless, if she is looking at the third aspect and is taken by these, it is as if she were joined, or so astrologers guess. Likewise, if she has been seen by the Sun and is taken by him.

However, if we want to run through one by one all the powers and effects of these three and of similar stars, we will be taking on a long task, difficult in its quest, but most difficult of all in its observation. If we take ourselves to Venus in the right way, we will not get the Sun easily; if to the Sun in the right way, we will not get Venus easily.

So that we might therefore intertwine three Graces in one, let us escape, as it were, to Jove, who is by nature and effect in the middle of the Sun and Venus, and very tempered in his quality. Whatever we expect from Venus, or from the Sun, we ill get by our dealings with him, who is more magnificent and more honest than Venus and more tempered than the Sun. He is particularly agreeable with human nature in everything. Let us use, therefore, Jovial things when he and the Moon have their greatness, whether it is natural or accidental, and when they are together, or happily facing each other.

If sometimes this is not altogether possible, mix Solar things into one of them, and likewise Venereal things, and thus compose out of both a Jovial face. Do this when, for example, the Moon goes from coitus with the Venereal into the sixth aspect of the Sun, or is changed.

Remember, in making things which nourish and strengthen the heart and spirit, that the Moon is most powerful if together with these gifts of hers she is running through airy zodiacal signs, especially through Aquarius, which is thought to be particularly airy; or if she is in her house, or her exaltation, or in the house of Jove or the Sun. Wherever she is, if the station she is occupying is from one of these twenty-eight signs, it will be good for your work.

Chapter 6

*On the natural, vital, and animal powers, and which planets
agree or disagree with them*

The important thing is to hold on correctly to whatever spirit, whatever force, or whatever powerful thing it is that these planets signify. The Moon, for example, and Venus signify a force and spirit that is natural and genital, and they increase this. Jupiter, in the same way, but more effectively, governs both the liver and the stomach. He has no small part in the heart and spirit, and the vital power to the extent that it agrees in its own nature with the Sun.

By no means does the vital power do this through itself, or otherwise the heart would not receive vital spirit so particularly in the month of Jove. This is why the Greeks call Jove life, and say, "through him life."

The astrologers claim that he also has a power in the animal spirit, saying Jove leads one to find philosophy, truth, and religion. Plato claims this, too, when he says that philosophers come forth out of Jove. Even Homer meant this, in the opinion of the ancients, when he said, "The mind of men is whatever the father of Gods and men brings forth from day to day." There is nothing divine which goes before Jove.

The Sun has an especially vital spirit, and signifies the heart. He has some of it, including no small part in the head, on account of sense and motion, of which he is the lord. He is not lacking in natural force either.

Mercury has the brain and the instruments of sense, and thus the animal spirit.

The safest route, therefore, will be to do nothing without the help of the Moon, especially when she casts the heavens down, so easily and often, into the lower depths. This is why they call her another Sun, doing this every four months of the year. In the first of these four, the Peripatetics think she is warm and damp; in the second, warm and dry; in the third, cold and dry; in the fourth, cold and damp. Her light is without doubt the light of the Sun. The humors that rule over generation and all mutations of the foetus itself, in the stomach, are measured by her changes. As often as she is joined to the Sun, she receives life-giving power from him, which she pours into the humor.

In the same way, she mixes the force she gets from Mercury into the humors, too. Mercury brings this force into everything with his transformations and multiple gyres. In the same way, she receives a force from Venus, which she conducts to forms that are ready for birth.

It is important to remember that the daily course of the Moon is distributed into four quarters. In the first, she rises from the East to mid-sky, all the time increasing the humor and natural spirit. In the second, she tries to fall from mid-sky, and does the opposite in us. In the third, she arrives after her fall at the lower mid-sky, and again increases the spirit and the humor. In the fourth, she falls back towards where she rose from, and diminishes little by little, which is seen especially on the shores of the ocean, where the sea rises and falls very clearly according to her course, which is why vigor rises and falls in the weak.

It is probable that the Sun, through these same quarters of

hers, increases and diminishes the natural heat and the vital apirit. He increases the animal spirit too, insofar as he has Mercury for an ally. Knowing all this, a doctor will be able to wait for the right moment for the humor and natural heat, and for refreshing the spirit.

But enough about the Moon. It is not right to ignore Jove, in one of whose months we received life, and in the other, happily, we were born. He is between the Sun and Venus, and also between the Sun and the Moon, a middle, so to speak, in quality and effect. He thus embraces everything.

The Sun itself, as lord of heaven, we can hardly ignore either, and it would be dangerous to do so, unless someone were to say that if one had Jove one had the Sun, too, in Jove, and had him at his most temperate toward man. In the Sun, certainly, are all the powers of the heavens, as not only Iamblichus and Julian said, but everyone else too. Proclus said that in the face of the Sun all the powers of all the heavens were congregated and gathered into one.

That Jove is a certain kind of Sun tempered especially for us, nobody will deny. And you should hardly neglect the Moon as one tempered to Venus. For she helps much in obtaining a strong and healthy life. Venus makes a man fertile and happy, and you should watch her for that. Although if the Moon is like Venus, yet more balanced in humor, and just barely less warm, you can mix her with Jove or the Sun and you will have Venus exactly!

What to do? Well, in order to take the safest and most convenient path of all, observe the Moon when it faces the Sun and is joined with Jove, or at least when it faces Jove and the Sun, or certainly when after it has faced the Sun it proceeds to its coitus with Jove. At this time, make up or apply to yourself, in turn, Solar, Jovial, and Venereal things. But if necessity or difficulty forces you to flee to one of these, flee to Jove himself, or rather to the Moon along with Jove. For there is no star that nourishes and strengthens the natural powers in us more than Jupiter, none that promises more prosperous things.

And whenever it is fortunate to receive him, go ahead and receive the Sun, though it is not always safe to do so. For while

Jupiter always helps, the Sun often seems to do harm. Venus, however, is almost weak. Thus Jupiter, alone, is called the helpful father.

Ptolemy confirms this when he says that hardly any drug can move nature when the Moon is in congress with Jove. But I have found that when the Moon is joined with Venus hardly any medicine works. Nonetheless, when we are very afraid of phlegm, we should especially watch the Moon when it faces the Sun, and in the same way when we fear bile and dryness we should watch it when it faces Venus.

The direction of the Moon toward Jove is good for all of these and especially good for getting rid of black bile and for restoring and strengthening the general complexion of man. For just as licorice and rose oil cool things off, and wine likewise, because it moistens the dry elements from above and dries the damp ones, so Jupiter is harmonious with human heat, as are wine, rose oil, camomile, and licorice. Albumasar said, therefore, "There is no life in living things beyond God, unless it be through the Sun and Moon."

I hope you realize how much one must look to the general influx into everything. The proper and most accomodating influx is from Jove. There are, however, in the nature of the body, powers for attracting, retaining, digesting, and expelling. Jupiter himself helps all these, especially the power of digesting, or dividing, and likewise the power of generating, nourishing, and increasing, on account of his airy and large humor and his ample heat, mildly dominating the humor. Certainly when the rays of Jove are diffused everywhere, the light of the Sun gets especially tempered for the health of man, and the rays of Venus and the Moon, too.

Since the rays of Venus and the Moon are somewhat damp, they need a certain tempering, and just as the rays of the Sun are somewhat warm, they need a tempering of something damp. The rays of Jove, however, need no tempering. For what else is Jupiter but the Sun tempered from the beginning for the health of things, especially human things? What else is Jupiter but the Moon and Venus made warmer and more powerful? So the astrologers predict from Jove a fertile year, a hard one, or a healthy one, and from him they hope for remedies for diseases that threaten. Empedocles was imitating Orpheus when he discussed the particular merits of each planet and called Jove the Prince of Generation.

Besides Jove, they say that the Moon must be watched diligently for all tasks, as if she were struggling between heavenly and earthly things. Let the Moon therefore be in an appropriate stage, position, and aspect for the best work to be done. Let it not be in an ecliptic, nor under the rays of the Sun through the twelve stages and beyond, unless it be in the same diminished stage with the Sun.

There are many who claim that all the planets are strong when they stand in unity with the Sun. They measure this unity by thirty-two minutes, numbering sixteen ahead and sixteen back.

Let the Moon not be impeded by Saturn or Mars, nor in the descendant. Let it be in the latitude of the meridian when it enters these twelve stages. Let it not be opposite the Sun, nor diminished by its light, nor slow in its course, when, for example, it does not pass through the twelve stages in one day. Do not let it be burned on the way leaving the twenty-eighth stage of Libra for the third of Scorpio, nor in the octave, nor in the ascendant, nor in the limits of Mars or Saturn.

They say the Moon should especially not be in the sixth, the twelfth, or the ninth, when in quarter. They approve of it being in the other regions of the sky.

When you are unable to embrace all these things, wait for Jove at least, or Venus in the ascendant or tenth stage, for they operate to the detriment of the Moon.

Do not forget that to the extent that the Moon is increased in light, not only our humor but our spirit and strength are increased too, and these are dilated when the Moon is at circumference, especially in her second quarter. When she is diminished, things go opposite, especially in her final quarter. Her first third to the Sun is present at her second. Her sixth is present at her first. In this stage, the Moon refills with heat as much as light.

There are some, therefore, who observe not so much how the

Moon looks to the Sun (for she always looks), but how much light she has, especially when she is increasing.

She is meanwhile in her third or sixth looking at Jove or Venus. At this time, fiery things help her attractive power, earthly things help her retentive power, airy things help her digestive power, and watery things help her expulsive power. If you want all these things to help in you, you can especially strengthen the attractive power through fiery things, when the Moon, standing in fiery signs or stations, is facing Jove—for example, when she is in Aries, Leo, or Sagittarius.

The same goes for her retentive power through earthly things, especially when she is facing Jove and stationed in earthly places like Taurus, Virgo, or Capricorn. You can strengthen her digestive and degenerative power through airy things like Gemini, Libra, and Aquarius, when she is taking Jove under airy signs or going under. Her expulsive power is strengthened through watery things: Cancer, Pisces, Scorpio. When she is positioned under watery signs, she is lighted with the rays of Jove. She will be especially well pursued in all of these if she will be possessing in her house Jupiter or some similar sign, or at least not a dissimilar sign.

To stimulate the stomach with solid medicines, take Pisces, the watery signs, or Scorpio. With medium medicines, take Cancer. To purge the lower tracts, take Pisces and Scorpio. For the upper tracts, take Cancer. You should avoid the evil face of Saturn or Mars looking at the Moon. For the former vexes the stomach, the latter dissolves the intestines. Stay away from Capricorn and Taurus, for they bring on nausea.

Know that a limb should not be irritated when the Moon takes a sign that is favorable to that limb (and moves the humors) but rather it should be nourished.

Those which are principally dominating in the liver, and concern the natural power and spirit, are divided into four areas, as we have said, and they have been sufficiently described.

As far as the vital power and spirit flourishing in the heart is concerned, what can we say? This has already been noticed enough. For these are helped through fiery and airy things, when the Moon, in its house or similar domicile, takes Jove, especially if she embraces Jove and the Sun.

You can strengthen the animal power through the sense and movement dominating in the head, through airy things, and secondarily through fiery things, when the Moon takes Jove in her house or similar seat, especially if she embraces Jove with Mercury. Let me warn you about this, lest you think Mercury is watery or earthly (which I have sometimes suspected, except for the fact that these do not confer motions or quickness of mind). Realize that he is airy. This is why he is so mobile, so easily changeable, and does so much for the mind.

He is especially airy when he stands in Aquarius. The humor is tempered in him, and heat is lessened. When he is positioned under the Sun, the humor is said to dry out. When he is far from the Sun, it is thought to be moistened. He gets much of his heat then from the nature of the Sun, and it is more in his own nature to dampen than to heat. He does not yield to Venus in his heat, and he exceeds the Moon's, but in humor he yields to both.

Haly said that Mercury mixes the qualities of the heavens because he is so easily changed. He is changed first into the quality of the terminus which he enters, then into the nature of the star which he faces.

I think that he is easily changed because he does not have the excellent power which Jove has, nor the further quality, which many heavenly bodies have, of being able to resist alteration. It is probable that Mercury is the faithful Achates of the Sun, since he has many of his powers, and thus it is possible to expect certain Solar things from Mercury.

They say Mars sometimes imitates the Sun in some of his gifts, and that Venus bestows things which belong to the Moon. Remember these things, then, in doing all this.

Never ignore the terminal positions. For they say that the planets in their different terminal positions make things opposite to light or dark. Thus, when you fear Mars, place him against Venus. When you fear Saturn, stick to Jove.

Do this work so that you are turning in perpetual motion with these powers, avoiding fatigue, so that you will set the right motion against the external motions that are secretly harmful, and so that you will imitate the heavenly movement for the sake of its powers. But if you are able to go through very large spaces with these movements, you will be imitating the heavens even more and you will attain the many powers that the heavens have scattered here and there.

Chapter 7

How our limbs are nourished through agreement with the signs of the Moon and the fixed stars

As we have said, you can nourish virtually the entire body, and most of all the head, if you have observed the planets in Aries, or in its first house, and you can nourish the area around the heart, if in Leo; the stomach and liver, if in Cancer and Sagittarius, or at least in Virgo. You will thus receive those things which are suitable for each limb. It is good to know which planet contains which limb in its sign.

You will even be able to advise someone on the differences of age, through the four ages of the Moon. In the first quarter of a new moon it is childhood. In full moon it is youth and manhood. In its third quarter it is manhood and old age. Then, at its final conjunction, it is old age. You will apply the age of the Moon best to the age in which you are caring for your body if you treat its face like the Three Graces. For the face of the Moon is always and graciously bestowing things. Nevertheless, this is not easily done for any length of time or to the utmost unless, before looking at the Moon, the Graces themselves mutually look at each other, or are nearly about to look at each other, either the three of them, or two of them anyway.

Furthermore, they offer fixed signs for long periods of time: Leo, Aquarius, Taurus, Scorpio. If you are not able at present to direct the Moon to the gracious planets, select fixed stars that have the nature of the Graces, like Jove or Venus or the Sun, and direct the Moon to them.

It is safer, meanwhile, for the Moon to be entering Jove or

Venus. For the fixed stars, if they are alone, exceed too much the human proportion, that is, of one man. They hold this proportion in moderation when they are with their fellow citizens.

Chapter 8

On the powers and uses of the fixed stars

The astrologers say that certain greater stars have learned from Mercury, and these have great authority. One such is the center of Andromeda in the 22nd degree of Aries, very Mercurial and Venereal. The same for the head of Algol in the 18th degree of Taurus, which possesses the nature of Saturn and Jove. They say this one is at the root of iron and mugwort too, and exceeds them both in boldness and power. The same for the 22nd degree of the Pleiades, a Lunar and Martial star. This one is behind crystal, the herb diacedon, and fennel-seed. They think it is good for improving the vision, and though some people say it is even used for the summoning of demons, in my opinion this is a fiction.

The first or third degree of the double star Aldebaran is Martial and Venereal. The goat in their 13th degree, Jovial and Saturnine. Under this are sapphires, white horehound, mint, mugwort, and mandrake. Unless these people are wrong, it is supposed to bring dignity and grace. They say that under it also are rubies, the tit-mallow, matrisylva, and that it increases your wealth and glory.

In the sixth or seventh degree of Cancer, Canis Major is Venereal, excelling in beryl, savina, mugwort, and dragonwort. It excels in grace, and the same in the 17th degree of the same Canis Major, which is Mercurial and Martial. They say that under it are the agate, the herb heliotrope, and pennyroyal, and it bestows grace.

In the 21st degree of Leo, the Heart of Leo, a royal star both Jovial and Martial: they think granite is subject to it, and swallowwort, and mastic-gum. It is supposed to repress melancholy, and make one balanced and gracious.

In the 19th degree of Virgo, the Tail of Ursa Major is Venereal and Lunar. They think the magnet is its stone and its herb is chicory. It protects against robbers and poisons.

In the seventh of Libra, the wing of the Raven on the right. The same in its 12th degree, and perhaps its 13th. Its left wing is Saturnian and Martial. Its herb is sorrel and henbane, and they think it increases boldness with the tongue of a frog. It would be harmful, in the 15th or 16th degree of the same, its brightest star being Venereal and Mercurial. It is in charge of the emerald, sage, trefoil, mugwort, and mandrake. It increases your wealth and power and saves you from distress.

Another one is in the 17th or 18th degree of Alcameth. They put plantain under this one. They hope that it strengthens the blood and rids all fevers.

Another, in the fourth of Scorpio, is Venereal and Martial. According to another computation, in the fifth degree of the same is horn, and perhaps it also presides over topaz, rosemary, trefoil, and ivy, and increases grace, chasteness, and glory.

In the third of Sagittarius, the Heart of Scorpio is Martial and Jovial, ruling over Sardonic amethyst, the long birthwort, and saffron. They think that it brings good color, makes the soul happy and a man wise, and that it repels demons.

In the seventh degree of Capricorn, the falling Vulture is in charge of chrysolite, savory, and smoke-of-the-earth. This star is Mercurial and Venereal, and temperate. It does best in the ascendant and in mid-sky. They say that it brings the authority to work charms or enchantment, which I doubt.

In the 16th of Aquarius, the tail of Capricorn is Saturnian and Mercurial. It is in charge of chalcedony, marjoram, catnip, mugwort, and mandrake. It is supposed to be good for grace, increasing wealth, and for keeping a man and his house safe.

In the third of Pisces, the shoulder of the Horse is Jovial and Martial. The philosopher Thebit teaches that to capture the power of some star like the one just mentioned, you must take its stone and its herb and make a gold or silver ring, in which you insert the stone with the herb under it, and then wear it around, touching it. You should do this, however, when the Moon is under the star, or is facing its third or sixth aspect. The star should be crossing in mid-sky or in its ascendant.

I would, myself, put together the things that pertain to these stars in the form of a medicine rather than a ring, a medicine to be used internally or externally when the predicted time is observed for its best use. Nevertheless, the ancients made terrific rings. For Damis and Philostratus tell us that Hiarchas, the leading wise man of India, in a similar way made seven rings, each one named for one of the seven stars, and he gave these to Apollonius of Tyana. He wore a different one each day of the week, distinguishing the days of the week by these names. Hiarchas said to Apollonius that his grandfather, the philosopher, lived a hundred and twenty years, perhaps because he was supported by this heavenly gift. Apollonius, using this, even in his hundredth year, they say, seemed young.

So if these rings have some power from on high, it does not seem to be applied to the soul, in my opinion, or to the thick body, so much as to the spirit. The spirit seems warmed little by little with the ring, having thus some affect there that makes it stronger, or brighter, or more violent, or kinder, or more severe, or happier. These affects go into the body mostly, and into the sensual soul somewhat, which is very indulgent towards the body. The idea, however, that these rings work against demons or enemies, or that they offer some important grace, is either a fiction or it is deduced from the fact that they make the spirit intent and firm, or even mild, lovable, and gracious.

Now, really, if I were to say that something is conferring these celestial things beyond just bodily strength onto thought, art, and fortune, I would not be saying anything that Thomas Aquinas did not already say. In his third book *Contra Gentiles* he claims that something in our bodies is imprinted by the heavenly bodies, whose gift we can then use to decide what is good, even if we do not know its reason or purpose. Because of this, he says, we are very fortunate and (agreeing with Aristotle) well born.

He goes on to say that with this heaven-borne power some people are gifted with certain aspects of their arts (to use his words), such as a soldier in conquering, a farmer in planting, or a doctor in healing. But just as herbs and wonderful stones have these heavenly powers beyond any natural element in them, so also does man have some of these in his arts.

As for me, they will have done enough if these celestial powers somehow confer good health through their medicines (either internal or external) at the same time that we, pursuing the health of the body, are careful not to neglect the health of the soul. Let us try nothing, of course, that is prohibited by holy religion. Above all, in whatever thing we are working on, let us hope for and seek the fruit of this work from him who made the heavenly bodies and the things that are contained in them, and who gives their power, moves and preserves them always.

Chapter 9

Observing the merits of the planets in their signs for the use of medicines

The house of Saturn is Aquarius and Capricorn. Its exaltation is Libra. The house of Jove is Sagittarius and Pisces. Its exaltation, or kingdom, is Cancer. The little house of Mars is Scorpio and Aries. Its exaltation is Capricorn. The seat of the Sun is Leo. Its regnum or kingdom is Aries. Venus' habitat is Taurus and Libra. Her exaltation is Pisces. Mercury's building is Virgo and Gemini; his kingdom is Virgo. The house of the Moon is Cancer; her exaltation is Taurus.

Saturn and Jupiter have their triplicate in fiery and airy signs. The Sun has his mostly in fiery signs. Mercury's is only in airy ones, Mars, Venus, and the Moon in watery and earthly ones.

Other than the Sun and Moon, certain planets, in whatever sign, possess certain ends, which we call their terminus. Thus, in Aries, Jupiter has his six first termini, Venus has the six following, Mercury a later eight, Mars then has five, and finally Saturn has five. In Taurus, in a similar order, Venus has eight ends, Mercury six, Jupiter eight, Saturn five, and Mars three. In Gemini, Mercury has six, Jupiter six, Venus five, Mars seven, Saturn six. In Cancer, Mars has seven, Venus six, Mercury six, Jupiter seven, Saturn four.

In Leo, Jupiter has six, Venus five, Saturn seven, Mercury six, and Mars six. In Virgo, Mercury has seven, Venus ten, Jupiter four, Mars seven, Saturn two. In Libra, Saturn has six, Mercury eight, Jupiter seven, Venus seven, Mars, two. In Scorpio, Mars has seven, Venus four, Mercury eight, Jupiter five, Saturn six. In Sagittarius, Jupiter has twelve, Venus five, Mercury four, Saturn five, Mars four. In Capricorn, Mercury has seven, Jupiter seven, Venus eight, Saturn four, Mars four. In Aquarius, Mercury has seven, Venus six, Jupiter seven, Mars five, and Saturn five. In Pisces, Venus has twelve, Jupiter four, Mercury three, Mars nine, and Saturn two.

The Sun and Moon have their ends by a different system. The Sun has six signs for his ends: Leo, Virgo, Libra, Scorpio, Sagittarius and Capricorn. The Moon has the rest: Aquarius, Pisces, Aries, Taurus, Gemini, and Cancer. They say the Sun and Moon therefore have the foremost place and effect in these signs, which the other planets have in their ends.

Besides their ends, the planets have in their signs their faces, which the Greeks call their Decans, since they occupy ten degrees in a sign. In Aries is the first face of Mars, and the second face of the Sun, which follows Mars in the sky in the Chaldaean system. The third face of Venus is here, since she follows the Sun in the sky. In Taurus is the first face of Mercury, following Venus. Here, also, are the second face of the Moon, who follows Mercury, and the third face of Saturn. At this it turns back, because the number of the planets is complete. In Gemini is the first face of Jove, following Saturn, the second face of Mars, the third face of the Sun, in the same order and so on.

Chapter 10

How we should use the planets for medicines

We have mentioned the merits that planets have in their signs so that, as often as we must do or compose something that pertains to some planet, we might know where to place it in its merits. This is especially useful when a planet has its foremost place at our birth.

Even Saturn and Mars, otherwise depressing us, might nevertheless be constructive for us if they should stand as the sign-factors of our birth.

It is extremely important in doing all this, when we are making something to use as a medicine that will bring us the help of the Moon, Venus, and Jove, that we be careful that these are not standing in the termini of Saturn or Mars. For then we would be forced to prevent dissolution through Saturn and to repress heat, and to warm the coldest things through Mars and take on numbness. Otherwise, we should go for the termini of Jove and Venus, and take the termini of Mercury.

Mercury's are among the most promising for man. Nor should we hide, being very Mercurial men, things that favor art, mind, and eloquence, no small part of which is Solar. For Mercury is always full of Apollo.

Here is how we describe the figures in the sky: when a sign rises from the East, we call this the first house, or the house of life; when it has risen, the second house, and the third, and so on, up to the seventh house, which is a sign that is descending into the West opposite to its ascendant. Here it takes its eighth house. The ninth is when it falls from mid-sky, which makes the tenth house. Following this is the eleventh. But the twelfth falls from the ascendant.

For the planets to be powerful, therefore, they must be had at their corners, either East or West, or mid-sky. This is especially true in the corner or angle of ascending, or in the middle of the tenth house, over the head, where it holds the sky, or at least in regions which follow upon the angles. Nevertheless, they say the Sun in the ninth house, which falls from mid-sky, enjoys the Moon falling in her third.

The astrologers tell us to keep in mind these two rules. One is for the ill person, the other is for the doctor. When, for the ill person, the seventh house through Saturn and Mars is unfortunate, or his house is unhappy, you should separate the sick person from his doctor, if you believe Ptolemy. In choosing a doctor, furthermore, it helps if Saturn and Mars are in decline. Ask your doctor if at his birth the sixth house was in sight of the Sun, or Venus, or Jove, in which case things will be fortunate.

We say that a sign is unfortunate if it goes through Saturn or Mars, unless these are its proper houses or reigns. They are proper when, for example, they belong there, or from there they look to the opposite or to the quartile. We say the opposite aspect is between those which are separated by a small interval rather than by some great one. A quartile is where something is in a fourth part of the sky, that is, distant by a space of three signs. Saturn and Mars, nonetheless, are less harmful to the other planets during a conjunction of opposite quartiles, when, as it were, they are guests in a house or when they receive them in their reign or terminus.

The planets are more happily favorable to someone when they withdraw through the sixth or third aspect or even a conjunction, as we have said. A conjunction of the Sun with a planet is to be feared, while an aspect of the Sun is to be enjoyed, for example with a third or sixth.

It is necessary, then, to remember that Aries is in charge of the head and the face; Taurus the neck; Gemini the arms and shoulders; Cancer the chest, the lungs, the stomach, and the arms; Leo the heart and stomach, the liver and the back, and the posterior ribs; Virgo the intestines and the lower stomach; Libra the kidneys, thighs, and rump; Scorpio the genitals, vagina, and womb; Sagittarius the thighs and groin area; Capricorn the knees; Aquarius the legs and shins; and Pisces the feet.

Mindful of this order, you will be careful not to touch a limb with iron, or fire, or a cupping-glass, when the Moon is passing under its sign. For at that time the Moon increases the humors in the limb, whose excess both prohibits consolidation and weighs down the power of the limb. If you observe this order, however, you can then treat the limb with certain friendly remedies inside or outside, and nourish it properly.

It helps to know what sign was rising when you were born. For, besides Aries, this sign also signifies the head for you, and in this sign the Moon is looking at your head.

When the Moon goes under Aries, it is a good time to try baths and showers. When under Cancer, take very little medicine for the blood, especially in the form of melt-in-the-mouths. When it is in Leo, do not try vomiting. When in Libra, enemas are appropriate. In Scorpio, do not take any baths. There are some who would neither prohibit nor recommend taking laxatives then. In Capricorn, it is dangerous to take medicine. Likewise in Aquarius. In Pisces it is okay.

Which limbs go with which planetary sign for someone, even though it is necessary to know, is nonetheless a nuisance to list.

Nor is it a good idea in purifying the stomach to forget Ptolemy's rule: take purging medicine when the Moon is in Cancer, Pisces, or Scorpio, especially if the house of the ascending sign attaches itself to a planet that is going under the earth. If, however, the house is rising and is joined, meanwhile, overhead with a planet holding mid-sky, nausea and vomiting will immediately be aroused.

Finally, let us conclude with Galen that astrology is necessary for the doctor. Galen, arguing about critical days, once said, "There is a certain saying of the Egyptians, that the Moon marks the affections from day to day, both for the sick and the healthy, so that if the rays of Jove and Venus are mixed with the Moon, both the sick and the healthy will be helped. If, on the other hand, they are mixed with Saturn and Mars, you will have the opposite result."

But we have wandered way off course. Let us return now to the spirit and life and the Graces.

Chapter 11

In what ways our spirit can draw in a lot of the spirit and life of the world; and which planets create and refresh the spirit; and the things that pertain to each planet

Everything we have been talking about comes down to this, that our spirit, when it is correctly prepared and cleansed through the things of nature, can receive from the spirit of worldly life a great deal through the rays of the stars. Since the life of the world is based in everything, it is propagated plainly in herbs and trees, as if they were hair on its body. It is propagated in stones and metals, as if they were its teeth and bones. It is produced in living shells, adhering to rocks and earth.

These are no more different than if they were all living life in common. This common life flourishes even more, however, above the earth in the subtle bodies, as if these bodies were nearer the soul. Through its intimate vigor, water, air, and fire possess their living things and are moved. This life nourishes and agitates in perpetual motion air and fire even more than earth and water. It particularly makes the heavenly bodies flourish, as if they were the head of the world, or the heart, or the eyes. Through the stars, as if they were its eyes, it diffuses rays that are not only visible, but visual. With these, like sparrows, as we have said before, it sees the lower things, and seeing them nourishes them, and even generates them with its touch, forming and moving everything.

Therefore, you receive the movement of world life in the movement of shining water and serene air, in fire that is reasonably distant, and in the movement of the sky, if you are yourself also moved, softly, and in a similar way, driving those gyres for their powers, avoiding dizziness, beholding the heavens with your eyes, turning them over and over in your mind.

In the same way, by this frequent use of the planets and living things, you will be able to draw a great deal from the spirit of the world, especially if you do this with living things that are fresh from Mother Earth, as if you were being nourished and taken care of by things sticking in her.

You should walk as often as possible among the plants that smell nice, or at least that do not smell bad. For all the herbs and flowers, all the trees and fruits are fragrant, though one often does not pay them any attention. With their fragrance, as if with the breath and spirit of world life, they will refresh you and make you flourish. I say that your spirit, with these odors, becomes like nature, and through the spirit that is between the body and the soul, your body gets easily refreshed by them, and your soul is marvelously helped.

You should spend a long time every day among these things,

under the sky, to the extent that it is safe or possible for you, in high, serene, and temperate regions. For up there the rays of the Sun and stars can more readily, more purely, touch you all over, and fill your spirit with the spirit of the world through rays that are particularly rich. Above all, the natural movement itself of the air, which is perpetual over the globe, although hardly perceived by anyone on account of its gentleness and our having got so used to it every day, freely licks you as you walk under the day sky and as you dwell in lofty, pleasant places, penetrating you purely and marvelously presenting the world movement and vigor to your spirit. I say the day sky, because I have found night air to be hostile to the spirits. Daily use of this is what is good, especially if you walk about a lot in the open. Avoid too much intemperate air, and move around often at a time when not only the air is temperate and serene but the position of the stars, too, is more healthful for you.

It is a good idea to choose the place that is the most fragrant, and keep silent there from any kind of searching, but move yourself around continuously and gently. I advise you to keep changing the location, although always with delight, because the good things of the heavens and of nature's universe are in various different things and places, and distributed in different things so that we will come to enjoy everything there is. I will not bother to add that variety also prevents boredom, that enemy of the spirits that is Saturn's special property. It brings pleasure, through which, as I have said, Venus herself, that friend of pleasure, comes into the spirit, because it is her duty, once she has got in there, to propagate it.

One should think of Paradise, and of the Tree of Life in Moses, or the similar way of life that was described by Plato in the *Phaedo,* and what Pliny said about people living on smell alone. Then you will know that I am right in all this.

But let us bring our spirit down to nature. The quality of spirit is without doubt Jovial, at whose time it is poured into us. It is also Solar. For Jupiter pours it in, to the extent that he can temper in himself the enormous power of the Sun. It is Jovial for other reasons too: because it is warm and damp, and abounds in heat rather than humor, and because it is born in blood, called in fact a vapor of the blood. It is Solar because it boils up, and is very subtle and shining, and arises in the heart.

It also has within it a Venereal power. For it overflows with Venereal motion, pours out, is transferred, and propagates off-spring. With its pleasure the senses dilate themselves, and it rids you of sorrow.

In sum, the spirit, to the extent that it brings the body to life, and motion, and propagation, is thought to be Jovial, Venereal, and Solar. To the extent that it attends to the soul in the senses and the imagination, it is thought to be Solar and Mercurial, and it is Mercurial whenever it is so mobile, so easily changeable, so formable.

The healthy spirit does not have much in it of Saturn, Mars, or the Moon, or it would be stupid (Saturn), furious (Mars), and obtuse (Moon). This is why Lunar things are very foreign to it, being thicker and damper than the subtle and volatile nature of the spirit. A lot of Saturnian things and too many Martial things are like poison to the spirit—its natural enemy. These have extreme cold and dryness or are in need of dryness and heat.

The nature of spirit, therefore, is said to be Jovial and Solar most of all, and then Mercurial and a little Venereal. The important distinction is this: the natural spirit is dedicated to Jove, the vital spirit to the Sun, and the animal spirit to Mercury.

When, therefore, you seek some help from one of these three spirits, if the patron spirit himself is indisposed or sick, you will not easily get help for his little client. It is very difficult for the animal spirit then, when Mercury is unhappily affected. Mercury has so much authority in the animal spirit that he can put animals to sleep with his wand, then call them awake; that is, when he has his aspect one way or the other he can stupefy the mind, or sharpen it, or weaken it, or strengthen it, vex it or calm it marvelously. So, as often as you try to cultivate some spirit, do not just observe whether its patron is happy and powerful, but see whether the Moon is favorably directed toward it, too.

The substance of the spirit is not created or refreshed at any

time through the influx of Saturn alone, but it is always called back
from the farthest out to the innermost place, and often from the
lowest to the highest. This is why it leads us to the contemplation
of more hidden and deeper things. It is possible, nevertheless, even
though it is rare, for the force of Mars and Saturn to be of service
to the spirit as a kind of medicine, either by heating it up when this
is necessary, exciting and amplifying it, or at other times by con-
straining it from being too flighty.

The natural spirit is very much created and refreshed through
these things, when such things are in agreement with these four
planets. So if you lean at random to Solar things, you will sharpen
the spirit, dry it out and dissolve it. If, in the same way, you lean
to Venus, you little by little liquefy it or dull it. If you trust very
much in Mercurial things, you will not really get very much out of
it. Therefore, it is most valuable to use Jovial things, and to mix the
others a little with these, and to use things frequently which these
others share in common with Jove, or which are proper only to
Jove.

They all have something in common. The things they have in
common are things which have substance, are not too fiery, nor too
earthy, nor simply watery, a quality that is not very sharp, nor very
dull, but modest and light to the touch, and somewhat soft, or at
least not hard, not bitter, its taste somewhat sweet, pleasant smelling, its sight pleasing, its sound mild and jolly, something happy to
think about. So a pleasantness of flavor is common to all of them.

If this pleasantness is almost watery, and at the same time fat,
it belongs more to Venus, and if it is almost insipid, or sometimes
austere, it belongs to Mercury. These are not very good for the
spirit, though they are necessary sometimes to weaken an excess of
the spirit's sharpness.

If the pleasantness is open and subtle and contains a little of
the styptic and the sharp in its flavor, it is correctly called Jovial.
This is the sort of substance you get in sweet almonds, pine nuts,
filberts, pistachios, starches, licorice, eggs, egg-yolks, the meat of
hens and pullets, peacocks, partridges and the like, as well as
behen root and elecampane; also, clear, fragrant wines, slightly

sweet, and styptics, the brightest sugars, the whitest wheats. Even grain belongs to Jove, if it is strengthened with the power of balsam; otherwise it belongs no more to Jove than it does to Venus. These, then, are substances and pleasantnesses special to Jove, which make the spirit lively and refreshed beyond all else. All those things are Jovial which, in our book on *How to Prolong Your Life,* we said were healthy for old people and good for preserving youth.

If, on the other hand, the pleasantness is rather limited, and the thing has a lot of styptic and sharp quality to it, or is even somewhat bitter, it is called Solar.

The classification and distinction here works the same way as the one for odors. For these are the sisters of flavors. The same goes for colors. Watery colors, or white, green, and sometimes saffron, violet, rose, and lily colors are colors that refer to Venus, the Moon, and Mercury, while sapphire colors, which are even called airy, much fuller of purple, mixed with gold and silver, and perpetually green, belong to Jove. The more ardent colors of saffron, pure golds, and clearer purples, belong to the Sun. If the colors are even more alive or like silks, they belong to the stars. They are strong in metals and stones and glass because of their likeness to the heavens.

But, to return to Jove, his flavor or fragrance is almost like what you get in a golden peach, or a pear, or an orange, and in very light mallow wine, or a light vernacea wine, or like what you get in green ginger, or cinnamon, or sweet fennel, or wolfsbane, if these are tasted with a lot of sugar mixed in. These latter four, along with fresh nutmeg, if they are alone, are rather Solar, and musk is Solar, too, for its odor but not for its taste or sight. Amber is very Solar and Jovial. Saffron is Solar in everything, even if its color and odor, according to the astrologers, is devoted to all the graces. Its flavor belongs to the Sun.

So, all fragrant and aromatic things, to the extent that they bear a pleasant odor, belong to Jove, Venus, and Mercury, as well as to the Sun, although among these those that are sharper belong to the Sun, those that are duller to Venus and Mercury, and to Jove belong things that are temperate in smell, taste, hearing, sight, or touch. But mild sounds and pleasant songs belong to Mercury. Threatening and lamenting ones prefer Mars and Saturn.

Nor should you be surprised at how many colors, odors, and sounds we attribute to all these. For flavors pertain in particular to the natural spirit; odors more to the vital and animal spirit; colors, figures, and voices to the animal spirit.

The movement of the soul, when it is either happy, sad, or constant, strongly drives the spirit to its own likeness. It first drives the animal spirit, then through this the vital spirit, and through this the natural spirit. All spirit, because of its fiery, airy, lucid, and mobile nature, is similar to light, and thus through colors and airy voices, odors and movements of the soul, it is moved and formed suddenly in every part. Wherever it goes it makes some affect of the soul and some quality of the body.

Finally, when one is first exposed to the Graces or pleasures through those things which are their specialties, inasmuch as one is then himself naturally in agreement with them, one is immediately bestowed the marvelous gifts of their favors through their rays that flourish everywhere.

Chapter 12

When we say that our spirit is put forth by Graces through things that contain the properties of these Graces, we think this is done not only through qualities which are seen, heard, smelled, or tasted, but even through those that are touched. Remember, therefore, that it is warm in the first stage of Jove, in the second stage of the Sun with Jove, in the third of Mars with the Sun, and in the fourth of Mars. It is cold in the first stage of Venus, in the second of the Moon, in the third of the Moon with Saturn, and in the fourth of Saturn. It is humid in the first of Mercury with Jove, in the second of Venus with the Moon, in the third of the Moon with Venus, in the fourth of the Moon, when it is joined with Venus and Mercury. It is dry in the first of Jove, in the second of Mercury with the Sun, in the third of the Sun with Mars, and in the fourth of Mars with Saturn.

In sum, from the qualities of the planets, as Ptolemy writes in his *Quadripartito*, we gather a harmony from their all coming together which is directed to heat and the humor. For the enormous heat of Mars and the Sun and the temperate heat of Jove overcome the enormous coldness of Saturn and the thin coldness of Venus and the Moon, so that heat exceeds cold there. Likewise, the humidity of the Moon and Venus, when near us and temperate, overcomes much of the dryness of Jove, Saturn, and Mars, and the temperate dryness of the Sun. When, therefore, the humor is dominated by cold and dryness, heat is dominated by the humor.

Someone who is healthy in body and tempered by this heavenly harmony from heat and dryness of the heart, and from heat and humor of the liver, and from cold and humor of the brain, will be of strong complexion, inclining to heat and humor, with heat mildly ruling. For heat of the heart and liver overcomes coldness of the brain. Likewise, humor of the liver and brain exceeds dryness of the heart.

I do not want us to omit the fact here that the same common harmony exists among the fixed stars that we said existed among the planets, for the astrologers think these are similar. Why mention this? So that you will remember that our spirit and body turn to some kind of tempering of heat and humor, either constantly from nature, or in an attempt at accommodating this through the heavens by obtaining the heavenly things for themselves.

Nevertheless, we are not saying that our spirit does this only through the heavens, prepared only through the qualities of things known by the senses. It does it much more through certain properties inside the things of heaven hidden from our senses, things hardly known to reason at all. For when properties of this kind and their effects are unable to exist with an elementary power, they have to go forth from the life and spirit of the world through rays of the stars one by one, affecting the spirit very much through

them. They are put forth with the heavenly influxes very powerfully. So we get the emerald, the amethyst, the sapphire, topaz, ruby,
unicorn horn, and especially the bezoar stone, as the Arabs call it,
all endowed with hidden properties of gifts.

These gifts come not only from taking such things internally,
but even if they just touch your flesh, and thus produce on it their
warm power. They then bring their heavenly force into the spirits
which protect against poison and plague itself.

What exactly these things do with this heavenly power is a
matter for argument, because even when you take just a tiny
amount of them the effect it has is far from tiny. Because they
hardly ever give up their elementary quality, it is like a heavenly
fire. For a Martial power, in order to do much, needs a lot of
matter. When it has a certain kind of form, however, even when
there is very little matter, it works very strongly.

There is a similar power in Phoebus' peony, when it touches
the flesh, arming the spirit against some dread disease when its
vapor is drawn in. Coral and chalcedony likewise work against the
illusions of black bile, with the power of Jove and Venus, and other
things work their properties in the same way, balsam protecting
one's youth, sharpening one's old age, and stimulating the mind
and memory, thanks to Jove who tempers Saturn and to Mercury,
the friend of the senses. Someone might even think he had come
upon the Tree of Life in Paradise.

They consecrate to Mercury the agate-stone. Physicians agree
that it is good for vision and powerful against poison. Serapio
writes that whoever wears an amethyst, or a seal made from it, will
be safe from lightning, and that its power is very widely spread
around. If it has this power, we think it has it from Jove.

The eagle-stone or aquiline has a power from Lucina, that is,
from Venus and the Moon, to move the womb and to bring speedy
delivery in childbirth. Rhasis, with Serapio confirming him, says
that he himself frequently found this to be true.

Perhaps from Phoebus who shot the Pytho, the Cretan plant
called dittany has a power to block poisons and to draw iron from
a wound. Ginger, with the power of the Sun, when taken at meals,

wards off fainting spells. Gentian calms the madness of a dog and drives away snakes. Vervain is said to stimulate prophecy, as well as happiness, satisfaction, and vision. Rue and setwall work against theriaca poisoning. Incense cultivates the vital and animal spirit against weakness, forgetfulness, and fear. Sage and mint, with the power of Jove, drive away paralysis and with their odor strengthen the soul.

With the same power, cinquefoil resists poisons, and one of its leaves drunk twice daily with wine cures One-day Fever, while three leaves cure Three-day Fever and four leaves cure Four-day Fever. The ancient priests used to use this herb in their purification rites because of its purity.

A chaste lamb, through the power of Saturn, will stop you from getting an erection, and jasper will stanch blood.

The marvelous effects can come forth when, in its hidden property, some elementary property is kept, too, just as in balsam's strengthening the spirit and body it has not only the heavenly power that does that but a styptic power, too, and an aromatic one that marvelously prevents putrefaction and looseness and strengthens the spirit. Just as saffron seeks the heart, so that it might dilate the spirit and provoke laughter, it does this not only by a marvelous hidden power of the Sun, but the nature itself of the saffron that does this is subtle, amplifiable, aromatic, and bright.

But since I am talking about medicinal plants and simples, I want you to know what has been said about their compositions. Come on, you say, tell us how theriaca helps us against poison.

It does not bring the poison out, since it tightens the stomach. It does not change altogether so quickly the nature of the poison, for this is not so weak and changeable. Rather, it makes the vital spirit very thin and changeable. Suddenly, in a certain proportion that conforms to it, it strengthens itself so much that this state of strength, as it were, does the work, and together with the theriaca as its instrument it partly overcomes the poison, partly changes it, and partly protects the heart area from it.

But in what proportion of powers does the theriaca do this? It seems to lay claim to Jove and Phoebus through a mixture of many things thrown together in a certain proportion. There is a triple power in it. I say this is itself heavenly, for the reason I gave.

The other heavenly property we mentioned before, too, in herbs and aromatics, with whose selection it is properly composed, and it has a power, as we said before, which works for this same purpose. There is yet another power in many of its parts, elemental rather than heavenly, nevertheless such that it leads to the fortifying of the spirit, a quality I call styptic and aromatic. The one strengthens the spirit, the other nourishes it.

Theriaca is thus gifted with a marvelous force against an early old age and against poison, its three powers conspiring, as it were, for the same purpose, of which one is heavenly, acquired through an artificial mixture, another is heavenly, but naturally inside its parts, and the third is elemental.

But what I said before about its being heavenly acquired suggests that it would be even more admirable if it were not only mixed of a proportion of Jovial and Solar and things of this kind, but if a time were chosen that was opportune for this, through an observation of the heavens. For whatever the body has at a certain place and time, its movement and action have at that time.

Just as certain bodies and their forms grow and are kept in certain places and times, so their proper actions obtain an effectiveness from these proper times. So Socrates notes in the *Alcibiades*, and Proclus explains. Pythagoras paid attention to it too, calling this an opportunity, the good itself, and the perfection of things. Thus the first principle of all things, according to Pythagoras and Plato, is measure, that other places and times might be apportioned to other bodies and actions. Wherefore, just as a certain thing is nowhere but here, nor other things anywhere but where they are born and grown and kept, so also material action, fear, this event or that, is given its efficacy and perfect effect nowhere else but when a heavenly harmony is in agreement with it everywhere. This harmony is thought to have such a power that it bestows marvels, not only through the labors of farmers, or the

125

artifices made by doctors with herbs and aromatics, but even through images, which according to the astrologers are made from metals and stones. But images will require their own chapter here.

How important choosing the right hour for action and works is, is strongly confirmed by Ptolemy when he says, in the *Centiloquium,* "He who chooses what is better seems to differ in no way from him who has this by nature." In these words he seems to confirm the importance of our choice and judgment of the heavenly powers.

Albertus Magnus said in the *Speculum,* "For a liberty of judgment that is forced in the choice of the hour is not praiseworthy; it is haste in judgment, not liberty, when you forget about the choice of the hour for beginning great things."

Chapter 13

On the power of images according to the ancients, and on acquiring medicines from the heavens

Ptolemy said in the *Centiloquium* that the images of lower things are subject to the celestial faces. Ancient wise men used to fabricate certain images, therefore, similar to the faces of the planets when they are in the sky, as if these faces then entered into examples of the lower things.

Even Haly approves of this, saying one can make a useful image of a snake when the Moon goes under the heavenly Snake, or happily faces it. Likewise, you can make an effective effigy of Scorpio when the Moon enters the sign of Scorpio, and this sign holds one corner of its four. He says it was done in Egypt in his time, and that he was present when a seal of Scorpio on bezoar stone was impressed onto a figure of incense, and this was given in a drink to someone whom a scorpion itself had stung. The person was suddenly cured.

Even the physician Hahameth agrees that these are useful to make, and Serapio agrees too. Furthermore, Haly tells us that a famous wise man known to him made images with a similar industriousness, and these were made to move, which effect (I do not know how) we read of in Archytas.

Trismegistus tells us of such things too, which the Egyptians made out of certain things of the world in order to get strength. He says they used to bring the souls of daemons into these to good effect, including the soul of his ancestor, Mercury. In the same way, they used to make the souls of Phoebus, Isis, and Osiris descend into statues, to be for men's use or even to be harmful to men. Likewise, Prometheus snatched life and heavenly light into a certain figment of clay.

But the Magi who were followers of Zoroaster, in summoning spirit from Hecate, used certain gold javelins marked with the characters of the heavens, on which a sapphire was inserted, and a whip made of bull's hide was whirled around, during which time they chanted. But I will pass over their chants. For the Platonist Psellus disapproves of them and mocks them.

The Hebrews, when they were in Egypt, learned how to set up a golden calf, as the astrologers thought this would bring the favor of Venus and the Moon against the influxes of Scorpio and Mars that were unsafe for the Jews.

Porphyry, in his *Letter to Anebo,* declares that images are effective and adds that, at certain times, those who exhale with proper fumigations are immediately made strong by taking the airy daemons into their chests. Iamblichus agrees that in materials which are in natural agreement with the heavenly bodies, and which are properly and correctly gathered from all over and brought together, the powers and effects are not only celestial, but are able to take on the daemonic and divine, too. Proclus and Synesius say the same.

The wonderful works that can be done for health by doctors who are learned in astrology through stuff that is made up of many things, for example, powders, liquors, unguents, and tablets, seem to have a more likely value and reason in themselves than images: first, because powders, liquors, unguents, and tablets, made correctly, take on the heavenly influxes more easily and quickly than the harder materials from which images are usually made; second,

because either the heavenly effects are taken inside us and converted into us or at least they inhere more and penetrate deeper; and
third, because images are constructed from only one kind of thing,
or from a few. The powders, and so forth, can be more selective
because they consist of many things. So that if there were a hundred gifts of the Sun and Jove scattered over a hundred plants and
animals, you could make up these hundred known to you and put
them into one form, and then you would seem to have nearly the
whole of the Sun and Jove.

You realize, of course, that the lower nature cannot capture
all the powers of the higher nature in one thing, and so these are
scattered about us through many natures, and they can be more
conveniently gathered through the works of doctors than through
images. Images made from wood, therefore, have little power, for
wood, even if it is very hard, is easily taken for a celestial influx,
and if it will receive it, will retain it less. Anything that is ripped up
out of the bowels of Mother Earth loses, in a little while, all the
vigor of its earthly life, and is easily converted into another quality.
Stones and metals, even if they seem too hard to accept a heavenly
gift, nonetheless retain it longer, if they receive it, as Iamblichus
agrees. Their hardness, the vestiges and gifts of worldly life, qualities they had when they were sticking to the earth, are held by
them after being dug out. For this reason they are considered at
least suitable material for taking and holding the celestial powers.

It is likely, as I said in the **previous** book, that things that are
this beautiful could not have been formed under the earth except
by a great effort of the heavens, and the power of this effort, once
impressed on them, endures. For heaven has worked a very long
time on these things, cooking and shaping them.

Indeed, since you cannot easily put together many things of
this kind, you must try diligently to discover which metal, among
all those on your list, belongs most to some star, or which stone is
the highest in rank, so that at least in knowing where this one ranks
you might know the others for their powers, too. With this little
undertaking you might even change the heavenly things into being
in agreement with it.

128

For the sake of an example, in the Solar ranking, under a man of Phoebus, the hawk or rooster holds the highest place among the animals, balsam or laurel among the plants, gold among the metals, carbuncle or ruby among the stones, and boiling air among the elements, for fire itself is considered Martial. As we have said, however, to increase the influx of the Sun, or Jove, or Venus, we know from common sense that one should not, from birth, appear the destroyer of these.

Chapter 14

On the order of things that depend on the stars, and how the spirit becomes Solar

As I have said elsewhere, from whatsoever star there is above (to speak Platonically), there hangs a series of things that is special to it. Under the heart of Scorpio, after its daemons and men, and the animal scorpion, we can even place the herb Asterion, the star-flower that shines at night like the figure of a star, which doctors say has the quality of a rose and possesses a marvelous power against diseases of the genitals.

Under the celestial Serpent, or serpentary, they put Saturn, and sometimes Jove. After that, the daemons, who sometimes take on the forms of serpents, the herb called snake-weed, the stone called Draconite that is born with the head of a dragon, and Serpentine, with which it shares the name, plus other things which I will describe later.

Under the Solar star, namely Syrius, first the Sun, then also the daemons of Phoebus, who sometimes occur to men under the form of lions or roosters, as Proclus tells us; the men under this, and the Solar beasts, then the plants of Phoebus, the metals and stones, and vapor and boiling air. For a similar reason, when this star moves from some firmament through another planet, they say things joined there descend step by step under its property.

If, therefore, as I said, you correctly understand all the Solar things through each step of its order, for example its men, or a certain kind of man, its animals, plants, metals, stones, and everything that belongs to these, you will drink in the power of the Sun to this extent, and even somewhat the natural faculty of the Solar daemons.

Likewise, think of what we said about the other things. For they are Solar men too, as I said before, who are born with Leo ascending, and with the Sun either holding it or facing it, and likewise those born under Aries. Blood that is taken from the left side of these people is Solar and benevolent. Solar, too, are the crocodile, the aster, the lion, the rooster, the swan, and the raven. There is no other reason why the lion fears the rooster, but because in the order of Phoebus the rooster is superior to the lion.

For the same reason, says Proclus, an Apollonian daemon who sometimes appeared under the image of a lion immediately disappeared when confronted with a rooster. The heart in these animals is particularly Solar.

I think even the sea-calf is under the heart of the heavenly Leo, and for this reason its naked hide, belted around you with a clasp made from its bone, cures you of pain in the kidneys. Against pain of this kind, the astrologers used to employ influxes from this star. Perhaps for the same reason, this hide is said to protect us from lightning.

Among plants, the palm is Phoebean, and especially the laurel, whose power repels poisons and lightning. The ash-tree has a similar faculty for protecting us from poisons. The persimmon tree is Phoebean, as its round fruits bear witness, and so also for the fact that it unfolds its leaves during Phoebus' day and folds them back up again at night. The peony is Phoebean, not only as its power indicates, but even its name (paeonia). To Phoebus as well belong all those flowers and herbs which draw back at the setting of the Sun but open up again when it returns, and those that are continually turned to the Sun.

Gold, of course, is Phoebean, and Elis stone with its golden rays imitating the Sun. This stone, which is called the Eye of the Sun, has the figure of a pupil from which light shines forth. The carbuncle is Phoebean, too, turning red at night, and the ruby, containing in itself all the powers of gems, as gold does of metals, and the Sun does of stars.

With many of the things which we mentioned previously, if you want to, you can make powders, unguents, and tablets that would be under the rule of the Sun by using their blood, the hearts of such animals, the leaves and fruits of such trees, such flowers, herbs, gold leaves, and even pupils. Add to these saffron, balsam, aromatic calamus, incense, musk, amber, wood-aloe, ginger, mastic-gum, spikenard, cinnamon, wolfsbane in a citrus syrup, setwall, nutmeg, mace, Indian spice with golden honey, or a golden balsam, mastic, laurel, or nard-oil solution. These are good for nourishing the heart, the stomach, and the head, inside or outside, so that the spirit of the Sun might enter into them. From all of these, I tell you, or at least from many of them, something can be made in which the Sun will be dominant.

It will be a good beginning in the use of things under this dominance if you put on Solar things to wear, if you live in Solar places, look Solar, hear Solar, smell Solar, imagine Solar, think Solar, and even desire Solar. Likewise, if you will imitate in your life the dignity and gifts of the Sun. Hang around with Solar men and plants, and carefully touch the laurel.

It will be very safe for your health if you mix in with the Solars some Jovials and some Venereals. Venereal humidity is the best modifier of Solar heat—for example, water and juice of roses and violets. But I have already mentioned medicines of this kind in Book One, *On Caring for the Health of Men of Letters*, and in Book Two, *How to Prolong Your Life*, books which I composed in part from my own ideas, in part from others, and even in part modified from others.

The herbs from the Sun and Jove, which have wonderful powers against epidemics and poisons, I have already given in my book *Against the Plague*, among which is Perforata, also called the Demonkiller, which has no other faculty but to protect us from the harmful vapors of evil demons, and a few other herbs or stones, like coral, which seem to do the same. One, a Lunar herb, given by Mercury, with blue and round leaves, produces one leaf each day as the Moon increases and takes them away as it decreases, and it offers to the user many Lunar years. But let us return now to images, introducing them in a slightly different way.

Chapter 15

On the power of images and medicines according to the ancients, and how medicines may be much stronger than images

If you obtain these Phoebean stones which we have been talking about, you will have no need to impress images on them. You should hang them, encased in gold, around your neck, on a yellow silk cord, when the Sun passes through Aries or Leo and rises, or when it is mid-sky, and facing the Moon.

Proclus tells us that the stones in the Moon series are much more powerful. First of all is moonstone, which not only imitates the Moon in its shape, but in its movement, too. It moves around with the Moon. If you are lucky enough to find one, and you hang it, encased in silver, on a silver cord around your neck, when the Moon is going under Cancer or Taurus, holding itself in the right corners, your spirit will return to you and it will be Lunar. When you rub this Lunar stone to warm it up, it will busily work its power into your spirits.

Another stone you might check out has the name Sunmoon, which, naturally, has the image of the Sun and Moon joined together by the Sun. Anyone who encases it in silver and puts it on his neck on a gold cord—while the Moon is in her house or in the same minute of the Sun when she passes with the Sun, and when she holds her corner—will get a Solar and Lunar spirit together, or at least what there is when the Moon goes through the center coupled with the Sun. Here you see the scattered gifts of Phoebus, as if they were the limbs of Osiris, being gathered by his sister Phoebe, as if she were Isis.

But I wish it were that easy to find somewhere a Solar or Lunar stone, for they are as powerful, in their rank, as the magnet and iron are in the North Pole series. Apollonius of Tyana says they found a Solar stone in India, a stone that was perhaps a ruby, blazing like fire, formed twenty feet under the earth. It contained so much spirit that it swelled up, and tore the earth a great deal where the stone was formed. It drew the other stones to it the way a magnet draws iron. Why this Herculean stone grabs us very strongly even now, in the present, making us contemplate it!

We see how sailors on watch use a magnet with a needle balanced to move to the Bear Star as an indication where the Pole is, the magnet drawing them there, because the power of the Bear Star is still in this stone. It is transferred into the iron, drawing both back to the Bear Star. This power is infused into it from the beginning, but it is also continuously fed by the rays of the Bear Star.

Amber, perhaps, does the same for the other Pole. But ask yourself, meantime, why a magnet attracts iron from all directions? It is not because they are alike, other than the fact that a magnet can attract another magnet much more than iron can attract iron, and it is not because it is superior in the order of bodies. No, it is even more superior a metal than a stone. Why then? Because both are included in a ranking that follows the Bear Star, but the magnet holds a higher rank in what it contains of the Bear Star, while iron holds a lower one. What is higher in the same context of things draws that which is lower, and converts it to itself, or does whatever else it wants, or affects it with the power that was infused into it before. The lower thing, on the other hand, is converted to the higher by the same infusion, or otherwise moved by it, or affected further.

Thus, in the series of the Sun, a lower man admires a higher one. In the Jove series, a lower man venerates a higher one. In the Mars series, he fears him. In the Venus series, the lower one is seized with a burning love for the higher one and abandons himself. In the Mercury series, he always learns or is persuaded by the superior one. In the Moon series, his movement is very often begun by the higher one, while in the Saturn series, his sense of quiet is very often begun by the higher one.

I myself, once, when I had explored these things up to this

point, congratulated myself, and decided that since I was a young man I would carve the figure of the heavenly Bear on a magnet, for its powers, and wear it on an iron chain around my neck when the Moon was looking at the Bear. I hoped in this way that I would at last be the master of the power of this star. But when I had tried this for a long time, I found the influxes of this star very Saturnian and Martial.

I knew from the Platonists that the very Northern daemons were evil, as even the Hebrew astronomers admit, who put harmful, Martial daemons in the North, and kindly, Jovial ones in the South. I learned from the theologians and from Iamblichus that evil daemons often take on the illusions of images and deceive us.

I once saw a stone that had been brought to Florence from India, where it had been dug out of the head of a snake. It was a round stone, in the shape of a coin with many small holes, as it had been naturally marked by the stars. When you poured vinegar on it, it moved back a little; it even moved sideways. Then it would start to spin, during which time it gave off the vapor of vinegar.

I assumed that since a stone of this kind had the nature and almost the shape of the heavenly snake, and got its movement through the spirit of the vinegar or strong wine, it would return to that snake or to its more usual place in the ground. Therefore, whoever wore this stone, and poured vinegar on it, would get some power perhaps from that Snake which, with its twin coilings, winds around the Greater Bear and the Lesser Bear. It stands snakelike near Scorpio, almost like a man wrapped in a snake, holding the head of the snake in his right hand, its tail in his left, with his knees almost bent and his head bent a little back.

Of course, I had read the Persian Magi who advised that this image be impressed on a stone—on bloodstone, in fact, which is set into a gold ring, and designed so that a little snake-weed root is placed between the stone itself and its gold setting. Wearing this on a ring would be a good precaution against poisons and poison diseases, especially if you pick the snake-weed when the Moon is on it. Pietro d'Abano approves of this image, too.

As for me, if this ring has any of this power, it is my guess that it is not the shape but the materials which do it. They are made in such a way and at such a time that they obtain the heavenly gifts. Keep in mind, then, that the stones which are born in animals, and not in weak ones but snakes, roosters, and swallows, are as effective as other stones. Like stones born in the earth, which refer back to their stars, these stones refer back to stars, too, through their animals.

The gem that is often extracted from the stomach of an old rooster has grown strong with a Solar power, which is why Dioscorides said he often found that a man who carried this stone in his mouth would fight and never be beaten. He also says that a red swallow-stone, dug out of a swallow, cures melancholy and makes one lovable and himself again. It has this power from Jove, for the reasons we have said, undoubtedly one of those stellar things that exist beneath the Moon.

There is a Platonic saying that confirms this, too, that this machine of the world is so connected that heavenly things are on earth in an earthly condition, and earthly things are in heaven in a heavenly dignity; and heavenly things are present in the hidden life of the world, and in the mind, the queen of the world, where they are its vital and intellectual property, its excellence.

Through these bodies overhead, some people even think that magic can somehow draw down these heavenly things at the right times to men, making the lower things in agreement with the higher, and that magic can even unite the celestial bodies to us through the celestial things overhead, or work them inside us, where one can finally see them. This is done with a certain art, gathering many things into one, correctly and appropriately. It seems to be sufficiently probable that they are able to do this, for those reasons which I outlined above, and because many things of this kind, when they are gathered, chopped up, mixed together, and digested under a certain star according to medicine and astrology, start the rays acting inside, and thus these things become heavenly.

When, because of the cooking and fermenting, these things little by little take on a new form, they acquire this form under the star by a kind of poultice from heaven. At the moment when metal or stone is sculpted, it does not seem to take on a new quality, but a new shape. The same for the motion that goes through the required stages of digestion, stages which natural change and generation are supposed to observe. Since heavenly nature, like a model of the lower nature, is accustomed to proceed with a certain natural tenor and smile on all things that are proceeding so, many things actually scatter, and their images in this way have a heavenly power.

I, too, am very often sceptical, and would deny that they have this marvelous power except for the fact that all authority and all the astrologers thought they had it. I would certainly not deny it altogether, for I am of the opinion (unless someone can persuade me otherwise) that these things have at least some power for good health, especially because of the material selected. For this reason, I think there is much better stuff in drugs and ointments when they have been put together with the favor of a star.

What I have to say, by the way, about the selection of this material I will postpone until the following pages.

These things can be mentioned, in the opinion of the Maguses and the astrologers, in order to interpret Plotinus on images, which I will briefly bring up if I can first, however, warn you: do not think I am approving of the use of images, I am only telling you about them. For I make use of medicines tempered in heaven, not images, and so I consult with others daily. If you admit that God has put marvelous powers in things beneath the Moon, admit that they are even more marvelous in heavenly things; and if you think that it is all right for a man to use the lower things for his health, think, too, that it is all right to use the higher things. The rule should be, from the lower to the higher, tempering them with the art of the doctor, as they were tempered from the beginning by God.

Chapter 16

On the power of heaven, and on the powers of the rays from which images are thought to obtain their force

The staggering magnitude of the heavens, their immense power and motion, work in such a way that all the rays of all the stars penetrate immediately and easily right into the center of the earth, which is barely a pinpoint in the heavens, as all the astronomers say. Here, as the Pythagoreans and Platonists say, the rays are extremely strong, because they can touch right down to the center, and because they are all gathered in a narrow place. Their violence down there makes the earth ignite, it is so dry and far from any humor, and having ignited, it is thinned out and dispersed through its passages all over the place, spuming out lava and sulfur.

But they think this fire is very smoky, and almost a fire that does not have any light, just as in the sky there is a light that does not have any fire. This is a fire, however, that is between the celestial and the infernal, its light combined with a raging heat. They think, however, that this fire flowing up from the center is a Vestal fire. They think Vesta is the goddess and life of the earth. That is why the ancients used to construct a temple to Vesta in the middle of their cities and place a perpetual fire in the middle of it.

But lest we go further off the track here, let us conclude that if the rays of the stars penetrate the whole earth, it cannot easily be denied that they penetrate metal and stone, too, when they are suddenly engraved with images, and whatever marvelous things one is able to impress on them. Indeed, in the bowels of the earth these rays produce the most precious things.

But who would deny that these things are penetrated by such rays? Even air and quality, and sound, less effectively, pass through solid things suddenly, and affect them with a certain quality of their own. Indeed, if hardness were able to resist penetrating rays, light would pass through air much more quickly than water, and water much more quickly than glass, and glass more quickly than crystal. But when they pierce through solid spaces as if they were liquid ones, it is apparent that no hardness can resist such rays.

137

They say metals receive heavenly rays and influxes, and even keep them for a time, binding such things to heaven. They keep, I mean, a certain power created by what is drawn out of the rays all running together. But why should this be, that a material not as hard as something can resist blows that the harder material cannot? Well, a sword cuts through wood under wool but will not cut the wool. A ray of lightning will strike a leather skin without hurting it but will dissolve the metal that is inside it.

Since the heavenly nature is incomparably more preeminent than our kind of fire, it should not be thought that it is the duty of the heavenly ray only to do the work that we see manifest in a ray of fire, such as to illuminate, to heat, to dry out, to penetrate, to thin out, or to dissolve the things that are most known by our senses. No, the heavenly ray has many more marvelous powers and effects, although in other respects both the lower material and the frail senses are made equal with the divinity of the heavens inside.

Who will deny that the hidden powers of things, which the doctors call special, are not accomplished by an elemental nature but by a heavenly one? Such rays, therefore, can impress on images (or so they say) hidden and marvelous powers beyond what we see, in the same way that they put their powers in other things. For these rays are not immediate, like the rays of a lantern, but like wines, and like sensual things they shine through the eyes of living bodies.

They bring miraculous gifts from the imaginations and minds of the heavens. They drive a force that is extremely violent because of their strong affect. They drive the body with an extremely rapid movement. They especially drive their heavenly rays into the spirit. Down from on high they drive into bodies the hardest things, for these are the weakest things to the heavens.

There are, however, in different stars different powers, and even in the rays themselves there are differences. In the blows of these rays that fall in one place rather than another, different powers are born. In the mutual falling of rays in one place or another, here or there or wherever, different powers arise suddenly with effects on one kind of thing, effects that are greater and faster than on another kind, and on other mixtures of elements and the qualities of elements, even much faster than in Music, where different tones and numbers are struck in different places.

If you have considered these things carefully, perhaps you will not be sceptical when it is said that with a certain hurling of rays these powers are impressed onto images, and different powers with a different hurling.

How do they do this so quickly? I will not go into the enchantments that are done with a sudden glance. I will skip also the extremely poignant cases where love is suddenly kindled by the rays of the eyes—these, too, a kind of enchantment—which I recommend you get from my book on love. I will not mention how quickly a red eye infects someone looking at it, and a menstruating woman looking in a mirror. Were there not supposed to be certain angry families among the Illyrians and the Triballi who could kill a man with a glance? And certain women in Scythia who used to do the same thing? There are certain kinds of bulls and snakes that killed men by shooting rays from their eyes. The touch of an electric eel can stun you even at a distance through the staff in your hands. The sea-urchin is said to be able to stop a great ship just by its touch. There are certain spiders in Apulia who with either a bite or some hidden thing suddenly transform your spirit and soul into a stupor. What does a rabid dog do, or is it not apparent from his bite? What does the scopa plant, or the wild strawberry do? Do they not stir up poisons and madness at the slightest touch? How can you deny, therefore, that the heavenly bodies touch with the rays of *their* eyes, with which our own see, and so immediately do wonderful things?

A pregnant woman, after all, with her touch, immediately leaves a mark on the limb of the child being born, a mark that is much to be wished for. Do you doubt that rays, touching different places, do different things? When you are gathering the herb, hellebore, and you carry the leaf down or up, suddenly touching it, are you not made into hellebore, so that your humors flow down or up accordingly? At the beginning of something or the birth or someone, do not the heavenly influxes, with their concoction and digestion of material, bestow their marvelous gifts in an instant, not over long periods of time? Is it not true that when the face of the heavens is favoring them, countless frogs and other creatures come leaping off the beaches in a second? There is so much celestial power in these materials, so much speed.

If the kind of fire we have is one that can be made instantly, why should the heavenly kind take so long? Would anyone doubt that the sky can ignite great things in a moment, even in materials less ready for it, when its flame is so much bigger? Why do you doubt, then, that the heavens can likewise make things that are shaped into images? You will say, I suppose, what I myself used to say, that these things have undergone the natural stages of change. But one has to be pretty dumb to diminish this heavenly gift and not receive it inside.

The Physics people do not want an image fabricated on just any old stone or metal, but on certain ones in which the heavenly nature has naturally started the kind of power they want—and not just started but perfected, like a flame in sulfur. It has finally perfected this power when this material is driven, forcefully, through art, under a similar kind of heavenly influx. Once driven, it heats up.

Art, therefore, arouses the inchoate power there, and while it renders this into a figure, similar to its own heavenly figure, it exposes further the Idea of itself, which, when it is exposed, is a completion of the heavenly power which had begun at first like a flame in sulfur. Thus there is a certain power in amber, given to it by the heavens, for seizing chaff. No matter how weak the amber is, though it is often made stronger by friction or heat, it suddenly does this.

Serapio writes about a similar power given to the stone *albugedis*, which looks like a sapphire, but it does not draw off the chaff until you have rubbed the stone on your hair. It is like the Jovial stone bezoar, too, which saves you from death, as we have explained in our book *Against the Plague*. It receives this power against poisons from Jove, at first, but it does not get very strong until you have worked it up with other materials. When under the heavenly influx of Scorpio you get an image of this supernal figure, it is said to contain a complete force against scorpions, a force which is strengthened when mixed with mastic or incense. The same thing happens with a sapphire, a topaz, an emerald, and other stones.

The art of such images is never effective unless its material is in agreement with the star and the effect for which the artist chose to make it, and not unless this same material returns through the image the same affects which it had at its beginning. They say that no materials should be used for images except the ones that are known to you to have the force which you want.

They caution you to scrutinize very carefully the powers of stones and metals, and to keep in mind, meanwhile, that among stones a certain carbuncle shimmers in darkness, and the ruby is especially subject to the Sun, the sapphire to Jove, the emerald to Venus, Mercury, and the Moon. Among the metals, hardly any have power beyond gold and silver. It would be a safer bet with these to refer pure gold to the Sun *and* Jove, to the Sun because of its color, to Jove because of its temperate mixture, nothing being more temperate than Jove and gold; likewise, if you refer pure silver to the Moon and Jove; to Venus, gold mixed with silver.

Above all, it would make the image more effective if the element power in its material were in agreement with its special power that is inside it naturally, and this other special power thus helped capture the heavenly things through the figure, too.

Finally, you must learn thoroughly how to make the lower figures and forms conform to the heavenly ones, as they say, as Perseus, with the cut-off head of the Medusa, was accustomed to predict the future beheading of some people, and many similar things. Remember, nobody doubts that the Moon and other planets under certain signs move certain things in us.

Chapter 17

What power is possessed by figures in the sky and figures under the sky

But lest you distrust figures too much, the ancients say you should keep in mind that in this region under the elemental Moon, they can also have a very great elemental quality, changing into one element or another, like heat and cold, humor and dryness. Those qualities, however, which are less elemental or material are, for example, lights, colors, numbers, and figures. They are perhaps less able to change into these, though these are very strong, they say, in heavenly gifts. For in the heavens, lights, numbers, and figures are virtually the most powerful of all things, especially since there is no matter there, as the Peripatetics and many others think.

Figures, numbers, and rays, therefore, since no other things are sustained there in matter, seem to be almost substantial. Since in the order of things mathematical forms come before physical ones, as if they were simple and less in need of anything, they rightly obtain great authority for themselves in the stages of the world that come before them, that is, in the heavenly stages, so that there will not be anything less in number, figure, or light than there is in some elemental property. The sign of this authority is seen even under the Moon.

For material qualities are shared with many species of things, so that when these are slightly changed, species are not themselves altogether changed. The figures and numbers of natural parts, however, possess a property that is inseparable and peculiar to the species; namely, those heavenly things which have been destined to be with the species. They have a special connection with ideas in the mind, the queen of the world. When these same numbers and species are delineated there with their proper ideas, it is no wonder that their proper powers are thus strengthened. Thus the species is drawn together in certain figures of natural things. Then movements and generations, and mutations, with certain numbers, are drawn together.

As for light, what can I say? It is either an act of the intelligence, or an image. Colors, however, are certain kinds of light. This is why the astrologers say that where there are lights, that is, colors, figures, and numbers, in material things, they can very easily prepare us for heavenly things, so that, they say, you should not deny these things. You should not ignore the harmony that exists through their proportions and numbers, which has a marvelous power for strengthening, moving, and affecting the spirit, the soul, and the body.

Proportions, however, that are constituted of numbers, are almost like figures, not only because they are made out of lines and points, but because of their motion. Also, with their movement the heavenly figures maintain themselves, and with their harmonies, their rays, their movements penetrating everything, they thus affect the spirit, in a hidden way, from day to day, as Music, above all, can affect it in a more open way. Look how easily the figure of a mourner moves many people to misery. And how much the figure of a lovable person suddenly affects and moves the eyes and the imagination, the spirit, and humors. Well, a heavenly figure is no less alive and effective. Does not the kind and smiling face of the prince of a city exhilarate everyone? The fierce or somber face just as suddenly scare everyone? What do you suppose, then, the heavenly faces can do, those lords of all earthly places?

When you think that people who are making babies often imprint on their faces not only their own actions but even what they were imagining, and this gets imprinted in turn on sons born long afterward, well, by the same token, the heavenly faces immediately infect matter with their marks, which seem sometimes to hide for a long time, but which emerge in time. The faces of heaven are the celestial figures. You can call figures that are more stable there than others, faces. Faces, however, are figures which change there frequently. The aspects of the stars which are made among themselves with a daily motion, you can call their faces and their figures. For they are called hexagons and tetragons.

Okay, someone might say, we want heavenly figures that are powerful at doing things, but how do we make figures with the art of images? The ancients would answer, not to worry about what is powerful—our figures are powerful in themselves to do things—but whether they are ready for actions, and ready to receive the powers of the heavenly figures, to the extent that they are made properly with such things ruling them, and shaped for such things by the carpenter's ruler. For that figure forces the figure out.

When the lyre is sounding, does it not happen that another

starts making sounds too? It is enough if you make the figure the same and put it out of sight, putting your faith in it, and staying intent upon it. For what happens if one lyre suddenly yields to another, other than that you have changed a location, the form conforming to it being the same.

The gentle figure of a mirror, concave, shining in harmony with the sky, properly receives its heavenly gift that focuses collectively the rays of Phoebus into itself, and then burns even the most solid thing down to its core from this focus. So, they say, have no doubt, a certain kind of image can be made from matter, especially from matter that is harmonious with the heavens, a heavenly gift that is given through the figure made with an art similar to heaven's own. This gift is first conceived in the thing itself, then passed to the nearest person or the person carrying it.

When not only the figure, but even its disposition is pervious—what they call diaphanous—it is to a certain extent ineffective and passive in its own nature. Because a pervious disposition is a special presentation of light in heaven, then whenever under heaven this is natural, when this disposition obtains something, a sudden celestial light is acquired and conserved. The heat with this is either fiery, as in flame, or somewhat airy, or watery and glutinous, as in moonlight or lanternlight or carbuncles, and perhaps even as in camphor.

Pay close attention now to what follows on images.

Chapter 18

The figures of the heavens which the ancients imprinted on
images, and the uses of images

Someone might ask, which figures of the heavens do they imprint most on images? For there are forms there very conspicuous to the eye, many that seem almost paintings, like Aries, Taurus, and zodiacal figures like them; and some that appear to be even from beyond the zodiac.

There are very many forms there, not so much visible as

imaginable, through their signs' faces, and all have been examined by the Indians, the Egyptians, and the Chaldaeans. Or at least they have been contemplated by them, as, in the first face of Virgo, a beautiful virgin seated, holding twin spikes in her hand, and feeding a child. And the rest, which Albumasar describes, and certain others. There are certain characters, too, of the signs and planets, which have been marked by the Egyptians.

They say, therefore, that everything has been engraved with images. If somebody hopes, therefore, for some benefit that is Mercury's specialty, he should summon him in Virgo, or at least when the Moon there is with the aspect of Mercury, and make an image then from a silver and lead alloy or from silver, on which is the entire sign of Virgo, its character, and the character of Mercury. And if you have used the first face of Venus, you should even add the figure which was observed in the first face, and likewise with the others.

The authors of such images claim that their universal form, taken from a likeness to the heavens, is round. Older authors, however, especially the ones we read from the Arab group, always made the shape of theirs into a cross, because the power was worked through a more diffused surface then. The surface on the cross is first marked off. It thus has longitude and latitude. This is the first figure and is the straightest of all; it contains four straight angles.

The effects of the heavens work especially well through a straightness of the rays and the angles. For then the stars are enormously powerful, when they hold the four angles of the sky, the very hinges, like East and West and both middles. Set up this way, they cast their rays one after another onto themselves, so that they constitute a cross.

The ancients said that this figure was a cross, first because it was made by the fortitude of the stars, and second because it was a little container for this same fortitude, and so it has the greatest power among images to receive the powers and spirits of the planets. This opinion was either imagined by the Egyptians or particularly strengthened by them. Among their characters, the cross was

145

very prominent, signifying, according to their custom, future life, and they carved this figure on the chest of Serapis.

In my opinion, however, the excellence of the cross among the Egyptians before Christ was not so much a testimony to the gifts of the stars and a presentiment of its power, than that it was a figure about to be taken by Christ. The astrologers, however, who came immediately after Christ, seeing the marvelous things done by the Christians through the cross, not knowing, however, or not wanting to attribute such things to Jesus, attributed them to the heavens, although they should have considered if it were through the cross itself and that miracles were hardly accomplished without the name of Jesus.

Perhaps it is probable that they took it for their images because it bore the fortitude of all the planets and stars and had its enormous power merely for this reason, that it could, when joined with other things that are necessary, produce good health in the body. But let us go back to discussing the opinions of other people, as we had begun.

The ancients made an image of Saturn on the stone Feyrizech, that is, the sapphire, for the sake of longevity, making it at the hour of Saturn, with Saturn rising. Its form was an old man sitting on a high chair or on a snake, the man's head covered with a dark linen cloth, his hands reaching above his head, holding a sickle in his hand, or a fish, and dressed in dark clothes.

For longevity and a happy life, they made an image of Jove on a clear or white stone. It was a man sitting above an eagle or a snake, crowned, in the hour of Jove, when he is in his exaltation happily ascending, wearing yellow clothes.

They made images against timidity in the hour of Mars, with the first face of Scorpio rising, images of Mars armed and crowned.

For curing diseases they crafted an image of the Sun in gold, in the hour of the Sun, with the first face of Leo ascending with the Sun, an image of a king on his throne, with yellow clothes, and the horn and form of the Sun.

For happiness and strength of body, the image of Venus as a

146

little girl, holding fruits and flowers in her hand, wearing yellow and white, in the hour of Venus, with the first face of Libra, or Pisces, or Taurus ascending with Venus.

They made an image of Mercury for thought and memory, with the first face of Gemini. They carved the same image in marble to fight off fevers, imprinting it on some material taken from the sick person. They said this cured every kind of fever. They made this image when the Moon was in increase and rising in the first face of Cancer. The form was of Mercury. It was a man helmeted and crested, sitting on a throne, with wings on his feet, holding in his left hand a cock or fire, and he was winged, sometimes over a peacock, holding in his right hand a calamus reed, and wearing various clothes. The Moon was a girl with a horned head over a snake or a bull, with serpents over her head and under her feet.

For curing kidney-stones and troubles with the genitals, and for constricting the blood, they made an image in the hour of Saturn, with Saturn rising in the third face of Aquarius. For the same cures they imprinted Leo in gold, the stone turned by their feet into the shape of the Sun, in the hour of the Sun, with the first stage of the second face of Leo rising. They thought this was good for getting rid of diseases.

They made a similar thing for kidney diseases, when the Sun held forth mid-sky in the heart of Leo, and Pietro d'Abano approves of it. He proved it through experience, but with this condition, that Jupiter or Venus be facing mid-sky. Planets that are harmful might fall and be unfortunate.

I learned from the distinguished physician, Mengus, that an image made in this way, with Jove joined with the Sun, delivered John Marlianus, a great mathematician of our time, from a fear he used to have of being hurt by thunder.

For strengthening soundness of body and avoiding poisons, they made an image from silver in the hour of Venus, with the Moon holding her corners and Venus happily looking on, while the lord faced Venus in the sixth house, or with Jove in his third looking on, or opposite. Mercury, however, should not be unhappy. They do these in the last hour of the day of the Sun, so that the lord might hold as his heir the tenth region of the sky.

Pietro d'Abano said that a doctor can cure the sick through this image. Only he notes that in making this, the angles of the rising middle sky must be fortunate, and its lord rising, and the same for the second house, but the sixth and its lord may be unhappy. He even says that body-strength would improve and life made even longer than what is fated at the beginning of life if this image is made to encompass one's birthday, putting these fortunate things on it as if it were the signifier of one's life. These signs and lords are givers of life in the same way, especially the one that is rising and its lord. The same for the middle sky, the place of the Sun, which is the part of fortune, the lord of any conjunction or prevention made before a birthday. But bad ones fall and are unfortunate. He concludes that no astrologer would doubt that such things lead to a prolonging of life.

It would take a long time to go through all the signs and faces and stations of the Moon which the ancients observed as necessary for expressing images. For in a station of the Moon from the seventeenth stage of Virgo to its end they made images against diseases and dreadful things. In a station from the beginning of Capricorn to its twelfth stage they made images against diseases, discords, and captivity. In a station from the twelfth stage of Capricorn to the twenty-fifth stage, images against languor and prison. In a station from the fourth stage of Pisces to the seventeenth stage, images for curing diseases, for money, for fellowship, and for increasing the harvest.

They plotted other stations, too, with a vain curiosity. I have gone over here only those that smell of medicine more than they do of magic. For I suspect that much of this stuff would be worthless as medicine.

For other, more legitimate confections of medicine, however, I think the houses of the Moon should be selected, and even in the sixth stage of Aries, in the nineteenth stage, too, in the twenty-sixth minute. The same for the tenth stage of Gemini, the fifty-first minute. In Cancer, the nineteenth stage, twenty-sixth minute. In Libra the sixth stage, thirty-fourth minute. In Capricorn the nineteenth stage, twenty-sixth minute. In Aquarius, the second stage, twenty-seventh minute. Also in Aquarius, the fifteenth stage, eighth minute.

Above all, one should keep in mind the saying of Haly: As long as the Sun is in some sign, the sign is alive and will dominate others. You should therefore direct the Moon there to get the gift appropriate for some medicine. I mean, direct it to the sign and face and especially the grade or stage, so that if you strive for the good things of Jove, the Moon is directed or united to these, as long as the Sun is illumining the place where the Jovial property flourishes. The same goes for the rest of them.

It might be curious, and perhaps even harmful, to talk about those images that were made to join or unjoin souls among them, to bring happiness or to bring calamity onto someone or some house or country. I do not agree that they could do such things. The astrologers, however, think they were able to do them, and they teach you how, things that I would not dare tell.

Porphyry, where he describes the life of his teacher, Plotinus, says that such things are possible. He says that an Olympian astrologer and Egyptian magus tried to do such things against Plotinus at Rome, using images and things of this kind to put a star-spell on Plotinus. But because of the greatness of Plotinus' soul the attempts were turned back onto their author.

Albertus Magnus, a professor of astrology as well as theology, says in his *Speculum,* in the passage on how one tells the licit images from the illicit images, that images made correctly by astrologers acquire their power and effect from a figure of heaven. Under this he tells of their marvelous effects, which Thebith Ben Corath, Ptolemy, and other astrologers promised. He describes the images which bring calamity or prosperity to someone, which, on consideration, I will omit here. But, meanwhile, he confirms that they are able to have this effect, although adding that a good man condemns the abuse of this art, and a legitimate theologian detests orations and prophecies which evil daemons do from images.

Nevertheless, he does not reprove the figures, letters, and sayings inscribed on images as long as they are simply to receive some gift from a figure of heaven.

Pietro d'Abano has agreed, too, that you can get such things through images. In fact, he claims that even a whole region, I do not know how, was destroyed through the image that Thebith says was made by the astrologer Phedice.

Thomas Aquinas, however, our leader in theology, was more afraid of such things and attributed less to images. He thought that one could acquire only as much power from the figures of the heavens and their effects as one is commonly accustomed to do through plants and other natural things. He thought this not so much because there is something figural in this material, but because when such a thing was composed it was placed in a certain species of artifice which is in agreement with heaven. He says this in the third book of *Contra Gentiles,* where he mocks the characters and letters that are added to images. He does not laugh at images themselves, however, but only at certain signs which are to join them to daemons.

In his book *On Fate,* he said that the constellations give order to being and enduring, not only in natural things but even in artificial ones, so that images can be made under certain constellations. If something marvelous happens to us through these effects beyond what is natural, he rejects the idea that daemons are in them seducing men. He clearly says this in his book *Contra Gentiles,* and especially in his little book on the occult works of nature, where he seems to attribute little value to such images, no matter how they are made, and to which I, myself, to the extent he has said, would attribute no value either.

To attribute certain marvelous effects in images to daemons is a falsehood, and the Platonic philosophers knew this too. For Iamblichus said, those who neglect high religion and sanctity, and merely make images from which they expect divine gifts, are very often deceived in this matter by evil daemons who come by under the pretext of being gifts of the Gods. He does not deny that certain natural good things are obtained from images made with a legitimate sense of astrology.

In my opinion, it would be safer to commit oneself to medicines than to images, and to have the heavenly powers that are assigned to images have their effect in medicines instead. For it is probable that if images have some force they do not acquire it suddenly through the figure so much as they naturally possess it through the affected material. If this force were acquired while the figure was being sculpted, it would not so much be obtained through the figure as through the warming that comes from chiseling it.

This chiseling and warming up, when done in harmony, like the heavenly harmony which once poured power into the material, arouses that power and strengthens it the way wind does a fire, and makes manifest what was hidden before, as fire will bring out letters written in onion-juice that were previously invisible. Letters secretly inscribed on a stone in goat-grease will come forth if the stone is submerged in vinegar, the sculpted letters now being prominent. In fact, just as the touch of a branch of the wild strawberry will render you unconscious, so perhaps the chiseling and warming alone produce the power lying in some material, when it is done favorably. This favor of the heavens is of great help in making medicines.

If one wanted to prepare metals and stones, it would be best only to strike them and warm them rather than to shape them. For anything beyond this is, I think, but an empty image, and we ought to admit that this is close to idolatry. It is not by chance that the healthful stars are used for getting rid of diseases that are most like these. For they often increase them, just as the harmful stars sometimes lessen diseases that are unlike them, as Ptolemy and Haly clearly point out.

Chapter 19

On making a figure of the universe

Why not make a universal image, that is, an image of the universe itself? The ancients seem to have expected benefits from such an image. One who is a follower of these might be the sculptor then;

he could make a kind of archetypal form of the whole world, if you want, in the air, imprinting it in silver on gold plate.

When is the best time to imprint it? When the Sun has touched the first minute of Aries. The astrologers say this is, as it were, where the universe was when it first started, and they predict from here the fortune of the world for at least a year. The sculptor then could imprint a figure of the whole world on this, its birthday.

Do you see how elegantly it helps our argument if the world is reborn at a certain point in the year? Do not the astrologers measure the birth of man in the very sign, the stage, the minute in which the Sun is standing? It is here that they put down the foundation of the entire figure. Wherever it is in the year, when the Sun first goes under the same minute, they are saying man is reborn then, and they then predict the fortune of the year. So just as they are not strong enough to do this in man, unless he is, as it were, reborn, and he is not able to become reborn, unless at some time he was born already, so they conjecture the world, too, was born at some time.

When the Sun then is placed under the first minute of Aries, when it does this in some year, the lot of the world, as if it were reborn, has now gone a revolution. So, then, one has made a figure of the world.

He should be careful, however, not to carve or express the figure of Saturn on the Sabbath day. For on this day God, the creator of the world, is said to have rested from work, which he had begun on the ideal day, the day of the Sun. As much as the Sun is fitted for generation, Saturn is to that extent inept. He finished the work, however, in Venus, signifying the absolute beauty of the work.

But more on the reasons for making the world later. Our man Giovanni Pico della Mirandola has already divinely portrayed the divine mysteries of the world's birth in the days of Moses.

So let us return to our purpose, that one should not carve his world on a day or in an hour of Saturn, but rather in an hour of the Sun. He should draw it on the year's birthday, especially if Jupiter and Diana are happily approaching.

The ancients thought it was best, by the way, if you colored all the features of the work. There are three universal and singular colors of the world: green, gold, and sapphire, and they are dedicated to the three Graces of heaven. Green, of course, is for Venus and the Moon, moist, as it were, for the moist ones, and appropriate to things of birth, especially mothers. There is no question that gold is the color of the Sun, and no stranger to Jove and Venus either. But we dedicate the sapphire color especially to Jove, to whom the sapphire itself is said to be consecrated. This is why lapis lazuli was given its color (sapphire), because of its Jovial power against Saturn's black bile. It has a special place among doctors, and it is born with gold, distinct with gold marks, so it is a companion of gold just as Jupiter is the companion of the Sun. The stone ultramarine has a similar power, possessing a similar color with a little green.

The ancients decided, therefore, that it was a big help, if you wanted to capture the gifts of the heavenly Graces, to look at these three powerful colors frequently, and to color in, on the little wall-map of the universe that you are making, the sapphire color for the spheres of the world. They thought it was worthwhile, too, to add the color gold to the spheres of the heavens and the stars, and to dress Vesta herself, or Ceres, that is, earth, in a green mantle. In this way a follower of these ancients would either wear this little form of the universe, or look at it on the wall.

It would be useful, too, to look at a sphere with its motions, as Archimedes once did, and which recently a certain Florentine by the name of Lorenzo has made. Not just to look at it, but to reflect on it in the soul.

Deep inside your house you might set up a little room, one with an arch, and mark it all up with these figures and colors, especially the room where you spend most of your time and where you sleep. When you leave your house, do not pay so much attention to the spectacle of individual things, but look at the shape and colors of the universe. But makers of images will see to this.

You will make a more excellent image in yourself when you have learned that nothing is more orderly than the heavens, and that nothing more temperate can be contemplated than Jupiter. You can expect at last to obtain the benefits of heaven and Jove if you thus distinguish your thoughts, your feelings, and your actions, making your life itself orderly and temperate.

But now that we have mentioned heavenly temperateness, it would be good to keep in mind that there is in heaven no excess of the elemental quality (to speak like the Peripatetics), for if it were composed like that, it would now be lost after so many centuries, and if it were that simple, with such magnitude, it would have lost its power with the motion of some other thing. Instead, as if it were the most moderate thing there is, it moderates everything and mixes the different elements into one. Thus, with such temperateness as this, and the excellence of its form, it divinely deserves life. For we see that it attains life, through these things it composes, only with difficulty, when a perfect mixture of qualities seems to break up the previous contrariety, as in plants.

There is thus a more perfect life in animals, to the extent that their complexion is further removed from contrariety than it is in plants. In men, again, for the same reason, there is an even more perfect mixture. If, in fact, the human complexion has arrived at a heavenly temperateness, especially in the spirit, which beyond the subtlety of its own substance and temperate qualities is in harmony with those in heaven, it is fitted for heavenly light. Above this, where the heavenly is especially powerful, the human condition is divinely fitted, before all others, for heavenly life. To the extent that it makes and keeps itself this way in all its life and habit of life, to that extent it obtains the singular gifts of the heavens.

When we say, therefore, that there is in heaven no excess of an elemental quality, we know that either there is no quality of this kind there at all, but rather powers that are the temperate causes of qualities, or, if these are to a certain extent like qualities, they have an almost airy temper. When we call such things as these cold and dry, we are using Plato's reasoning; that is, cold is what you call something that has little heat, and dry is what you call something that shows us little humor.

Thus the astrologer, Abraham, said that Saturn leaves our body somewhat cold and dry, because he affects our heat and humor very little. For the same reason, the flesh of cows and rabbits are warm and moist in themselves, while ours are cold and dry.

From this deduction, however, draw these two corollaries: first, if the more a body is temperate, the more it lives, and heaven most exactly possesses in itself the most absolutely temperate life of all, then it can be assumed that to the extent that other things approach heaven's temper and life, they will obtain a more excellent life, too. The second corollary is this: heaven's life is a form perfect in itself, showing a proficient body and the basis of movement; an intimate basis of movement, I mean, that is first done internally, then carried out externally through every part.

If, therefore, this is what heaven's life is—a mind that is grasped through thought, which could not know that such a form exists in heaven, and a most excellent body, which goes around always with a perfect motion, giving life to everything—then more and more our own life should naturally approach nearer to this likeness of itself, and each day expose itself more fittingly to heaven's influxes.

Chapter 20

How much power images are thought to have over the spirit, and the spirit over them; and on the effect of using and doing them

We have discovered that if one correctly uses hellebore, it works powerfully, and changes to some extent with its excellent purge and hidden property both the quality of the spirit and the nature of the body. It moves the soul and rejuvenates one so that he almost seems to be reborn. This is why the maguses say that Medea used to bring back youth with certain herbs. (The balsams do not so much bring it back as conserve it.)

The astrologers thought propitious images had a similar power through which they change somewhat the nature and habits of someone who wears them. They restore him to an even better condition, as if he had escaped from his old self, or at least they keep one's health good for long periods of time.

For the one who wears them, images have a power against

harmful things, like poisons or plague, a power that even exceeds the art and potency of hellebore. Images, however, made and directed against somebody else to bring a disaster on him, could be cast back through a concave bronze mirror, by focusing and breaking the rays back in the opposite direction, and even at close range burning someone, or at a distance making him feel hot. This is where all those stories and rumors started about how the machines of the astrologers and the poisons of the maguses could put a spell on men, animals, or plants, and weaken them.

As to whether images have any force at such distances, I do not know enough to say. I suspect that they have some for the wearer, though not the kind, I think, that many people construe, and what power they have I think is from the material rather than the shape of the image; and, as I have said, I put medicines way ahead of images.

The Arabs and the Egyptians, nonetheless, attribute so much to images and statues that are invented with the art of astronomy and magic that they think the spirits of the stars are enclosed in them. Others believe that the spirits of the stars are certain marvelous powers of the heavens, still others say daemons, or even that the stars are footmen of the daemons. So the spirits of the stars, whatever they are, are thought to be inside statues and images in the same way that daemons are supposed to occupy some human bodies, to speak through them, to move and be moved, and to carry off miracles. Certain ones like these are thought, through images, to make the spirits of the stars.

They say that daemons dwell in a worldly fire, on fire up to their shoulders, and that in the same way, through igniting our spirits and affects, they work their way into our bodies. Likewise, the spirits of the stars can be brought inside through taking in their rays in the right way, as well as their mists, light, and powerful tones, all through the right material in images. These are able to do wonders for someone carrying them or just being near them.

As for what we think about what daemons are able to do, we think they do not so much dwell in certain material as they rejoice in being cultivated. But we will go into this more carefully elsewhere.

The Arabs say that our spirit is powerfully in agreement with this spirit when we correctly fabricate images, if it has been extremely attentive to the work through imagination and effect; if it has been joined to the stars with the spirit of the world itself, and with the rays of the stars through which the spirit of the world works; and if it is so joined that the spirit of a certain star, a certain vivid power, is poured into an image through the rays from the spirit of the world.

Suffumigations also help the stars that are fitted for this work, to the extent that such mists or suffumigations affect the air through their rays, and affect the spirit of the image-maker and the material of his image. I myself think that certain odors, so to speak, of the spirit, similar in nature to air, when they are raised up, are in agreement with the rays of stars. If they are Solar or Jovial, they affect the air and move the spirit powerfully to the gifts of the Sun or Jove, when these are correctly taken under their rays. The spirit is so affected, so enriched, that it is able with a certain more strenuous effect not only to drive the body to its own task but especially to that which conforms nearest to its own nature, and more weakly, to affect it with a certain similar quality. I think that the material of the image, supported by odors and by the imagination of the person making it, can hardly take on less of this.

The spirit itself, nevertheless, is so affected by the odor that it is made into one thing out of both of these. It is clear from this that an odor goes no farther in its smell once it has gone far enough. For smell and anything else from it or like it is not allowed to do this. But more on this elsewhere.

The point is, I think, that the intention of the imagination has its force not so much in images or medicines as in the act of applying them and using them. It is as if someone wearing an image correctly made, or using a medicine, strongly created a power from this, unhesitatingly and firmly believing and hoping that this and even a whole pile of things to come came about through this aid.

For where the power of the image, if it has one, is warmed up and penetrates the flesh of someone touching it, at least the natural power in its material, or the vigor of the medicine one swallows,

slips into the veins and the innards, carrying with it a Jovial property. The spirit of man is then transformed into a Jovial spirit with
this affect, that is, with love.

For it is the power of love to transform. Faith and hope, too,
now stand in the spirit of a man so roused by the Jovial spirit
inside, strengthening him. If Hippocrates and Galen taught that the
love and faith of a sick man made the work of a doctor much more
effective, both internally and externally (the pious Avicenna even
said that trust was more effective than medicine), how much more
should we realize that such trust in the heavenly influxes inside us,
working within us, penetrating right down to our guts, will lead to
a heavenly enrichment? Love itself, and faith in the heavenly gift,
is often the cause of the heavenly gift, and love and faith obtain this
perhaps sometimes because the kindness of heaven favors this in
us.

Chapter 21

On the power of words and songs in obtaining heavenly gifts,
and on the seven steps leading to the celestial things

They say that certain words, pronounced with a somewhat sharp
effect, have a great power around images, directing them to do
their own thing more effectively, effects to which words are intended. Therefore, to reconcile these two with a burning love, they
fabricate an image when the Moon is going under with Venus in
Pisces or Taurus, having observed many things in the meantime
very curiously about the stars and words, things which I am advised not to discuss. We are, after all, not teaching love-potions
here, but medicines.

It is more likely, however, that effects of this kind are done
through Venereal daemons, rejoicing in these works and words, or
simply through seductive daemons. For they say Apollonius of
Tyana often used to cast out lamias, those lewd and Venereal daemons who disguised themselves as beautiful girls and lured beautiful men. Luring them as a serpent does an elephant with its mouth,

they sucked them with vulva as well as mouth, and emptied the men out. Apollonius himself saw such things.

Origen asserts, against Celsus, that there is a great power in certain words, and Alchindus and Synesius, discussing magic, agree; likewise Zoroaster, who forbid the chanting of strange words, and Iamblichus, too.

The Pythagoreans used to do certain wonderful things in the manner of Phoebus and Orpheus with words, songs, and sounds. The ancient doctors of the Hebrews considered this most important, and all poets sing and make wonderful things with their songs. That very grave man, Cato, in his book *De Re Rustica*, used strange chants at times to cure the diseases of beasts. But it is best to forget about chants.

The music with which young David saved Saul from ill health—if it was not some kind of divine mystery—should perhaps be attributed to nature. Since there are seven planets, there are also seven steps through which harmony is drawn from the higher to the lower, with voices holding the middle step, dedicated to Apollo. Harder materials, stones and metals, hold the lowest step, and these seem to refer to the Moon. The second place, in ascending order, belongs to things which are made from herbs, the fruits of trees, gums, and the limbs of animals, and these answer to Mercury, if we follow the heavenly order of the Chaldaeans. In third place are the subtlest powders and the vapors selected from them, and the odors of herbs, flowers, and unguents pertaining to Venus. In fourth place are words, songs, and sounds, all of which are rightly dedicated to Apollo, the author of Music beyond all other things. In fifth place are the powerful concepts of the imagination, forms, movements, and affects, all having a Martial force. In sixth place are the discourses and deliberations of human reason, which belong to Jove. Seventh place is for more secret and simpler intelligences, almost separated now from movement, joined to divine things, and devoted to Saturn. The Hebrews appropriately call this last quiet place Sabbath.

What is all this about? Well, it is so that you might know that certain things that are made of herbs and vapors are made first

159

through the art of medicine, then through the art of astrology, resulting in a common form, just as a certain harmony is given by the gifts of the stars. Thus, tones are first selected for a kind of norm of the stars, then they are composed among themselves for the same kind of congruity, and become almost a common or shared form, in which a certain heavenly power arises.

It would be an extremely difficult task to decide which tones go with which stars, or which composition of tones goes with which stars and agrees with which aspects. But we can pursue this, in part through our diligence, and in part through a kind of divine chance, in the same way that Andromachus, exhausted after spending so much time inventing theriaca, discovered the power of theriaca, after such diligence, by a kind of divine luck, as it were. Galen and Avicenna agree that he came upon it divinely. In fact, the entire art of medicine had its beginning in prophecies, as Iamblichus and Apollonius of Tyana prove. This is why Phoebus is the high priest of medicine.

We shall offer three important rules for this, if we can first warn you not to think that we are talking here about adoring the stars, but rather about imitating them, and seizing them by imitation. Again, do not think the stars give their gifts by choice, but rather by a natural influx. It is a multiple and complex business, so we strive to fit ourselves to it carefully, just as every day, for the sake of our health, we fit ourselves to the open light and heat of the Sun. To fit oneself to his occult and wonderful gifts is the duty of a wise man.

But to come now to the rules for fitting our song to which stars: the first is, to discover what powers these have in themselves, which star, planet, and aspect has what effect on them, which ones take them away and which ones bring them. Then we add these to the significations of our words, detesting those which take away and approving those which bring.

The second rule is, to consider which star especially dominates which kind of place and which kind of man. Then to observe which tones and songs are used in these regions and by these persons, so that you might use similar words spoken with the same

160

significations, which you are wont to associate with these same stars.

The third rule is, pay attention every day to the location and aspects of the stars, and under these explore which speeches, songs, movements, dances, customs, and actions usually excite people, so that you might be able to imitate such things for the sake of the powers that are in these songs, which please some similar heavenly object. In this way you might receive a similar influx. Remember that song is the most powerful imitator of everything. For it imitates the intentions and affections of the soul, and words, and this matters for the gestures and movements of the body, the acts of man, and his customs. It imitates and does all these so strongly that, in order to imitate and do the same it provokes the one who is singing and then those who hear it. When the heavens are imitated with the same power, it provokes our spirit to the heavenly influx, and then, marvelously, it provokes the influx to our spirit.

Now, of course, this material of harmony is purer, and more like heaven itself, than the material of medicine. For it is an air, warm or tepid, breathing, and to a certain extent living, made with its own limbs and joints, like an animal, not only bearing movement, and presenting an affect, but even bearing, as it were, a meaningful mind, just as an animal can be called, to a certain extent, airy and rational. Harmony, therefore, is full of spirit and sense when it answers to a star according to its own signification, according to its limbs, and the form resulting from these limbs, and according to the affect of its imagination. It has no less a power than anything else that goes into the one who is singing. From him this power goes into the nearest listener, to the extent that the song keeps its vigor and keeps the spirit of the one singing, especially if this singer himself has a Phoebean nature, a strong vital spirit of the heart, and a strong animal spirit.

For just as the natural power and spirit, where it is very strong, softens and liquefies suddenly the hardest foods and changes the tough into the sweet, and the seminal spirit generates beyond itself an offspring, so the vital and animal power, where it is most effective, makes the most intense sort of things through the song of its spirit. It works powerfully, with conception and agitation, on the nearest body; then, spilling over, it moves the next body, and when it has affected its own, it then affects someone else with a certain property. It conceives this from its own form and from selecting the right time.

For this reason, at any rate, many Orientals and Southern people, especially from India, people for the most part who use Solar things, are said to have an astonishing power with words. I say it is not a natural force they have here but the vital and animal force that they have most of all, along with others who live in regions that are particularly Solar. Their singing is conceived with this power, opportunity, and intention. It is perhaps nothing other than a different spirit, conceived in you inside your spirit and made Solar, working then in you, then on those next to you, with a Solar power.

For if a certain vapor and spirit can sometimes stun through the rays of the eyes, or otherwise bewitch through what is spun off them, and can otherwise affect someone nearby, the spirit flowing out more richly and fervently from the imagination and the heart can do so much more and be more powerful in its movement.

It is not, then, altogether amazing that certain diseases of the soul and body can sometimes be carried away by it, or even brought on by it, because this Musical spirit touches and works in the spirit as a medium between the body and the soul, affecting either one with its outpouring of affection. You will agree that this force is marvelous, exciting and spirit-brightening, if you agree with the Pythagoreans and Platonists that this is a heavenly spirit, arranging everything with its movements and tones.

Remember that all Music comes from Apollo. There is a Jovial music only to the extent that it agrees with Apollo. Venus and Mercury also carry Music when they are in Apollo's neighborhood. Harmony belongs to these four alone, while the other three have voices but no song.

As for dull voices, heavy ones, hoarse ones, and whining ones—we attribute these to Saturn. To Mars belong hostile voices, quick ones, sharp ones, bitter ones, and threatening ones. The Moon's voices are in the middle.

The harmonies of Jove are to a certain extent grave and intense, or sweet and happy with their constancy. They are the opposite of Venus's, to whom we assign lascivious songs and songs voluptuous with softness. In the middle of these are those we attribute to the Sun and to Mercury. If the songs are venerable, with grace and smoothness, simple and intense, they are considered Apollo's. If the songs are to a certain extent relaxed and enjoyable, but nonetheless strenuous and multiplex, they are Mercurial.

You will be united by your own songs with any one of these four if you can produce competent sounds to go with the songs, so that when you cry out, singing and making sounds in the style of one of these, they will seem to answer you right back, either like Echo, or like the chords vibrating on your lyre. When one is vibrated, another is tuned accordingly. As Plotinus and Iamblichus say, it naturally touches you from the heavens, whether it is resounding back at you on your lyre, or in the vibration, or in the Echo from an opposite wall.

From doing this frequently, making Jovial, Mercurial, or Venereal harmonies, with these clearly reigning, your spirit, most attentively singing to this one or that one, will certainly become Jovial, Mercurial, or Venereal, having conformed to their harmonies.

Meanwhile, it becomes Phoebean, too, since the power of Phoebus as Lord of Music flourishes in all harmony. Furthermore, your spirit becoming Phoebean from Phoebean songs and sounds, you will also be acquiring for yourself the power of Jove, Venus, and Mercury. Again, since your spirit has been affected inside, you will likewise affect the soul and the body. Remember that what you say must be aptly and correctly composed and full of affect and feeling, and strong, to have a similar force in your songs.

How much power those Indian priests had in praying, it is no use repeating, or so say Damis and Philostratus. They do not even bother to tell us which words Apollonius used to summon the ghost of Achilles. For we are not speaking now about numinous figures that have to be adored, but about a certain natural power of speech, song, and words. There is a Phoebean medicine in song, and a power in it.

Just as people in Apulia, when they are touched by the poison spider there, become numb and lie down half-dead, that is what happens to people who hear Phoebus' song. For they dance to its sound, they play, and get well. If, after ten years, they should hear a similar sound, they are suddenly stirred to dance again. I guess that kind of sound is Phoebean and Mercurial.

Chapter 22

How we can fit ourselves to the seven celestial modes, and in what things Saturn is harmful, in what things propitious; in what things Jupiter defends against Saturn; how heaven works on the spirit, the body, and the soul

Because heaven has been composed by a harmonic cause, and because it is moved harmonically, and affects everything with harmonic movements and sounds, it is right that through this harmony alone not only men but all lower things are prepared to take the heavenly gifts for their powers. We divide up this vast harmony of higher things into seven grades of things: images that are harmonically constituted, medicines tempered with a certain consonance, vapors and odors that are made with a similar concinnity, and musical songs and sounds.

We want to add to this list the force got out of gestures of the body, dancing, and ritual movement, through concepts of the imagination, harmonious movements, agreeable discourses of reason, and tranquil contemplations of the mind. For just as we expose the body through its daily harmony (that is, through its habits and customs), and its image, to the light and heat of the Sun, we also acquire the spirit that is hidden in the powers of the stars through a similar kind of harmony. This is acquired with images (as some claim anyway) and certainly with medicines and odors harmonically composed.

Then, finally, through the spirit that is thus prepared in the planets (as we have often said) we expose the soul and the body to them. We expose the soul, I say, to the extent that it is inclined to the spirit and body through affect. We can now truly place imagination, reason, and the mind in the soul. At any rate, either because of the quality and movement of the spirit, or through our own choice, or even both, our imagination can be so arranged, composed, and strengthened by Mars and the Sun, that there is a special influx of Phoebus or a little contribution from Mars.

Likewise our reason, either through the imagination and the spirit together, or through deliberation, or through both, can, by a kind of imitation, put itself in agreement with Jove. Our reason then might take on Jove for his dignity and nearness to us, and receive the gifts of Jove much more than even the imagination or the spirit. In the same way, the imagination and the spirit, for the same reason, receive much more of the heavenly gifts than certain lower things and materials.

Finally, the contemplative mind, to the extent that it calls itself away not only from those things which we feel but even from those which we imagine and which we prove in human affairs, calls itself away in affect, intention, and in life, and calls itself back to separate things—to this extent it exposes itself to Saturn. For this alone Saturn is propitious. For just as the Sun is the enemy of certain night animals but the friend of daytime ones, so Saturn is the enemy of men who lead an open, public life, and the friend of those who choose to escape the company of the public. He is against people whose affections are public. He grants this public sort of life to Jove, and takes for himself a separate and a divine life. In fact, he is such a friend to the minds of men who are set apart that he is almost their kinsman.

To the spirits who inhabit sublime air (to speak Platonically), Saturn himself comes before Jove, just as Jupiter is the helpful father of those who live a public life.

There is no Saturn more unfeeling than the one for men who only pretend to the contemplative life, not really doing it. For Saturn does not recognize them as his own, nor does Jupiter, the moderator of Saturn, help those who flee from the common laws and customs of men and from commerce. Jupiter has had to claim possession (as they say) of these, with Saturn tied on, while Saturn takes the separated ones. This is why those Lunar people whom Socrates describes in the *Phaedo*, living on the highest surface of the earth, higher than the clouds, seeing things soberly and content with only fruits to eat, with the zeal of a secret wisdom and a religion devoted to Saturn, enjoyed happiness. They lived such a prosperous and long life that they were said not to be mortal men at all but immortal daemons, whom many heroes celebrate, a golden race enjoying Saturn's time and reign.

This is, I think, perhaps what the Arab astrologers meant, when they said that beyond the equator, to the South, there are certain extremely subtle daemons living, who seem neither to be born nor to die, and who have there Saturn's power, and the tail of the Snake. Albumasar seems to confirm this, in his book *Sadar*, saying that certain regions of India are subject to Saturn, and that men there are very long-lived, and they die only after a very long old age. He gives a reason for this: that Saturn does not harm those in his house, his domestics, but only outsiders.

Be sure then that you do not neglect the power of Saturn. The Arabs say he is the most powerful of all, that the planets submit their powers to him; they all accede to him, rather than the opposite. The planets have been joined to him, and to his nature. For he is indeed, among the planets, the head of an enormous orbit. No matter what planet is the head of its orbit, both the heart and the eye is Saturn.

The same goes for the innumerable stars it is near, and for the Primum Mobile which it is most like, in that this has a long circuit. It is the highest of the planets, which is why they call a man happy if Saturn has happily breathed on him.

Although they fear Saturn as a very great stranger to the common life of man, they think he is nonetheless even placated towards the common life when he has much of his power and dignity in the ascendant, or his Jupiter is happily looking at him, or he has excellently taken his ends. Otherwise, his influx having been received, it becomes especially thick in material, as if a poison, like

166

a rotten egg, or it becomes a poison with burning. At this point there arise or escape certain unclean, dumb, sad, envious things, things exposed by unclean daemons, from whose dealings you should run as far away as you can. For the poison of Saturn hides away somewhere as if it were asleep, or as if it were a sulfur far from flame. In living bodies it often explodes, and like sulfur, once it is ignited, it does not just burn but fills everything around it with a noxious vapor and infects whatever is near it.

Against such an influx, which is so foreign and dissonant to the common life of man, Jupiter arms us, first with his own natural quality, then with his foods and medicines, and even (so they say) with his images, and then with his customs and his business, and with studies and things that pertain especially to him. These make the noxious influx of Saturn go away, and they bring a kind influx instead, not only for those who are escaping to Jove but even for those who bring themselves with their whole mind to the divine contemplation that is signified by Saturn himself.

By this arrangement, the Chaldaeans and Egyptians and the Platonists thought one could avoid the malignity of fate. For when they did not want the heavenly bodies to be empty, but divinely animated and directed by the divine minds above them, it is no wonder that they not only wanted to obtain the many things that pertain to man's body and spirit there, but the many good things as well that overflow for the soul, not from bodies into the soul, but from souls. Many more things of this kind, however, flow forth from the higher minds in heaven.

If you want to assign all the reasons among these, which Moses did, giving the Sabbath as a day of leisure to the Hebrews, perhaps you will find the very sublime and secret allegory that the day of Saturn is useless for civil and military actions, but useful for contemplation, and that on this day there is a divine injunction against discussions of defense and business. Abraham and Samuel, and many Hebrew astrologers, trying to work against the threats of Mars and Saturn, used offerings and sacrifices, their minds elevated to God, clearly confirming that precept of the Chaldaeans: if you set the mind to a serious work of piety, you will keep the body also from falling.

The precept of Iamblichus is worthwhile, too: what the higher things have of heavenly, worldly, numinous powers, the lower things have somewhat. Since through the former we overcome effects that are fatal to us, through the latter we break away from fate, as if they had keys, as Orpheus said, for opening and closing. The higher divinity in the world, therefore, saves us much more from fatal necessity.

It would be extremely worthwhile to explore that Hebraic idea, that in animal sacrifices, and in the other things we sacrifice to disperse the imminent bad things of the heavens, they are dedicated by us toward us. But we will leave these matters to our man Pico to explore.

Finally, whenever we say that gifts descend to us from the heavens, know that first of all these riches of the celestial bodies come into our bodies through our spirit being prepared correctly. This happens before they even flow naturally into the spirit through their rays, or however else the spirit is exposed to them. Then the good things of the celestial souls come in too, partly by leaping into the spirit through rays to abound in our souls there, and partly by their souls, or by angels that men's souls are exposed to. By exposed, I mean, not so much by some natural arrangement, as by free choice of judgment or by feeling.

In sum, whoever imitates the beneficence, action, and order of the heavens, with vows, with study, with life and habits, will be, I think, like the higher beings themselves, and receive from them even more abundant gifts. Men, however, who are unlike the disposition of the heavens in their art, men who are discordant, will be secretly miserable, and will soon become publicly unhappy.

Chapter 23

In order for you to live and work prosperously, above all know your mind, your star, your Genius, and a place that is fitting for them. Live here, and follow your natural profession

Whoever is born of sound mind has been naturally intended by

Whoever is born of sound mind has been naturally intended by heaven for some honest work and some kind of life. Whoever, therefore, wishes heaven to be nice to him, will go after this work and this kind of life, and doggedly pursue it. For heaven favors things it has itself begun. You were made by nature for this purpose beyond anything else. What you do from your tender years on, what you talk about, mould, fit, dream, imitate, what you try very often, what you can do easily, what you are most of all good at, what you love beyond all else, what you would be unwilling to leave—this is clearly what heaven and the rector of heaven bore you for.

To this extent, therefore, heaven will favor your beginnings and will smile on your life, as much as you pursue the signs of this creator, especially if that Platonic saying is true (in which all antiquity agreed), that there is a certain daemon guardian of life for everyone who is born, bound by one's own star itself. In order for him to help someone in this duty of life, the heavenly beings assign him to each person being born.

Whoever, therefore, scrutinizes his mind, through the kind of discussions we have just described, will find his own natural work, and will find likewise his own star and daemon, and following their beginnings he will thrive and live happily. Otherwise, he will find fortune to be adverse, and he will feel that heaven hates him.

There are two kinds of unfortunate men. One of these is the guy who, having professed nothing, does nothing. The other kind is the type who takes on a profession that is wrong for his mind and contrary to his Genius. Such people languish in idleness, though heaven is always in the meantime trying to drive them to action. When they work at something that is foreign to their celestial patrons, they labor in vain, deprived of heavenly patronage.

The first type confirm the ancient proverb that the Gods help those who help themselves but are deaf to those who are lazy. The second type confirm a similar proverb, that you should do nothing if Minerva is unwilling.

I guess it was for this reason that the Pythagoreans prayed to Jove in their hymns, that either he would remove many of the evils on the human race, or at least show the way for us to use our daemon as guide. It would thus be useful for you to search for which region would be the best for you to live in and cultivate, the one your star and daemon has marked for you from the beginning, because there they will smile on you all the more.

This is the place in which your spirit is advanced and refreshed, where your senses remain thriving, where the disposition of your body is healthier, where many things nourish you, and where your wishes succeed. So find such a place, choose such a region, cultivate it happily! It is a place you would be unhappy to have to leave unless you could return and continue there.

Meanwhile, exercise yourself in this region with frequent motion, make yourself into an image of certain celestial gyres. For, given to a motion and circuit of this kind, you will conserve the things that they resemble.

It will be useful for you to think over how much pertains to your habitation. The countryside, like a food necessary for life, is a help to the city-dweller. The city certainly takes it out of you, so get a lot of rustication into your life, especially when tediousness begins to bother you and the rush and business of the city begins to grind you down.

How much one has to look to one's habitation as well as one's profession is something the Oriental astrologers would have been the last to deny. They said that a change of name, profession, appearance, food, or place changed our heavenly influx for better or worse. The Platonists even thought that our daemons were traded in, or that we got the same ones but that they were sometimes here and sometimes there.

The astrologers agree with the Platonists that we can have twin daemon guardians: one that we get at birth, the other with our profession. As often as our profession is in agreement with our nature, the same daemon is certainly very much like us and makes our life more concordant with his, and thus more tranquil. But if, however, our profession clashes with our mind, the daemon we get with this is discordant with our natural Genius, one that will be laboriously hard on us and worrisome.

However, to those who want to find out which daemon they

got at birth, Porphyry discovered a rule from the planet dominant at one's birth. Julius Firmicus said that the dominant one at your birth is either the one which has many of its dignities or merits then, or better, the one whose house is about to be sought by the Moon. That is the sign a man gets at birth. But he thinks one's daemon is not to be discovered by the same rule, but rather, in the opinion of the Chaldaeans, by the Sun or the Moon. By the Sun if you were born in the daytime, by the Moon if you were born at night, paying attention to an interval computed between these: you go through an equal space descending from the ascendant grade, and to which you limit a terminus. For whatever star that terminus is, they say that is your daemon.

In sum, the tenor and fortune of life depends on your dominant sign at birth and on your daemon. I have added the word fortune here because some people figure that part of one's fortune is due to the same cause. The ancients used to wish that their daemon would be one who descended from some pole in the heavens, from the East or the West, or mid-sky, or at least from the eleventh or fifth region. The eleventh in fact passes in mid-sky over our heads, and is called a good daemon, and sees from the sixth the ascending grade from the East. The fifth succeeds the antipodes in mid-sky and is called good luck, and looks at the ascendant grade from the third. Their third choice for a daemon was one who might at least come from a falling region, or one that had come from a ninth or a third. The ninth is called God, the third is called Goddess. The former looks at a descending grade from a third, the latter from a sixth. They hated to get the twelfth when it was falling, or the sixth. They called these two 'evil daemon' and 'bad luck,' respectively.

Since we, however, think that it is utterly useless to wish for these, we would advise you simply to observe those regions, which they preferred for daemons and luck, as planets and stars fitted for getting work done, and see to it, then, that they are at the corners, or in the two succeeding grades which we said, or at least only in the two falling ones which we said.

They say they do not like the Sun in a ninth house, the Moon in a third, Jove in an eleventh, or Venus in a fifth. For these all look at a grade that is ascending. But let us return to our subject. If, through experience and the diligence which I talked about before, or through this art which I just told you about, you discover the first trace of your nature and your daemon, I think you would be unfortunate if you did not then profess some honest calling in life. For, really, a man does not have a guiding daemon in his profession if he does not do honest work, and nature is not much of a guide for him either. It is always the duty of stars and daemons, or guardian angels, to be divinely disposed to guardianship, excellently and completely.

A man would be unfortunate, as I said before, who, contrary to nature, takes a daemon who is different from his own Genius. Remember that, depending on the worthiness of the professions, you gradually receive worthier daemons, or if you prefer, angels, and in public government even worthier ones. You will be able to receive one that is not contrary to nor very different from your Genius and your mind and suitable to the art and tenor of your life even if you advance to higher things.

Remember, again, to work up a familiarity with them, whom the Graces accompany. On this depends the good of your soul, your body, and your fortune: for just as an odor comes off musk, so some element of good exhales from something good onto the nearest thing, and often continues to the point of absorption. It would be a marvelous combination of three happy things, or two, anyway, miraculously flourishing between themselves.

Remember, finally, to steer clear of unrestrained, impudent, malign, and unhappy people. For these people are full of evil daemons or rays, and they are evil-doers; they are like lepers, harmful not only if they touch you, but even if they are just near you and in sight. Just being near such animate bodies is thought to be contact enough, on account of the effectiveness of their vapors and exhalations dripping from their heat, spirit, and feelings. Familiarity with these disgraceful and unfeeling people will be particularly sickening if it is absorbed by us after vegetal life in the month of Jove, that is, the second month. Whereas, in the month of Mars, that is, the third month, the sensual soul is freed from absorbing such disturbances. For they are so full of this disturbance, so full of Mars, that they infect those nearest them with Martial contagion.

For the opposite reason, frequent association, contact, and commerce with happy and excellent people, as we have said before, is marvelously productive.

Apollonius of Tyana, they say, detected an old man at Ephesus, under whose figure was hiding a daemon, who, just by his presence alone, contaminated the whole city with disease. Xenophon and Plato, on the other hand, have testified to how beneficial Socrates was, just by his presence alone.

Chapter 24

How men of letters may know their own mind and follow it; a way of life that is in agreement with spirit

Because I am speaking to students of letters, I want to remind you that anyone who is taken by a love of literature is first of all Mercurial, and then Solar, to the extent anyway that Mercury is himself Solar. This is a common condition for all such people. It is also true that, beyond just a Mercurial nature, anyone who shows graceful eloquence, charm, dignity, and loveliness, recognizes the Apollo in himself, and the Venus. Someone who is more inclined to law, or to natural and social philosophy, should not ignore that he has Jove for a patron. But the man who is driven with curiosity to scrutinize the innermost secret things should realize that he is not only Mercurial, but Saturnian. Under his dominion are all those people who get involved in some study that will take them until the end of time, especially those who are oblivious of daily life.

Finally, if it is true what some natural philosophers and astronomers say, the soul that descends into human conception in the month of the Sun, that is, the fourth month, is endowed with intellect. These people live with great intellect and show this from the very beginning, and they go forth every day as Solar people. These planets are a vent for medicine to flow through. One should make his home in their regions.

But most of all, o you cultivators of the Muses, you men of

letters, most of all I summon you to Apollo, guide of the Muses. My dear sweet brothers in the love of the Muses, some among you have much more strength of mind than of body. Well, you should know, then, that as soon as she was born, Phoebe, the sister of Apollo, had to supply him with a little material for nourishment and with a lot of spirit at his own birth. Indeed, the humors and foods in the body are easily broken down into such spirit. Your entire spirit, therefore, is made of some such material.

A man is spiritual, I say, who is living on this earth in the mask of a spare body, tiring his spirit before anything else with constant labor, so that his spirit more than anything else has to be carefully refreshed. In old age, in which it usually becomes very thick, it has to be called back to its proper subtlety. You know after all that a thick body is nourished by its own four, sort of thin, elements. The earth supplies wine for it, the odor of wine is carried by water, song and sounds move the air, and light prefers the element of fire. With these four, then, the spirit is nourished, I mean, with wine, smell, song, and light.

I do not know how I started this chapter talking about Apollo and now we are already into Bacchus! Anyway, it is right that we should proceed from light to heat, from ambrosia to nectar, from a glimpse of the truth to a burning love of the truth. They are certainly brothers and individuals, those pals, Phoebus and Bacchus. One of them gives you two of the most powerful things, light and the lyre. The other one gives you two more to refresh the spirit, wine and the odor of wine, with whose daily use the spirit itself becomes Phoeban and liberated.

For this reason, prepare yourselves daily for taking the light of the Sun. Do this in such a way, of course, that you avoid a certain distilling of yourself and a drying out, but, as often as possible, live under the light of the Sun, or at least in its sight, either at a distance from it or right smack under it, either covered up or bare to it, tempering your use of the vital power of the Sun all the time.

Do not forget that at night you can bring the Sun in with you with a fire, and with singing on your lyre. Whether you are asleep or awake, always breathe air that is alive, air that is living in light.

Likewise, it is really necessary for you to accept Bacchus' gift of wine, made after all with the help of Apollo. Accept his wine, therefore, in the same proportion that you accept Apollo's light. Too much, of course, to the extent of distillation and drying out, as I said about the Sun, and you are drunk.

Beyond just the substance of wine, which you should take twice a day, let your mouth frequently suck in its odor, which is a good way to refresh the spirit. Wash yourself in wine, in part by washing your hands with it, and in part by putting it in your nostrils and your temples.

Now we brothers have talked long enough, and now we have drunk enough, too. Be well.

Chapter 25

Using your astronomical knowledge for bearing children, for preparing meals, in housing and domestic matters, and for clothes; how much one can care for such things

But it is a good idea if we speak, just for a moment here, to the grave overseer of religion. Come, tell us, high priest, what is it that you condemn in the use of the stars? You say there is something in it that takes away our free will, something that goes against the worship of one God? Well, I not only condemn the same things you do, I even detest them.

I know that you curse those (and I shudder to even think of them) who, when they want to acquire something from God, go flocking to Jove in mid-sky as he goes under that vast head of the Serpent which once tumbled from heaven, taking a third part of the stars with it. These people are as miserable as they are stupid, and they will only be devoured in the end by this Serpent themselves.

But you do agree, do you not, that one should choose the right hour for contracts, marriages, meetings, journeys, and similar business?

I see that you are not going to consent easily to this, though I do not know what you are afraid of in regard to free will.

But okay, even if a theologian like Albertus Magnus will back me up on this question of choosing the hour and its relevance to free will, even if reason itself dictates that the heavens are subject to the use of our good judgment when they offer a doctor their herbs, even so, I will, for now anyway, take your word for it and believe you instead. Even though you brook these things only with great difficulty, I will give them up with no problem.

You have permitted for a long time now (at least I think so) observations of the Moon, and even other stars as long as this involved curing diseases and preparing remedies. You have also conceded, and approval came down from on high, the idea of an increasing Moon and its increment of light as a good time to sow seeds in the fields and to plant vines. Why not, then, for the planting of man (if I can speak like a Cynic), let us use the Moon's help, too, and Jove's, and Phoebus'? After all, we have always used Venus for this purpose anyway!

But, and I will be straight with you now, these Gods are always being used. For Diana is my Venus.

And as for food, what can we say? Is it not permitted, and is it not useful, to make wine under some happy autumn star, and, from day to day, to make bread and have feasts that way, too? If we cannot, in preparing these things, wait for the aspect of some star, it will at least be useful to receive the Sun, Jove, Venus, and the Moon when they are ascending or otherwise angular. For thus everything which we use is happily affected by heaven, and happily affects us.

Well, I see that so far you are ready to yield in this controversy, except that you still worry that our lives, in all this, would be nothing but perpetual slavery. I would myself add to this, that mortals who are slaves to accumulating wealth and honors do so in vain, and they are going to be perpetually liberated from such stuff if in the meantime they do not take care of their health so that they have long lives. If, therefore, they serve God alone, which is the best thing to do, or if their lives are in service to something else besides, their lives will be strong, and long, more so than if they indulge themselves in vain honors and wealth.

So we agree.

But one more thing: do people build houses just any place, do they choose to live in unlucky places? Where some contagious calamity infects someone living in a building, and the poisonous vapor of the disease even stays in the walls for up to two years, some residue of the epidemic even hiding in one's clothes, it can long afterward infect the user who is not careful and it can kill him.

But now that we have brought up this subject of clothes, would you forbid me, pious father, in making such clothes, to first look carefully to Venus' little breathing-hole, so that it might almost be Venus herself who is making the clothes for me, and thus have her affect my body and my spirit with a little of her pleasant quality? Do not doctors, after all, forbid you to wear the skin of foxes, but approve the skin of lambs? It is not different with the stars from day to day, making clothes for us as if we were born that day, as they have done for us from the time we were babies. Certain clothes, and other works of art, receive a certain quality from a star.

Thomas Aquinas agrees, in his book *On Fate*. You, therefore, will agree too.

Indeed, infected clothes infect the wearer, as any leper will tell you. If you will only talk to people about life, you will, I think, permit these things. And I, with your permission, will talk about what should be observed.

But if, however, while you do not actually condemn my kind of care for those whose lives are death-bound, you should nonetheless warn me to give it up, I will indeed give it up, relying on the confidence of a better life, and I will advise others to do the same. Good-bye.

Chapter 26

How the things below, exposed to the things above, draw down the things above; and how the most powerful worldly gifts are received through worldly materials

But lest we digress even further from what we started to do in the beginning, which was simply to interpret Plotinus, let us briefly sum it all up.

The world is effected by the good itself (as Plato teaches, along with Timaeus the Pythagorean) as best as it can be effected. It is therefore not only corporeal, but sharing in the life and intelligence above. This is why, beyond this body of the world familiarly clear to the senses, there hides in it a certain spirit-body, exceeding the capacity of the fallen senses. In its spirit the soul thrives; in its soul the intelligence shines.

Just as, under the Moon, air is not mixed with earth except through water, nor fire mixed with water except through air, so in the universe there is a certain food or kindling for the soul that couples it to the body, and this is what we call spirit. The soul also is a kind of kindling in the spirit and the body of the world, divinely following on the intelligence, just as oil is used to penetrate a deep dryness in wood. The oil that it drinks in is food for the fire. I call it the next thing to heat. Heat, itself, is the vehicle of light, and if this wood is of such a kind that it shines with the present fire, it does not burn, which is the way it is when we see it.

Now in this example we see that for a man or anything else under the Moon vital things can be received as long as there are certain preparations, in part natural, in part artificial. Even certain good intellectual things somehow come down, too.

What pertains to religion here, let us discuss some other time, though Plotinus himself brings that subject up right here in the middle.

As for what pertains to natural influxes, the kind that are coming down from above, realize that they can be acquired in us and in our materials at any age, when nature supplies us with its poultices, and when heaven conspires to bring them. Does not nature, the creator of the foetus itself, when it affects the little body with a certain kind of arrangement it has, and shapes it, does it not bring forth spirit from the universe immediately with this preparation, right in the foetus itself, as if it were a kind of food it was giving it? And through this poultice, as it were, does it not draw life and soul?

Finally, through a certain species and disposition of the soul, the body is so alive that it is worthy now of a mind as if this were a gift of the heavens. Nature, therefore, is everywhere a magician, as Plotinus and Synesius have said. It clearly entices certain things with certain foods, just as gravity draws heavy things to the center of the earth, or the curve of the Moon draws light things, or leaves are drawn by heat, or roots are drawn by water, and so on.

The wise men of India say that by this same kind of attraction the world is bound to itself, saying that the world is sometimes a masculine animal, sometimes a feminine one, and that it is everywhere copulating with itself out of this mutual love of its own limbs. They say that it exists in such a way that the bonds that hold these limbs together are inside its own mind, which, going through its limbs, works the whole mass and mixes with the great body itself.

Orpheus called this nature of the world, and Jove's world, both masculine and feminine. It is so because the world is everywhere hot to make love to its own mutual parts. Everywhere it is mixed between the masculine and feminine sex, as the order of signs declares, where, in perpetual order, the masculine goes first, the feminine follows. The trees and herbs prove this too, which have both sexes the same as animals.

I will pass over the fact that fire goes to air, and water goes to earth, like man to woman, because there is nothing surprising in the fact that the world's limbs, among themselves and all its parts, lust for copulation with each other. The planets are in accord with this, too, part of them being masculine, part of them, in fact, feminine, and Mercury in particular is both masculine and feminine, as the father of Hermaphroditus.

If we turn to agriculture, one prepares a field and seeds for heavenly gifts, and with certain graftings one propagates the life of a plant, leading to another and a better species. Doctors, physicians, and surgeons do similar things in our own bodies to nourish them and to make them acquire more richly the nature of the universe. A philosopher learned in natural and astral matters, whom we call therefore a Magus, does the same thing, with certain earthly enticements drawing the heavenly things when he does it properly, sowing no differently than a farmer who is knowledgeable in grafting, who starts a new shoot off old stock.

This is exactly what Ptolemy said, too, agreeing that a man who is wise in this way can help in the work of the stars just like a farmer can in working the power of the earth. A magus subjects earthly things to the heavens, the lower to the higher, so that everywhere things that are feminine are made fertile by things that are masculine, as iron is drawn to a magnet, as camphor is sucked by boiling air, as crystal is illuminated by the Sun, as sulfur and sublime liquor are ignited by fire, as the empty shell of an egg, filled with dew, is lifted by the Sun; in fact, as an egg itself is nourished by a hen.

Just as some nourish their eggs, others bring life from the universe even without such animals. By preparing certain materials for them, they create animals without eggs or apparent seeds, like the scorpion from clover, bees from a cow, blackbirds from sage, getting life from the world with certain materials at the right times.

Thus, the wise man, when he knows a certain material, or those partly worked on by nature, partly finished by art, gathers them even if they are scattered, and knows which heavenly influx they are able to receive. He gathers these with the planet reigning whose influx they contain; he prepares them, uses them, and obtains for himself, through them, the heavenly gifts.

For whenever a certain material is exposed to the higher beings, the way a mirror is to your face and a wall is to the echo of your voice, it falls out, obviously through some extremely powerful agent everywhere present by its power and its marvelous life, that it acquires a passionate power, exactly the way a mirror reflects an image from your face and a wall represents an echo from your voice.

Plotinus himself uses these same examples, where he says that the high priests or maguses, imitating Mercurius, were accustomed to receiving something divine and wonderful in their statues and sacrifices. He says, however, along with Trismegistus, that through these materials nothing numinous was received separate from the material inside, but only something worldly, as I have said from the beginning, and Synesius agrees.

By something worldly, I mean a certain life, or something vital from the soul of the world, and from the souls of the spheres and stars, or even a certain movement, a vital one, as if brought on by daemons; in fact, those same daemons who sometimes get into materials.

Mercurius himself, whom Plotinus follows, says that he made, through airy daemons and not celestial or sublime ones, statues from herbs, trees, stones, and aromatics, that had some natural force of divinity (as he says) in them. He adds that songs are like the heavenly things, from which he says they delight us, and that the heavenly things are present longer in them than in statues, both for the good or the ill of man.

He says, too, that Egyptian wise men, who were also priests, when they were unable once to persuade the people that there are Gods, that is, certain spirits above men, thought to use this kind of illicit Magic to entice daemons into statues to appear to be Gods. But Iamblichus condemns the Egyptians for this, that they accepted daemons not only as certain steps to be used in discovering the higher Gods, but even more, that they adored them. He prefers the Chaldaeans, in fact, for not employing daemons.

The Chaldaeans, I say, were masters of religion, for we suspect that the astrologers of the Chaldaeans, far more than those of the Egyptians, tried to draw daemons through the celestial harmony into earthen statues.

This is what the Hebrew astrologer, Samuel, seems to mean, supported by the authority of David, his fellow astrologer, that the ancients clearly were makers of images and statues that would predict the future. He says that the harmony of the heavens was arranged in these. They would melt some metal into the shape of a beautiful man, on a day of Mercury in the third hour, and certainly on a day of Saturn, when Mercury goes under Saturn in Aquarius, in the ninth region of heaven, which designates prophecy. Gemini is rising then, a star that signifies prophets, they say, and Mars is burned by the Sun; but Mercury is not looking on, and the Sun is looking at the place of its conjunction. Venus, meanwhile, is obtaining some corner in the West and is powerful, while the Moon looks at an ascending grade from her triangle, and Saturn does the same. This is what Samuel says.

I myself, however, first of all, following the opinion of blessed Thomas Aquinas, think that if they really did make statues that talked, they found these words not simply through the influx of the stars but through daemons. And secondly, if by chance it happened that they got into statues of this kind, I do not think they were bound there through a heavenly influx, but rather they yielded to the will of their worshippers and were finally trapped there. For a higher nature, sometimes, can be united to a lower one, but it cannot be confined. And that disposition of the stars, which I described just a moment ago, cannot, perhaps, come about.

Although daemons can be enclosed in statues through astronomical business, nevertheless, where they appear because worship is shown towards them, Porphyry says, they speak oracles according to astronomical rules. These are frequently ambiguous, and rightly so, because, as Iamblichus agrees, true prophecy and certain prophecy come about not through daemons or human arts nor through nature, but by a divine inspiration in minds that have been cleansed.

But let us get back to Mercurius—in fact, let us get back to Plotinus! Mercurius said priests received a power that was from the nature of the world, and that this was mixed. Plotinus, following him, thinks that everything can be easily conciliated in the soul of the world to the extent that it generates and moves the forms of natural things through certain seminal reasons divinely inside it. He even calls these reasons Gods, because they are never apart from the ideas of the supreme mind.

Therefore, through reasons of this kind, the soul of the world easily applies itself to materials which it formed from the very beginning through these. Some magus or priest will then use the forms of these things, collecting them correctly and at the right times. These forms belong properly to this or that reason, like the magnet to iron, rhubarb to bile, saffron to the heart, agrimony and scoria to the liver, spice and musk to the brain.

This can be done at any time, as long as you apply these reasons to the forms. The sublimer gifts will then descend, to the extent that their reasons in the soul of the world are joined to the intellectual forms of this same soul, and through these to ideas in the divine mind. Iamblichus approves of this too, where he deals with sacrifices.

But this is a subject we will discuss more appropriately some other time. Then, far from seeming the impure superstition of pagan people, it will seem, quite the contrary, pure Evangelical piety. We have already in fact shown this in great part in our book *On the Christian Religion.*

Finis

The Apology Of Marsilio Ficino

in which he deals with medicine, astrology, the life of the world,
and the Magi who greeted Christ immediately after he was born

M arsilio Ficino, the Florentine, sends greetings again and again to his most beloved brothers in the search for truth, the three Peters: Nero, Guicciardini, and Soderini. I should more appropriately call you 'Tripeter' than three Peters. For just as the hand is one, and its many fingers do not make it many, so though you have three bodies, my friends, your one will makes you a Peter. Christ, the creator of the heavenly kingdom, created a huge rock and built the immense edifice of his Church upon it. I, too, am given such huge rocks, by some divine fate, that these three Peters will be enough now for my own arduous edifice.

Now, my friends, if you do not already know it, you will need the fortress of Minerva if we are to hold off from us the savage, giant force of these evil people. This is why I have shrunk your first fortress, constructed of three rocks, to one, to defend the life of my *Three Books;* to save, that is, their public life. You know, I assume, that I composed my *Book of Life* in a division of three little books. The first was called *On The Healthy Life,* the second *On Long Life,* and the third *On Heavenly Life.* The food of the title is pleasant in order to entice many people to taste it.

But in such a large audience there will of course be many ignorant people and not a few who are downright evil.

Someone, for example, will say, "Is not Marsilio a priest? He certainly is. Well what do priests have to do with medicine? And furthermore, what business of his is astrology?"

Someone else will say, "What does a Christian have to do with magic and images?"

Someone else, someone unworthy of life itself, will deny heaven its life.

All those who feel this way will be extremely ungrateful for our help to them, and contrary to our kindness, with which we counseled them publicly for the prosperity of their lives and for their faculty of mind, they will not hesitate to be cruel.

Our struggle in this will therefore be shared, and thus a little lighter, for there are three of you against these three enemies. Your battle stations are assigned. But do not refute invective with further invective (you see how much I know what is on your mind.) You must suck their bitterness out (your own pleasantness is marvelous for this) and overcome them with the sweetness of your own honey.

First of all, splendid Nero, you answer to the first charge: the priests of antiquity used to be doctors, and astronomers, too. The histories of the Chaldaeans and Persians, and the Egyptians, all testify to that. Nothing is more pertinent to the pious priest than the singular duty of charity, which is exactly what one does when he offers the greatest help of all, and in this the ancient priests were especially brilliant. There can be no question that the most magnificent service of all, one that is very necessary, one that is most sought by humanity, is the work that gives mankind a healthy mind in a healthy body. And even we can be good at this, if we join medicine to the priesthood. But because medicine without the favor of the heavens (as Hippocrates and Galen confessed, and as we have discovered, too) is very often worthless, in fact, very often harmful, it is no wonder that Astronomy belongs to this same charity of the priest's to which we said medicine also belongs. This kind of doctor, in my opinion, the sacred books compel us to honor, because the Almighty, out of necessity, created him.

Christ himself, the bestower of life, ordered his disciples to cure the sick throughout the world, and taught his priests that if they could not heal with words they should at least heal with herbs and stones. And if these were not enough, he told them to do this with a certain breath of heaven. For he would himself at times move animals to his medicine with this same breath of heaven, to provide them abundantly with life. Thus, divinely aroused by an impulse of heaven, serpents are healed with fennel, swallows heal their eyes with swallow-wort, eagles troubled with birth find eagle-stone through divine providence, and with it they immediately force out their eggs comfortably. Thus God himself, who, through the heavens, stirs the animal world to find medicines, certainly permits his priests to expel diseases; not for money, I mean, but for charity, using medicines that have been strengthened by the heavens.

You can add to this anything more that would help that your own mind can come up with to sting them.

Then you come on strong right after this, Guicciardini, and answer the curious, saying that magic and images are not so much recommended by Marsilio but described by him, and that he is simply interpreting Plotinus. Which the writings plainly show, if they are read with an open mind.

Nor is Ficino talking about the profane kind of magic which uses the cult of demons—assert this strongly—but the natural kind of magic which seizes, from the heavenly bodies through natural things, benefits for helping one's health—be sure to mention that. This faculty seems so much more helpful to the minds that legitimately use it than even medicine or agriculture do in their way, and even more helpful depending on our industry in joining heavenly things to the earthly.

In this work the first people of all were the Magi who worshipped Christ at his birth. Why, therefore, should you be afraid of the name 'Magus,' as if it were terrifying? It is a name pleasing to the Gospels, not something wicked and venomous, but signifying a wise man and a priest. Was not such a Magus the first worshipper of Christ? If you will permit me to say it, he was like a farmer who cultivates a field, only he was a cultivator of the world. He did not worship the world, any more than a farmer worships the earth. But just as a farmer, for the sake of human food, tempers his field to the weather, so this wise man, this priest, for the sake of human health, tempered the lower things of the world to the highest, and like the eggs of a hen, subjected the earthly things to the warmth of the heavens. This is something that God himself always does, and teaches us to do, and persuades us to do, that the lower things might be generated by the higher, and be moved and ruled.

So, there are two kinds of magic. One, with a certain ritual, works with demons and often makes predictions. This is driven out when the Prince Of This World is driven out. The other kind, which subjects natural materials to natural causes, works miraculously. There are two types of this artifice. One is curious, the other is necessary.

The former manufactures worthless omens for public display, as when the Persian Magi, using sage that has rotted under excrement while the Sun and Moon take the second aspect of Leo and hold the same grade there, produced something like a blackbird with a serpent's tail, and then reduced this to ashes, poured them into a brazier, and made a house seem immediately to be full of serpents. One should run from such silly and even health-endangering stuff.

The necessary kind of artifice should be held onto, however, which joins medicine to astrology.

If someone is really persistent and presses this further, Guicciardini, this is the way you must take him on: tell him that no man should read these harmful things, nor know them, nor remember them, nor use them, if he is unworthy of such benefits. There are many other things which you will be able to come up with out of your own head in tackling this ungrateful ignorance.

And now what is there for you to do, our nimble Soderini? Whether or not you will lift up the superstitious and the blind, those who see life in the most abject animals and the vilest herbs but do not see it in heaven or the world, I do not know. If these little manikins allow life only in the least particles of the world, what madness, what contempt they will feel toward us! They will not want to know the whole world, they will not want it to live, that whole in which we live and are moved and exist.

Aratus once sang about this, saying that Jove was the shared life of the world body. I do not know what luck made me come upon these words of Aratus now.

Remember Luke the Evangelist, and remember to use freely the words of the Apostle Paul, in which those wise men did not tremble at the life of the world.

But some superstitious person might object to these, and not easily be convinced by these words that Paul himself said of the world—that it has soul, but that it is only under God, and that we live in this same God. That is all right. Let us not give it a name in the world, then, if soul does not please them. Let the name 'soul' be profane. Will it be okay at least to call it some kind of life? Which God himself, the shaper of the world, so happily and kindly breathed on as his work when it was finished, since he was not eager for just the vilest things to have such life, and since he daily presents this life through the heavens and through many things which are so generously in the heavens.

Speak, my love, do you not see cows and donkeys—O cow! O donkey!—who, with a sort of touch bring forth living things from themselves to be alive? If these can bring forth living things just from some look, would you not assume that these other things live much more? This must be true, if there is such life.

The sky is married to the earth but does not touch it (in most people's opinion, anyway). He does not copulate with his wife, the earth, but he beholds his wife through the pits of the stars, as if with the rays of eyes that are everywhere, and beholding her, he impregnates her and creates living things. Now does not one who bestows life just by looking have a certain life of his own? Are you going to tell me that what gave life and a living aspect to a bird like the sparrow is worse off than a sparrow? Bring all this up—unless you are not convinced yourself—and you will knock the superstitious out; in fact, you will knock them dead!

In order to get as many patrons for our cause as we can, Peter Neri, I want you to recruit that Amphion of ours, Cristoforo Landino, our orator and poet. Our Amphion will quickly demolish the stone walls of our enemies with the wonderful smoothness of his music.

You, dear Guicciardini, my other chief, go now, go quickly, and rouse our Hercules, Poliziano. Whenever Hercules was in a particularly dangerous fight, he would call for his Iolaus, so you now likewise go get our Hercules, that this Hercules Poliziano might attack these barbarian monsters now devastating Latium and chew them up, murder them, maul them viciously, and safely defend us. He will then grab his club and bludgeon this hundred-headed Hydra that is now threatening our books, and he will burn it up in flames.

Hey, my sweet Soderini, come on, rise up, go get Pico, our Phoebus. I often call him my Phoebus, and he calls me in turn his Dionysus, his Bacchus. We are therefore brothers! Tell my Phoebus that the poisonous Pytho is after us, emerging once again from his swamp. Please, beg him to bend his bow! Have him fire his arrows right now! Once he starts shooting, he will kill the whole poisonous pack with one shot, and I know what I am talking about.

Farewell now, my dear lovely brothers, not just strong in health, but worthy of happiness, too. Care for the health and happiness of my books as they are now being brought into the light.

15 September 1489, in the field at Careggi.

What Is Necessary For Composure In Life
And For Tranquility Of The Soul

M arsilio Ficino, who enjoys more than anyone the hunt for truth, to his brothers, Bernardo Canigiani, Giovanni Canacci, and Amerigo Corsini, greetings.

Since I began now with the word 'hunt,' it is appropriate that I am writing to my hunting-dogs and my chasers. We rightly call philosophers hunters, always panting away on the track of truth. Are they not, after all, hunting-dogs? Socrates, in the *Republic*, says this is the perfect word for them. Philosophers are either legitimate or frauds. Both kinds are dogs. Those who wisely search for truth modestly hold onto some discovery. The others bark for the sake of public opinion, and bite and tear. There are dogs among philosophers, not only because they follow some sect or path, but even some who have a sect with the name 'Dog-like,' or Cynic.

Our Academy has its own dogs. Here, you wise dogs of the Academy; here, I am calling you for the chase. There are three of you. I am begging you now, defend my three tender children who I am afraid are about to be thrown to the wolves. Run, I say, quickly, I have fine work for you now, not troubles.

You know my friend, Giorgio Benigno Salviati, who for a long time now has wisely pursued that truth which you now run on the track of. He is an image of the Sun to his brothers; he, the older, illuminating the younger. Call on him, if you want to hear the howling of the wolves. This George is so brave he will easily chase away all the wolves when he has slain the giant dragon. He will help me. He will lighten your worry and concern.

Some of you often used to say that you could find nothing in life more healthful than to gulp down time in great composure. Others among you used to laugh at anyone saying this. But come, tell me, Canacci, is this not what you often used to say, to devour time this way? What did you mean by it? It means nothing, you say, other than to drink up, not to chew but to chomp, to gorge oneself with jaws full.

Time is by nature something fluid (as I have said before) and slippery. Its condition is liquid in the sense that if you confine it in a narrow place, you suddenly lose it. Its forces flow away and quickly scatter. If you compress water into a sponge and squeeze it, you immediately lose it. If you give it more room you will retain it, and this goes even more for air, fire, and aether.

These are discussed in vain by the Poets, who struggle to grab the images of Gods and spirits by the elbows. They must be received instead in the widest possible way. Liquid, and extremely abundant, they must be possessed abundantly.

Now a narrowness heavily presses us when we return the soul itself and its naturally ample movement into some narrow place. Those who ponder heavily on their studies and business and always work very exactly on tiny matters wear out their lives, or miserably waste away their lives in private. Pythagoras seems to have been right, therefore, in what he taught: Beware, lest you get boxed into some narrow space where there is no more sky for you and nothing more that is vital. The narrowest piece of earth still has life in the world, though it is the least life. So if we live in heaven and in time, the more widely we absorb the one, the more we live.

O my friends, live your lives happily, far from narrowness. Live happy. It was the happiness of heaven that created you; and with a kind of laughter, that is, with a dilating, a movement, a splendor, it declared you, as if it were rollicking. The happiness of heaven will protect you. So live every day happy in the present. For worry in the present steals the present away from you and steals the future, too. Curiosity about the future quickly turns it into the past. Therefore, I implore you, again and again, live happy!

The fates allow it, as long as you live without care. But, to live without care, do not allow one single care. Never worry about anything! Be extremely diligent in escaping from cares! For all it takes is one care for the heart of miserable mortals to burn with all cares. Neglect, therefore, your diligence, and love, in fact, your negligence, and even in this it is fitting to be negligent, I mean to the extent it is allowed us.

I am telling you all this, my friends, not as a priest, but as a doctor. For without this one thing—the life of all medicines, as it were—all medicines used for the benefit of life would die.

16 September 1489, in the field at Careggi.

GLOSSARY

I have not included in the Glossary names of stars or planets mentioned by Ficino, nor any botanicals

ABRAHAM   the patriarch of the Hebrews in *Genesis.*

ABRAHAM THE ASTROLOGER   Abraham Avenares, or Aben Ezra, a 12th c. A.D. Hebrew astrologer who wrote several treatises on astrology which were translated into Latin by Pietro d'Abano.

ACHATES   the faithful companion of Aeneas (*fidus Achates*) in Virgil's *Aeneid.*

ALBERTUS MAGNUS   (1193–1280 A.D.) born in Swabia, a Dominican priest and naturalist, taught in Paris, where he was regarded as the most learned man in the Middle Ages. His medical writings were influenced by Aristotle and Maimonides. His *Summa naturalium* deals with the therapeutic value of plants. His *Speculum astronomiae* discusses talismans, magic, and the occult. He was the teacher of Thomas Aquinas.

ALBUMASAR   Djafar ben Mohammed ben Omar el Balkhy (d. 885 A.D.), an Arab writer on astrology, meteorology, and divination.

ALCHINDUS   Abu Yusuf Ya'Qub Ibn Ishaq Al-Kindi (d. 873 A.D.), an Arab physician, astronomer, mathematician, and philosopher at Baghdad. He was the translator and author of over two hundred works, mostly on medicine, but also such works as *On the Rays of the Stars*, etc.

ALCIBIADES   A dialogue which Ficino attributed to Plato but which is now considered spurious.

ALEXANDER (AND NICOLAS, THE PERIPATETICS)   Alexander of Aphrodisias (ca. 200 A.D.), a celebrated commentator on Aristotle. Archbishop Nicolas of Methone was a 12th c. A.D. opponent of the neo-Platonists.

ALI THE ASTROLOGER   Aboul Hassen Ali ben Abi Erradjel, or Ali ben Radjel, an 11th c. A.D. Arab astrologer from Cordoba, whose treatises on astrology were widely disseminated in Latin translations.

AMPHION   in Greek mythology, he was given a lyre by Hermes. He and his brother Zethus then walled the city of Thebes, with Amphion drawing the stones after him through the magical music of his lyre.

ANDROMACHUS   Roman physician to Nero (54–68 A.D.). He was the inventor of a famous compound called *theriaca* (modern 'treacle'). Galen gives the formula in his tract *De theriaca ad Pisonem*. Its composition consisted of some 57 substances, and its preparation was considered so difficult and requiring such skill that at Venice in the fifteenth century it had to be prepared in the presence of the *Priori e Consiglieri*. A statute in Florence required that it be made with all the pharmacists and physicians together, and it could not be sold without the approval of the Consuls.

ANEBOS   an Egyptian prophet to whom Porphyry wrote an imaginary letter (*Letter to Anebos*) questioning divinations, incantations, and other theurgic arts. A reply exists, probably written by Iamblichus.

APOLLONIUS OF TYANA   a neo-Pythagorean sage (b. 4 B.C.) and ascetic teacher, who visited India and other places in the ancient world, and whose life is the subject of a biography by Philostratus.

APULIA   a province in southern Italy, north of Calabria.

AQUINAS, *see* THOMAS AQUINAS

ARATUS   Greek Stoic (ca. 315–240 B.C.) and author of an astronomical poem called *Phaenomena*.

ARCHYTAS   Greek philosopher from Tarentum, a mathematician as well as a general. He was a Pythagorean, and influenced Plato, his contemporary.

ARISTOTLE   celebrated Greek philosopher (384–322 B.C.) and founder of what became known as the Peripatetic School.

ARNALDO   of Villanova (1235–1312 A.D.), an alumnus of the Arabist school of medicine at Montpellier. A Catalan, he considered Avicenna "a professional scribbler," and was himself a devotee of astrology and Raymond Lully. He wrote much on diet and hygiene.

AVICENNA   a Moslem scientist and philosopher (980–1037 A.D.) from Persia, author of the most famous single book in the history of medicine, *The Canon of Medicine*.

CANACCI, Giovanni   member of the Careggi circle, Prior of Florence in

1492 and 1497, and one of the twelve advisers attached to the Signoria (the 'Buonomini') at the time of the condemnation of Savonarola, his bitter enemy.

CANIGIANI, Bernardo   had been a student of Ficino, was Gonfaloniere (senior executive officer) of Florence in 1472 and 1476, and one of the Buonomini in 1486.

CATO, Marcus Portius, Censorius   Roman moralist and militarist (234–149 B.C.) In his work *De Re Rustica,* he gives rules for libations and sacrifices as well as medical precepts.

CELSUS, *see* ORIGEN.

CHALDAEANS   An ancient Babylonian people. A poem in Greek hexameter called *The Chaldaean Oracles,* edited or composed by 'Julian the Chaldaean,' who lived under Marcus Aurelius, was regarded by the later neo-Platonists as a sacred book for its magical and religious practices, and its amalgam of neo-Pythagoreanism and neo-Platonism. About 300 lines from it are preserved in the writings of later neo-Platonists, from which Ficino knew them.

CORSINI, Amerigo   poet, (1452–1501 A.D.) and student of Ficino. In love with a certain Lisa, who rejected him, he wrote poems on this subject, and was consoled by Ficino in a long letter entitled "Whence Arise the Vicissitudes of Love." In 1488, Corsini was elected Gonfaloniere of Justice.

CYNICS   'the Dog philosophers,' a sect of Greek philosophers in the 3rd c. B.C. who followed the teachings of Diogenes, who was called a "dog" because he tried to live like an animal, against all conventions.

DAMIS   a contemporary Assyrian chronicler of Apollonius of Tyana's life, from whose account Philostratus wrote his.

DAVID   (ca. 1012–972 B.C.) King of the Hebrews, successor of Saul, for whom he played the lyre. He is said to have composed many of the Psalms.

DEMOCRITUS   Greek atomist philosopher from Abdera (b. 460 B.C.), called "the laughing philosopher" by the Roman poet Horace.

DIOSCORIDES, Pedanius   an army physician (1st c. A.D.) who wrote a distinguished study of pharmacological plants called the *Materia Medica.*

EMPEDOCLES   Greek Pythagorean philosopher (ca. 493–433 B.C.), scientist, poet, orator, statesman, healer, and miracle-worker.

FIFTH ESSENCE   in addition to air, earth, water, and fire, the Hermetic tradition believed in a 'Fifth Essence,' sometimes called "burning water," "the soul in the spirit of wine," and "the water of life." It was a strong alcohol that made man incorruptible and renewed his youth. One way of making it was by distilling wine "one thousand times." It is much like the modern drink *grappa.*

FIRMICUS, Julius Maternus   the 4th c. A.D. Sicilian author of *Eight Books of the Mathesis,* a theory of astrology, the final work on astrology of the classical world.

FOLIGNO, Gentile da, *see* GENTILE

GALEN   Greek physician (130–200 A.D.), author of over five hundred of the most influential treatises on medicine, diet, and hygiene.

GENTILE DA FOLIGNO   (d. 1348) student of Pietro d'Abano at the University of Padua, his medical case studies were a pioneering work of the kind.

GUICCIARDINI, Piero di Jacopo   (1454–1513 A.D.) member of Ficino's Academy, and father of the great Renaissance historian Francesco Guicciardini, whom Ficino baptized.

HAHAMETH   Abdallah ben Iahya, also known as Ahmed ben Thayeb, and as Sarakhsy. He was a 9th c. Arab author of many works on astrology and medicine, including a treatise called *Reply to Thebith ben Corath.*

HALY ABBAS   (d. 994 A.D.) compiled an influential Arab textbook on medicine, the *Al-Maleki,* which was the standard medical textbook until the *Canon* of Avicenna.

HECATE   ancient Greek Goddess of women often portrayed as the Moon.

HERCULES   the greatest of Greek mythological heroes, possessing great strength, usually portrayed as wearing a lion's skin and carrying a huge club.

HERODICUS   5th c. B.C. Greek physician and sophist, tutor of Hippocrates, he applied gymnastics to the treatment of disease.

HIARCHAS   Ficino's rendering of Iarchas. He was the chief of the Indian sages whom Apollonius of Tyana meets.

HIPPOCRATES   celebrated Greek physician of the 5th c. B.C. None of the books preserved under his name is genuine.

HOMER   8th c. B.C. Greek poet, author of the *Iliad* and the *Odyssey.*

HUNGARY, *see* KING OF HUNGARY

HYDRA   in Greek mythology, a serpent that lived in the swamps at Lerna, having numerous heads; when you cut one off, another appeared. To kill it, Hercules called in Iolaus, who brought torches, and whenever Hercules cut off a head, Iolaus cauterized the stump, so that no more grew and the beast died. Hercules then dipped his arrows in the blood to make them poisonous.

IAMBLICHUS   neo-Platonist philosopher (250–325 A.D.), studied under Porphyry in Rome. Among his writings on magic is his defence of ritualistic magic in *The Reply of Abammon,* a response to Porphyry's *Letter to Anebos.*

ILLYRIANS   a people on the Adriatic Sea, modern Yugoslavia.

IOLAUS   the nephew of Hercules in Greek mythology, see HYDRA.

ISAAC   Abu Ya'Qub Ishaq Sulayman Al-Isra'Ili, also called Isaac Judaeus, an Egyptian ophthamologist (850–941 A.D.) His principal work, *A Book of Diet,* was written in Arabic and translated into Hebrew. A Latin translation was published in Padua in 1487.

ISIS   in Egyptian mythology, wife of Osiris. When her husband is assassinated by their brother, Set, she searches for the coffer in which the body had been enclosed and cast into the Nile. When she finds it, Set cuts the body into fourteen pieces and scatters them. Isis then finds all the pieces (except the phallus), which she reassembles, performing the rites of embalmment for the first time in history to restore her husband to eternal life.

JULIAN, Flavius Claudius   called Julian the Apostate, a neo-Platonist Roman emperor (b. 332 A.D.) who restored paganism.

JULIUS FIRMICUS, *see* FIRMICUS

KING OF HUNGARY   Mattias Corvino, a friend of Filippo Valori, who had visited the King at his court at Buda. Valori had Ficino dedicate Book III of the *De Vita Triplici* to the King. In 1484, Ficino translated a work of Synesius on dreams especially for him.

LANDINO, Cristoforo   (1424–1498 A.D.) Professor of Oratory and Poetics at the University of Florence, friend of Ficino's father and of Cosimo de Medici. In 1456, as a budding Platonist inspired by Landino, Ficino wrote the *Institutiones Platonicae* for him. Lorenzo de Medici gave him the title of President of the Platonic Academy.

LATIUM   Ancient name for the region of Italy in which Rome was situated.

LORENZO, "a certain Florentine by the name of"   Lorenzo della Volpaia, who made an astronomical clock for Lorenzo de Medici containing representations of the planets. It is now in the Museo Fisico in Florence.

LORENZO DE MEDICI (1449–1492 A.D.) called Lorenzo il Magnifico, succeeded his father, Piero, in 1469, as head of the family and patron of Ficino.

LUKE early Christian, physician, and friend of Paul, regarded as author of the third Gospel.

MAGNUS, *see* ALBERTUS MAGNUS

MARLIANUS, John a famous fifteenth century mathematician from Milan. Giovanni Torella, in his *Opus praeclarum de imaginibus astrologicis,* published in 1496, calls John Marlianus "the most outstanding mathematician of our time" and says that he had heard from a physician of Venice (probably Mengus Blanchellus) how Marlianus was cured of his fear of thunderstorms by an image of a lion engraved in gold.

MEDEA In Greek mythology, the wife of Jason. To kill his uncle, Pelias, Medea tells Pelias's daughters that they can restore him to youth if they will first cut his body up and boil the pieces. They believe her.

MELCHISIDECH a Canaanite priest in the time of Abraham (see *Genesis* xiv), taken as a symbol of the priesthood. Saint Paul says of him (*Hebrews* 7.3), "He is without father or mother or genealogy, and has neither beginning of days nor end of life, but resembling the Son of God he continues a priest forever."

MENGUS Menghus Blanchellus (Mengo Bianchelli da Faenza), "a distinguished physician of our time," who wrote, among other things, a treatise on bathing following Michael Savonarola's work on mineral baths and their occult powers. He was present at a dinner, in June, 1489, at Lorenzo de Medici's house, with Ficino, Pico, Poliziano, et al.

MERCURIUS Hermes Trismegistus, putative author of various neo-Platonist writings of the 2nd–3rd c. A.D. Ficino, however, like everyone else in the early Renaissance, believed Hermes Trismegistus to be an actual person, living before Plato, and the source of Plato's own Platonism.

MESUES Yuhanna o Yahya Ibn Masawayh, also called Janus Damascenus, the first Syrian medical writer to use the Arab tongue. He was a Christian in Baghdad whom the Caliph put in charge of a school of translators to translate Greek medical manuscripts. He died in 857 A.D., leaving many works on dietetics and gynecology. His most important book, the *Aphorisms,* was first published in Latin translation in Bologna in 1489.

MIRANDOLA, *see* PICO

MOSES   Moses Maimonides, also called Rabbi Moses ben Maimon (1135–1204 A.D.), a celebrated Jewish physician and Aristotelian scholar, born in Cordoba, later court doctor to Saladin the Great in Egypt. His work greatly influenced Albertus Magnus and Thomas Aquinas, especially his *Guide for the Perplexed.*

MOSES   Biblical Patriarch. Like David and Samuel, Moses was considered an astrologer by those of the Middle Ages because of the secret incantations and rituals he employed to produce supernatural ends.

NATURAL PHILOSOPHERS   name given to the philosophers of antiquity whose chief concern was physics and phenomena such as light, heat, and sound, rather than the ultimate structure of substances.

NERO, Piero di Francesco del   member of Ficino's Academy, Prior of Florence in 1476 and 1492, Captain of Pisa in 1511, and friend of Machiavelli.

NICHOLAS, *see* ALEXANDER AND NICHOLAS, THE PERIPATETICS

ORIGEN   Origenes Adamantius (185–255 A.D.), early Church Father and Greek Biblical scholar. In 176 A.D. a certain Celsus, a neo-Platonist otherwise unknown, wrote an elaborate indictment of Christianity, to which Origen wrote the reply *Contra Celsum.*

ORPHEUS   legendary Greek singer of hymns in which the doctrines of a religion called "Orphism" are set forth. He is said to have attracted beasts and stones with his charms.

OSIRIS, *see* ISIS.

PAUL   Apostle to the Gentiles (d. 67? A.D.), author of the *Epistles.* Ficino wrote an extended commentary on his works.

PELIAS, *see* Medea.

PHEDICE   an otherwise unknown Chaldaean astrologer cited by Thebith ben Corath.

Philostratus, Flavius   Roman writer (b. 170 A.D.), author of the *Life of Apollonius of Tyana,* employing the earlier biography of Damis as his source.

PHOEBE   actually the grandmother of Apollo and Artemis, but identi-
fied with the Moon, and thus with Artemis, Apollo's sister. The
story that Artemis was born first, and had to assist her mother in
the delivery and nourishing of her brother, is first told by Apol-
lodorus.

PICO DELLA MIRANDOLA, Giovanni   the Count of Mirandola
(1463–1494 A.D.), educated as an Aristotelian in Paris and elsewhere, he joined the Ficino circle in 1484, then presented "Nine
Hundred Theses" to an audience in Rome, where he was accused of heresy. He fled to France, was arrested and imprisoned,
later acquitted. He knew Hebrew and wrote *Heptaplus*, a Cabbalist account of creation, as well as many other studies, including
a treatise against astrology.

PIETRO d'ABANO   also called Peter Ebanenses, and Pietro d'Apono
(1253–1316 A.D.), medical author of the School of Padua,
where he was called Peter the Heretic of Abano, because his
modern views of medicine collided with the Church (he denied
the existence of the devil). After he died, the Church burned his
bones. Influenced by Averroes, his most important work is the
Conciliator Differentiarum, one of the first works to reconcile the
Arab School of medicine with the now commencing humanist
Greek school.

PLATO   Greek philosopher (429–347 B.C.)

PLINY   called Pliny the Elder (24–79 A.D.), Roman polymath, author
of a *Natural History,* unique of its kind.

PLOTINUS   (205–270 A.D.) the most important of the neo-Platonist
philosophers; born in Egypt, lived in Rome, and wrote in Greek.
His writings were edited by his student, Porphyry, as the *Enneads.*

PLUTARCH   Greek Platonist philosopher and biographer (ca. 50–120
A.D.)

POLIZIANO   Angelo degli Ambrogini (1454–1494 A.D.), a native of
Montepulciano, hence his Latin name 'Politianus' (our 'Poli-
tian'), poet and member of the Careggi circle. Tutor of Lorenzo
de Medici's children. Poliziano's father, a supporter of the Medici, was murdered by conspirators plotting the death of Piero de
Medici. Lorenzo brought him to Florence, where he studied
Latin under Landino and philosophy under Ficino.

PORPHYRY   Greek neo-Platonist philosopher (232–305 A.D.), and ed-
itor of Plotinus' *Enneads.*

PROCLUS   Greek neo-Platonist philosopher, last great systematizer of the Greek philosophical tradition.

PROMETHEUS   in Greek mythology, he made man out of clay, and Athena breathed life into the images.

PSELLUS, Michael   of Nicomedia (1018–1078 A.D.), Byzantine philosopher at Constantinople, author of many works, including *De operatione Daemonum* (which Ficino edited).

PTOLEMY, Claudius   Greek astronomer, mathematician, and geographer of Alexandria (fl. 127–148 A.D.), author of the *Almagest*, a textbook on astronomy, and the *Tetrabiblos*. The *Centiloquium* was incorrectly ascribed to him.

PYTHAGORAS   Greek philosopher and mathematician (b. ca. 570 B.C.), held theories of the transmigration of souls and the mathematical base of musical intervals, but wrote nothing.

PYTHO   in Greek mythology, the serpent guardian of the Oracle at Delphi. Apollo killed him and took the oracle.

QUINTILIAN   Roman teacher of rhetoric and author of books on oratory (30–100 A.D.)

RHASIS   also Rasis, Rhases (b. 865 A.D.), a Persian pioneer in Arab medicine at Baghdad, author of 200 works, including an *Encyclopedia of Medicine.*

SALVIATI, Giorgio   friend of Ficino, regent of the Church of Santa Croce, and Professor of Theology at the University of Florence. He was present at a dinner in June, 1489 at Lorenzo de Medici's house (with Ficino, Pico, Poliziano, and Mengo Bianchelli) in which he dominated the evening by arguing that Adam's was not the greatest sin.

SAMUEL   Hebrew prophet, necromancer, and seer in the time of David and Saul.

SAUL   first king of the Hebrews (fl. 1025 B.C.) He went to the witch at Endor where his defeat and death were prophesied.

SCYTHIANS   ancient nomadic tribes from Northern Europe and beyond the Black Sea.

SERAPIO   Yuhanna Ibn Sarabiun, or John Serapion (d. 930 A.D.), a Syrian Christian who wrote works translated into Arabic; Ficino considered him an Arabic author. His principal works, the *Aphorisms* and the *Pandectae*, were translated into Latin by Gerard of Cremona in 1479.

SERAPIS   or Sarapis, a healing Egyptian divinity with cult at Memphis in the temple over underground chambers where the bodies of

Apis bulls were entombed, he thus represented the collectivity of these (Osorapis). The Serapeum at Alexandria was one of the Seven Wonders of the world.

SOCRATES   Greek philosopher of Athens (469–399 A.D.) who wrote nothing, his student Plato memorializing him in his writings.

SODERINI, Piero   (1452–1522 A.D.) member of Ficino's Academy and close friend. He was a poet and an ambassador, from a distinguished political family.

SYNESIUS   Christian neo-Platonist philosopher from Cyrene (370–413 A.D.)

THEBITH Ben Corath   Thabit ibn Kurra of Harran, 9th c. A.D. Arab astrologer whose principal work, *De imaginibus astronomicis*, translated into Latin in the 12th c., had wide influence.

THOMAS AQUINAS   the most famous of scholastic theologians (1226–1274 A.D.), student of Albertus Magnus, Italian philosopher and Doctor of the Church known as the Angelic Doctor, he became the supreme theological authority of the Catholic Church. His *Summa contra Gentiles* is a work that attacks paganism. His chief work, *Summa theologiae,* is an Aristotelian systematization of theology.

TIMAEUS the Pythagorean   from Locri, in Italy, said to have been a teacher of Plato. A spurious work attributed to him, *On the Order and Nature of the Soul,* was an abridgement of Plato's *Timaeus,* widely read in the Renaissance.

TREBALLI   an ancient tribe of Italy in the Sabine territory.

TRISMEGISTUS, *see* MERCURIUS.

VALORI, Filippo   a distinguished Florentine nobleman and friend of the Medici (d. 1494 A.D.). He paid the publishing expenses of Ficino's Plato translations, as well as for the *Three Books on Life.* A friend of the King of Hungary, he prepared "royal editions" of Ficino's works to be sent him.

VESTA   in Roman mythology, another name for Ops, Cybele, or Earth, the wife of Coelus and mother of Saturn.

XENOPHON   Greek general and military historian (428–354 B.C.) A student of Socrates, he wrote an *Apologia* and *Memorabilia* of Socrates after the master's death.

ZOROASTER   Zarathustra, 6th c. B.C. Persian religious reformer and prophet.

INDEX

(Compiled by Jay Livernois)

E

F

dry, 78

empty, 18, 19, 22, 26, 33, 56, 68, 77

incapacitated, 13

lower, 114

nature of, 13–14

soften, 44

stretch, 21

strong, 48

weak, 21, 45, 52, 65, 73,

student(s), 2, 3, 4, 11, 12, 13, 24, 25, 33, 39, 40, 99, 173

sublimation, 95

suffocation, 39, 40, 42, 44, 46, 50, 70, 76

suffumigations, 157

sulfur, sulfurous, 88, 93, 137, 140, 167, 180

sun, 1, 6, 28, 35, 49

Sun, Solar, 13, 14, 15, 17, 48, 50, 55, 56, 62, 72, 78, 81, 89, 90, 91, 92, 93, 94, 96, 97, 98, 99, 100, 101, 102, 103, 104, 105, 106, 107, 111, 112, 113, 114, 117, 118, 119, 120, 121, 122, 123, 124, 125, 128, 129, 130, 131, 132, 133, 134, 135, 141, 146, 147, 148, 149, 152, 153, 157, 160, 162, 163, 164, 165, 171, 173, 174, 176, 180, 181

sweat, sweating, 41, 48, 71

Synesius, 87, 127, 159, 179, 181

Syrius, 129

T

Tail of Aquarius, 109

Tail of Ursa Major, 108

taste, 64, 66, 77, 119, 120, 121

Taurus, 105, 107, 108, 111, 112, 114, 132, 144, 147, 158

teeth, 72, 116

temples, 24, 33, 34, 60, 175

Thebit, 109, 149, 150

theriaca, 22, 24, 25, 34, 50, 53, 54, 77, 124, 125, 160

Theologians, 2, 149, 150

Theology, 93, 149, 150

thick, thicker, thickness, 7, 8, 9, 11, 13, 14, 15, 16, 24, 26, 31, 43, 44, 45, 54, 55, 73, 75, 95, 97, 118, 174

thighs, 1, 114,

thin, thinner, thinness, thinning, 5, 7, 8, 9, 11, 14, 43, 44, 45, 46, 47, 49, 55, 56, 57, 62, 63, 68, 73, 75, 76, 95, 97, 122, 124, 137, 138, 174

thirst, 41, 72

Thomas Aquinas, 110, 150, 176, 182

thought, 8, 9, 10, 12, 13, 14, 15, 18, 19, 21, 22, 23, 25, 26, 27, 31, 38, 39, 44, 69, 70, 96, 110, 147, 154, 155

thunder, 147

Timaeus, 7, 30, 96, 178

tongue, 65

touch, touching, 13, 64, 65, 66, 116, 117, 121, 123, 131, 139, 151, 157, 172

Tree of Life, 54, 117, 123

Triballi, 139